University of Birmingham

URBAN AND REGIONAL STUDIES NO 5

II The Social Content of Planning

University of Birmingham

URBAN AND REGIONAL STUDIES

No 1. Recreation Research and Planning
edited by Thomas L. Burton

No 2. Experiments in Recreation Research
by Thomas L. Burton

No 3. The Urban Future
by John N. Jackson

No 4. The Social Framework of Planning
by J. B. Cullingworth

No 5. The Social Content of Planning
by J. B. Cullingworth

No 6. Planning for Change
by J. B. Cullingworth

Problems of an Urban Society

VOLUME II

The Social Content of Planning

J. B. CULLINGWORTH

UNIVERSITY OF TORONTO PRESS

First published in 1973 in Canada and the United States
by University of Toronto Press
Toronto and Buffalo

ISBN 0-8020-2084-4

Printed in Great Britain
in 10 point Times New Roman
by William Clowes & Sons, Limited
London, Beccles and Colchester

Preface

I owe a large debt of gratitude to the many friends who have helped me in the writing and editing of this work. The major debt is to my former colleagues—staff and students—in the Centre for Urban and Regional Studies at the University of Birmingham. No less valued have been the comments made by friends in local and central government. Consensus has not been achieved, nor attempted, and any shortcomings are entirely my own responsibility. In particular, it has proved impossible for me to bring all the chapters up to the same date. That the various chapters in Volumes I and II were written at different times during the academic year 1971–2 will be all too apparent. I am also extremely grateful to my diligent secretary, Mrs Gill King, who battled most efficiently with badly written drafts.

J.B.C.

Contents

Summary of Contents of Volumes I and III

Introduction

Few areas of debate have burgeoned in recent years as much as those concerned with urban problems. The reasons stem only in part from the growth of problems of urban decay, pollution, poverty, regional decline and the like. Of equal, if not greater importance are changing attitudes, changes in public awareness and in the limits of public toleration. As the complexities and interdependencies of modern life have increased, so has the resolve to combat the environmental and social ills to which these give rise. Concern for the quality of the environment is no longer the preserve of an intellectual minority of visionaries, administrators and politicians: it is a matter of concern to an electorate which is demanding greater 'citizen-participation' and more effective control over the vast and amorphous managerial institutions of contemporary society. At the same time the threshold of tolerability has changed. The number of the homeless and the destitute is certainly less now than it was a century or even a generation ago, but it is not the statistics which are currently 'shocking'; it is the fact that homelessness and destitution exist at all which has become intolerable. Of course, 'standards' have risen and concepts of poverty have changed beyond the wildest dreams of nineteenth century reformers. But this is irrelevant; each generation has to define for itself the criteria against which poverty is to be judged. Similarly with the physical environment. That towns are now relatively healthy places in which to live is a statistical fact, but this is of little relevance in the context of contemporary concern for the quality of the urban environment.

The point should not, however, be overstressed. The festering sores of slumdom still exist in some major cities and these bear a tragic resemblance to those described at length in the blue books of the nineteenth century. Further, they are hidden from—or, at least, are unseen by—the middle-class commuter and, therefore, do not shock the public conscience or precipitate the necessary public action. There are no longer cholera epidemics to overcome ignorance of the conditions that exist. At the same time individualistic moral philosophy has been given a modern twist with the perceived (yet unrealized) advent of 'the welfare state' and the defensive mechanisms rapidly and eloquently brought into play by the institutions of social welfare whenever major criticisms are made of their adequacy by social commentators. Curiously—and dangerously—the criticism of public and social service has become institutionalized to such an extent that 'direct action' is increasingly seen by some as being the only route to a change in 'the system'. At present the balance is heavily in favour of legitimized change within the system: by reform of institutional procedures, by consultative councils, by ombudsmen and, less surely, by neighbourhood groups. New styles of local government and new divisions of power are under serious discussion. Though there is a clear trend towards agreement on the need for large local authorities able to command substantial resources, responsible for meaningful areas of community interest, and capable of accepting a substantial devolution of power from central government, there is also a widely accepted need for truly local institutions able to express neighbourhood feelings and to undertake direct responsibility for matters which are of only local concern. The main debate, however, is sure-footed only in the former field where the issues are clear (though difficult to evaluate and balance one against the other): so far as 'community councils' (to use the term employed in the new legislation on local government) are concerned, the debate has barely progressed beyond recognition of the need.

Reference is made throughout these three volumes to these and similar issues relating to the distribution of power, and an attempt is made, in the last chapter of Volume II, to draw the threads together, but the main purpose is less ambitious; it is to provide an outline of some of the major urban problems of contemporary Britain. The qualifying 'some' is essential, both because of the competence of the author to discuss all the relevant issues and also because the field is limitless. The majority of the population live in urban areas. What then should be the criterion by which some issues are included as 'urban and regional problems', while others are excluded? There is no easy answer to this and no claim is made that this book demonstrates one. The 'solution' is personal but, hopefully, not idiosyncratic. The intention has been to provide an introduction to those issues which, on one view, are among the more important.

The three volumes complement *Town and Country Planning in Britain* which gives an outline of the apparatus of physical planning, but their focus is on problems and on social and (to a lesser extent) economic aspects. Some degree of overlap between the two works has been inevitable while, on the other hand, attempts to avoid this have led to a rather more slender treatment of some issues (such as 'amenity') than might have been expected.

14

A common thread throughout is the inter-connectedness of issues. This presents a perpetual—and probably insoluble—problem for government, which must divide its responsibilities into manageable parts. A similar problem faces an author who attempts to provide a broad picture of the issues, even when the field is narrower and, within that field, comprehensiveness is explicitly disclaimed. To illustrate: should the transport problems of elderly people be dealt with in a discussion of transport or in a discussion of the elderly? Should issues relating to the size and composition of the labour force come under the heading of 'demography' or 'economics'? Is it more appropriate to deal with housing subsidies in the context of housing or that of poverty?

In practice the solution adopted matters less than the awareness that there are always different, and possibly equally relevant, contexts for each aspect of a many-sided issue. What is totally inadequate is to approach a 'problem' in the terms of a discipline or a profession. Economics, sociology and, indeed, all the separate social sciences are abstractions which deal with parts of problems defined by the nature of their analytical tools. In a similar way, professions deal with parts of problems defined by the nature of their corpus of knowledge and their operational skills; and government departments and ministers deal with parts of problems defined by the nature of the responsibilities which have been allocated to them.

The development of multi-disciplinary studies, of generic professions and of non-departmental offices are all attempts to break down these artificial barriers. These three volumes are offered as a modest contribution to the same endeavour.

The intention in dividing this work into three volumes was simple and logical. Volume I would set the framework within which specific problems could be discussed in Volume II. Volume III would then provide a set of complementary readings. As with all good plans, implementation proved less simple. The subject matter refused to be so neatly packaged. Where does the 'framework' end and the 'problem' begin? By the time the plan had been finalized it no longer seemed to have the validity which it had at conception. Nevertheless, the underlying concept of a three volume series spanning major contemporary urban problems remained.

Volume I: The Social Framework of Planning

In the first volume there is a general discussion of the demographic, socio-economic and physical framework of 'planning', together with

15

an account of the problems of urban traffic and a note on the land values problem.

The starting point is the size and structure of the population, recent demographic trends and their implications. This is prefaced by a short discussion on the concept of an 'optimum' population. The fact that this is elusive and difficult does not detract from its importance. Recognition of this has developed markedly in the twelve months since the first draft was written.

Demographic analysis rapidly becomes indigestible, and no attempt is made to achieve a comprehensive coverage. The aim is to provide sufficient to demonstrate some of the more important implications of current trends. The chapter includes, as a 'case study' some detailed figures on the South East Region: chosen mainly because of the wealth of available material on this Region.

The second chapter, on the socio-economic framework, deals in the main with employment, regional problems and policies and urban growth policy. Again the concept of the 'optimum' is introduced, this time in relation to towns. But while the idea of an optimum population is viewed sympathetically, that of an optimum size of towns is severely criticized, particularly in view of the fact that controls over the growth of towns have formed a major plank of British planning policy, frequently with unintended and undesirable effects.

There is, of course, a clash here between a number of different objectives. This is more clearly seen in Chapter 3 which presents an even more selective treatment of the physical framework of planning problems and policies. The selected issues include urban growth, agriculture, forestry, water and natural resources. Since this chapter was drafted an important official study has been published on *Long Term Population Distribution in Great Britain*. An Appendix to Chapter 3 reproduces some of the main findings of this study. (A summary of the Report is reproduced in Volume III.)

Chapter 4 discusses urban traffic problems. This leans heavily (though by no means uncritically) on the writings of Professor Colin Buchanan. Emphasis is laid on environmental issues, road pricing and the development of public transport. Public support for these is currently growing. Unfortunately, no viable system of pricing has yet been devised and policy is therefore constrained to the narrower issue of parking controls.

Finally, a note is provided on the land values problem. This was forced to the fore of public debate just after the appropriate machinery for coping with it (the Land Commisson) had been abolished. Though there is some reference to the immediately current problem, the main emphasis of the chapter is on the broader issues. As with the majority of the problems discussed, practicable solutions depend upon public understanding and political leadership. The two schemes introduced by Labour Governments (in 1947 and 1967) failed politically and it is not easy to be hopeful that a third attempt will provide a long-term solution. Nevertheless there are, again, signs of changes in public opinion.

Volume II: The Social Content of Planning

Much of the second volume is concerned with urban poverty and disadvantage: the relative lack of command over resources and access to opportunity and power. Chapter 1 provides a review of the dimensions of poverty and serves as an introduction to the fuller discussion of selected issues in the chapters that follow.

Chapter 2 discusses the nature of housing policies, the special characteristics of housing, and a number of issues relating to tenure and choice. The issue of 'choice' emerges more clearly in the chapter on slum clearance and improvement. In both chapters, the differences between the institutional frameworks of 'public' and 'private' housing are underlined. Unfortunately, though justified in historical terms, these differences now create additional 'housing' problems which are further exacerbated by political approaches to 'council housing' and 'owner-occupation'.

Chapter 4, on 'race and colour' is a documentation of the emergence and recognition of a new urban problem which has its roots in human prejudice and fear. Government is here faced with a series of difficult and delicate political problems. The problems are complicated by the fact that they are inextricably intertwined with wider issues of social justice and equality.

The 'colour problem' has resulted in a greater awareness of the social objectives and social implications of physical planning policies. This forms the subject of an extended discussion, in Chapter 5, of the nature and scope of 'social planning'. Increasingly, however, it is being recognised that 'the social' is but a label for one aspect of planning, in the same way that 'the physical' or 'the economic' are labels for other aspects.

Throughout these chapters there is repeated reference to issues such as citizen-participation, the distribution of power, and the essentially political nature of all 'planning'. The final chapter attempts a broad review of these issues and stresses the crucial importance of the political process. 'Planning' is essentially not the fulfilment of plans, but a process of balancing conflicting claims on scarce resources and of achieving compromises between conflicting interests.

17

Volume III: Planning for Change

The third volume is intended not only to complement the first two volumes, but also to bring together a number of important papers on some crucial contemporary urban problems. The major theme is set out at length in Professor Mel Webber's challenging paper which lends its title (in abbreviated form) to the volume as a whole: what are the possibilities, the scope and the content of planning in a rapidly changing society? Some authors are more sure of themselves than others, though most raise more questions than can be answered.

The widespread interest raised by Webber's paper (originally delivered to the Bartlett Society and later printed in the *Town Planning Review*) is a result not only of the cogency of his argument and the felicity of his presentation, but also its particular timeliness. The 1960s saw the increasing rejection of deterministic, detailed 'development' planning and the increasing acceptance of flexible 'structure' planning. The impact was greater on thinking than on practice, but the new thinking underlay the planning legislation which was passed at the end of the decade. Moreover, Webber's 'permissive planning' approach was explicitly adopted in *The Plan for Milton Keynes* (to which Webber personally contributed).

The wider view of 'planning' has led to the creation of inter-disciplinary planning teams. Professor Alonso, in the second paper in this volume, questions the adequacy of these. He sees the inter-disciplinary team primarily as a source of innovation or dissent where new departures are called for. A new approach ('beyond the inter-disciplinary approach') is needed, in which urban and regional problems are dealt with by professionals who are first and foremost specialists in these problems and only secondarily members of traditional disciplines. This 'meta-disciplinary' approach is essentially problem-orientated—a point which arises again in the final paper of this volume.

The paper by Professor Donnison and his colleagues at the Centre for Environmental Studies, though focused on the Greater London Development Plan, demonstrates the inter-connectedness of urban problems and the way difficulties in solving them are exacerbated by definitions of areas of administrative and political responsibility.

This paper was submitted to the Greater London Development Plan Inquiry in November 1970, and has not previously been published.

One of the points raised at the end of this paper is the difficulty facing the public in participating in the debate on the Greater London Development Plan. Yet public participation is now supposedly part of the planning process. The Skeffington Committee dealt specifically with this issue. Its Report, *People and Planning* is the subject of further analysis in the fourth paper, by Levin and Donnison. The Report is shown to be only the beginning of an important debate, but though a number of proposals are put forward, Levin and Donnison necessarily conclude with more questions than answers.

With Peter Willmott's paper, modestly entitled 'Some Social Trends', we return to a theme touched upon in the second chapter of the first volume: the changing socio-economic framework. This broad review of social change in Britain argues that strong social forces are at work leading to a more homogeneous life-style.

A major element in current social change is demographic. Chapter 6 reproduces a short extract from the Crowther Report *15 to 18* which discusses demographic trends in the context of their educational consequences.

Much of the debate in the sixties was preoccupied with the problems of affluence, but each generation apparently has to 'rediscover' poverty. Adrian Sinfield's succinct paper (which extends the discussion contained in Chapter 1 of Volume II) reviews the state of knowledge on, and the awareness of, poverty in Britain. Originally published in 1968, its extensive bibliography has been updated.

Michael Thomson's paper on traffic provides a survey of the problems of a society which is about half-way to the 'saturation level' of around one car to every two people. The title is deliberately tendentious since it is argued that a fully 'motorized' society is neither possible nor, indeed, desirable.

The study which is summarized in Chapter 11 (*Long Term Population Distribution in Great Britain*) is perhaps the most important review since the Barlow Report. The fact that it was carried out by civil servants (rather than a committee of inquiry or a Royal Commission) affects the style, but not the message. In essence this is that the scope for government intervention, control and direction is limited. As with Webber the emphasis is on the need for flexibility. However, there remains a large area for political debate here, which an expansion of research effort could render more profitable.

Research is the subject of the final chapter which reproduces, without amendment, the editor's Inaugural Lecture at the University of Birmingham. This suffers from its brevity but, following the publication of, and debate on, the Rothschild and Dainton Reports (in *A Framework for Government Research and Development*, HMSO, 1971) it has an unexpected topicality. 'Planning for Change', if it is to be relevant and effective, demands a strong research base. But as the paper argues, research workers must be wary of over-enthusiastic politicians. Research can provide information, understanding and advice, but the responsibility for decision-making rests with politicians.

Chapter 1

The Dimensions of Poverty

THE RELATIVITY OF POVERTY

Poverty is a relative concept. The fifth of Americans who were officially described in 1964 as living in poverty conditions [1] had an objective standard of living very considerably higher than the *average* in many countries of the world. Their standard of living was also much higher—on an 'objective' measurement—than that of many in Britain who would be considered to be well above the poverty line.[2] Poverty can thus be determined only in relation to the general standard of living of a particular country. Furthermore, as standards of living rise so must the standard to be applied in determining poverty. The British standards of 1900 are irrelevant to the conditions of the nineteen-seventies. The 'necessities' of life are different. The poor are those 'individuals and families whose resources, over time, fall seriously short of the resources commanded by the average individual or family in the community in which they live'.[3]

It should be noted that this concept of poverty does not imply that 'the poor must always be with us'. It does, however, imply that poverty will be reduced only if there is greater equality. As Schorr has put it, 'if we are to overleap the relativity of our conception of poverty, then it cannot be only by modifying the absolute amounts of income that 15 million poor children receive but by modifying the *proportion of the total* that they receive'.[4]

Poverty is relative lack of command over resources and access to opportunity. It is, therefore, much more than an issue of money, important though this is. A family may have an average income but be unable to obtain access to good housing at a reasonable rent: their position would be disadvantaged in comparison with a family in a low-rent council house. Indeed they may be solely 'housing poor'. A family living in a rural area may have resources and costs equivalent to an urban family but be cut off from access to a wide range of services, facilities and opportunities because they do not have a car and the bus services have been axed: they are 'transport poor'.

Examples of these broad types of 'poverty' can be multiplied, but there are other quite different dimensions of poverty. A family may be provided with adequate financial resources for an officially-determined subsistence standard of living, but be so degraded and stigmatized by the manner in which this support is provided as to lose all sense of pride and competence. Policies based on a deeper understanding of social relationships and the character of human dignity may still fail to reach the roots of 'the subculture of exclusion and alienation'[5] because of cultural adaptions to relative depriva-tion. This dimension of poverty can be adequately tackled only by changing *relativities*. On this approach, the 'problem' of the affluent is as relevant as the problem of the poor; or to use an alternative formulation, the crucial issue is the total social structure, not that part of it which is seen as 'poor'. Thus the problem of poverty is essentially the problem of inequality. Given the acceptance of the relativity of poverty, no other conclusion is possible.

The implication is that the long-term aim of policy should be structural change in society. Poverty will always remain so long as a situation is tolerated in which anyone is unable to obtain an income significantly below the median. It is frequently argued that this can be achieved by policies of economic growth and increasing affluence. Unfortunately, evidence from the richest society the world has ever known convincingly demonstrates that this is not the case. Increasing affluence raises expectations, the general standard of living and the median income, but of itself has no positive effect on those below the median. Indeed, by raising general aspirations and at the same time failing to provide the means by which these can be achieved by all, it can exacerbate the situation. At worst it can lead to alienation and open conflict.

Much of the argument on the number of people 'in poverty' stems from fundamental differences in the concepts employed. The statements set out above are certainly not universally, or even generally, accepted. They involve beliefs and values which are not shared by all. In similar manner, of course, other approaches to poverty also involve beliefs and values. The overtly political nature of the issue is best explicitly stated.

Different viewpoints imply different policies. These are most clearly seen in relation to the question of income-related benefits and means tests. This is more than the typically polarized arguments on selectivity and universality recognize.[6] These arguments are commonly about the techniques of providing 'assistance'. Much more significant is the question of whether policy should be directed towards this end or whether it should not be aimed at a social re-organization in which the need for 'assistance' (with all its implications and overtones—as with 'welfare' in the United States) is reduced to the minimum.

POVERTY AND EMPLOYMENT

Perhaps the best example is employment. Full employment has been one of the basic explicit 'assumptions'[7] and policies underlying the British 'welfare state'. At the time of writing (February 1972) over a million people are registered as unemployed and a further unknown but significant number are unemployed but unregistered.[8] This represents a social, financial and economic cost of huge dimensions. It appears small in comparison with the massive unemployment of the inter-war years, but history is irrelevant. Over nearly three decades it has become expected (rightly) that such levels of unemployment would not be tolerated. Quite apart from its 'inefficiency', its social impact is too great to be acceptable. What is particularly worrying about the current unemployment is the suggestion that it is not frictional or cyclical, but structural: the beginning of a trend towards an economic structure in which there is a permanent 'excess of labour'. Hopefully, recognition of this may lead to action to prevent it.

Yet the experience of the United States advises against undue optimism. In that rich country, so wracked with poverty, the striving for economic efficiency has led to a long-term situation of large-scale unemployment which becomes more and more difficult to deal with as the 'efficient' structure becomes hardened and as the unemployed become increasingly demoralized and alienated. It is not without good cause that so much of American writing on poverty stresses the importance of measures to increase employment opportunities.[9]

The psychological impact of unemployment (redundancy, 'shake-out', or whatever) is well documented. Significantly, British documentation is now largely historical,[10] while a stream of publications is currently emerging from the United States.[11] There is much in the American situation which is significantly different from the British, in particular the importance in the former of the 'urbanized agricultural proletariat',[12] and the history and character of the American 'welfare' system. But there are similarities which may well be increasing, in relation for example to the coloured population (particularly in older urban areas) and decreasing job opportunities: 'The present-day poor . . . are seeking employment in a job market that is becoming more and more difficult for them.'[13]

As individual economic enterprises (both private and public) seek

23

after greater efficiency and as pressures for increasing wages in traditionally low-pay occupations achieve some success (slight though this has been to date) it is possible that Britain may face an increasing problem on this front. The classic economic argument does, of course, apply: as 'labour costs' increase, enterprises will seek cheaper (i.e. capital) alternatives. It does not necessarily follow, however, that this has simply to be accepted. Putting in automatic ticket barriers on underground and commuter stations or replacing two-man buses with 'pay-as-you-enter' vehicles may make good sense to transport operators, but on a wider view it may be nonsense. And even if it is justifiable in central London, can it be so in Glasgow?

Clearly such an approach is not compatible with one of profit-maximization or one of making public services 'stand on their own feet'. On the other hand, resisting technological change can be a counsel of despair. It is more fruitful to think in terms of 'local employment planning', the phasing of redundancies and the development of appropriate training programmes in conjunction with the stimulation of new jobs.

This is much more than putting the unemployed to work on the reclamation of derelict sites or the beautification of cities (though this is not necessarily to be despised). One of the paradoxes of the current employment situation (in both Britain and the United States) is a general 'excess' of labour accompanied by a severe shortage of workers in particular fields, especially the service trades. Gladwin has nicely posed the issue:

> Many questions need to be answered and wholly new strategies must be designed, tested and proven before the enormous employment potential of the service occupations can be fully realized. As long as the majority of service jobs pay less than their production equivalents and many of them are seen as second class employment suitable only for second-rate workers, and as long as neither security nor career potential exists in most of them and there are no effective organizations to serve and protect the interests of the servers, just so long as these conditions persist we in the affluent sector will continue to want to obtain the services we want and are presumably able to pay for, and at the same time multitudes of potentially available poor people will remain unemployed because the avenues for recruitment into the needed jobs are either non-existent or actively distasteful to them.[14]

As Gladwin recognizes, this is to pose the problem rather than to solve it; but it poses it in a helpful way.

The linking of poverty with employment opportunities is worthy of

24

much deeper analysis than has yet been attempted in Britain. Ornati has identified three broad types of causes of poverty linked with different poverty bands. Taking an annual income of $5,000 as the poverty line, much poverty is explained by the presence of low-paying industries. At a poverty line of $4,000, different incidences of poverty in different cities are related to their industrial and occupational structures. At a poverty line of $3,000 the different incidences of poverty between cities 'may be better explained by demographic composition'.[15]

Recognition of the importance of low pay as a factor in poverty has come only recently in Britain.[16] Partly this was due to the widespread belief that increases in real incomes and the various benefits of 'the welfare state' had abolished poverty in this area as in others. It is, of course, true that the real incomes of the low-paid have increased substantially since before the war, but, given a concept of relative poverty, this is not the issue. 'The position of low-paid workers in relation to better-paid workers has changed very little over long periods of time.'[17] The Report of the National Board for Prices and Incomes [18] and the DEP Report on *A National Minimum Wage* [19] demonstrate the complexity of the issues involved. Low pay is not confined to any particular industry or occupation: it is very widely spread, and the causes vary in a manner which is bewildering in the extreme. Since there is no single cause, there can be no single remedy:

In any one industry a variety of factors can be at work: the industry may be declining or may be faced with severe competition and falling profits; managements may be slack; the jobs themselves may be ill-suited to modern needs; workers may lack the skills necessary to do better-paid jobs, or they may simply prefer convenient and undemanding work; trade union organization may be lacking or ineffective; wage-fixing arrangements may be inadequate, and wage payment systems out of date....[20]

These occupational problems demand a large number of separate approaches but, for significant numbers of low-paid workers, employment opportunities are limited by ill-health, lack of training and counselling, and simple ignorance of available opportunities.

POVERTY AND INCOME

A new approach to the problems of low pay was made in 1971 with the introduction of the Family Income Supplement (FIS). This marked a radical departure in social policy. Previously, though certain benefits were income-related, no attempt was made to directly supplement low earnings. FIS provided a new non-contributory weekly benefit, payable to low-income families in which the wage-earner was in full-time employment. The FIS benefit is one half the difference between gross income and the 'prescribed amount'—a subsistence level of income taking into account the number of children. (Those in receipt of FIS are automatically entitled to a range of free benefits, e.g. welfare milk and foods, prescriptions, optical and dental services.)

This is part of the current policy to provide selective help to those in greatest need. Such an approach has serious drawbacks. In the first place, though it ensures that assistance is restricted to those in greatest need, it does not guarantee that all those in greatest need will, in fact, receive it. 'Take-up' depends upon knowledge of the scheme, willingness to undergo a means test, and acceptance of the benefit as a right carrying no implication of a 'poverty status'. Unfortunately, previous experience of highly selective benefits is that it is difficult to administer them in such a way that all who need them do in fact receive them, and receive them without loss of dignity.[21]

There are other drawbacks. It is costly in administration: the Financial Memorandum to the Bill estimated an administrative cost of £600,000 a year in distributing £8 million in benefits.[22] (This assumed an 85 per cent take-up: presumably the administrative cost of locating and aiding the remaining 15 per cent would be relatively much greater.) More important, it has severe 'negative' effects particularly when other benefits are taken into account. This follows, of course, from its selective basis. An increase in income of £1 a week involves a reduction in FIS benefit of 50p. But this is not all: it also results in a reduction in other benefits including the new rent allowance.[23] Combined with other income-related benefits, insurance contributions and taxes (which are becoming bewilderingly complex) the overall effect of an increase in earnings can be negligible. In other words, the marginal rate of tax on the low paid can be very high indeed.[24]

This points to a structural deficiency of FIS and income-related benefits. FIS meets only *half* the gap between actual income and the 'prescribed amount'. To meet the whole amount of this gap would drastically increase the 'negative tax' problem.[25]

The Reverse Income Tax proposal of the Institute of Economic Affairs [26] is even more objectionable on this account since it implies a marginal rate of tax of 100 per cent for those affected. Briefly, the scheme envisages automatic payments, via the tax system, to those whose assessed income falls below a prescribed poverty line. Though linked with proposals to dismantle many of the existing social services (including the social security system) it is conceptually separate. The scheme does, however, have the advantage (assuming that the administrative problems can be overcome—a not insignificant qualification)[27] of automatic 100 per cent 'take-up'.

All schemes such as these are based on the concept of channelling financial assistance to those below a poverty line. They ignore and implicitly reject the need to tackle the inequalities inherent in the socio-economic structure—inequalities which are not only of income but of educational and employment opportunities, health and environment, all of which interact on and reinforce each other.

Poverty is hydra-headed. Mere transfer of income cannot adequately cope with the type of situation succinctly described in the American 1971 *Manpower Report of the President*:

Disadvantaged city residents, particularly members of minority groups, have fared badly in competing for jobs because of a combination of obstacles that affects all aspects of their lives. Inadequate education, segregated housing, employment discrimination, and other barriers—both real and artificial—have isolated these workers from the mainspring of economic activity and have resulted ultimately in relegating them to a secondary labor market, where jobs are poorly paid and likely to offer only irregular employment.[28]

Being poor is more than having a low income. It involves an interlocking series of circles of deprivation:

One such is the circle of cause and effect in which being poor means living in a poor neighbourhood, which means going to a secondrate school, which means having an inadequate education, which means having a low-paying job or no job at all, and thus being poor. Or being poor means eating poor food and living in unsanitary housing which means having poor health, which means missing a lot of work or school, or perhaps being handicapped or not strong enough to handle the heavy manual work which is often the only kind available, and thus being unemployed much of the time, and so being poor. Being poor also means realizing that most of the other people in the world are more successful and are able to do things about which the poor person can scarcely dream, which means that the poor person sees himself as a failure, which means he has no confidence and gives up easily or perhaps does not push himself at all, and thus stays poor forever. All these circles begin and end with being poor.[29]

The poor have to come to terms with their poverty, and their

27

adaptions reduce their ability to break away from it. The term 'the culture of poverty' has been coined to describe this, though it is sometimes illicitly used as a psychological defence against the existence of poverty. After all, if poverty is not the fault of the poor it is the fault of the rich—and this is an uncomfortable admission to make.[30] The strength of the middle-class horror of 'spongers on the Welfare State' is an extreme manifestation of this.

The valid response to the interlocking circles of poverty is a series of policies which will bring about the real opportunity which is the pre-requisite of change. 'The major reason for the failure of most anti-poverty programs so far is that they require the poor to change their behavior before they have gained the resources that would change their situation.'[31]

This is not to imply that the poor should become 'conventional'; only that they should have equal access to conventional opportunities. What is done with those opportunities is irrelevant: the essential objective should be to ensure that the opportunities are real and equal. This implies social and economic restructuring on a large scale.

But these fine words are easier to state than to translate into policy; and it is easy to talk in general terms and to forget that there are different types of poverty of different incidence and severity. In drawing attention to the broader structural issues, sight must not be lost of specific elements which can (and must) be dealt with by different measures.

A TYPOLOGY OF POVERTY

A 'Poverty Panel', convened by the Social Science Research Council, attempted a typology of poverty.[32] This is well worth reproducing *in extenso*:

(a) The hardships that follow directly from bereavement, injury, illness, unemployment and other disasters may be thought of as *crisis* poverty.

(b) Some people never recover from these crises: they remain disabled or unemployable. Others are crippled, mentally or physically, from birth and suffer such handicaps all their lives. Their poverty is often the most severe of all. These *long-term dependencies* do not afflict large proportions of the population, but the numbers involved may be increasing.

(c) Recent studies have shown the continuing importance of *life-cycle poverty*, first clearly identified by Seebohm Rowntree as afflicting people during childhood, parenthood (when several children depend on one earner), and old age.

(d) *Depressed-area poverty* is as old as industrial progress; it still afflicts regions such as Ulster and the Scottish Highlands which have been left behind, economically speaking, by the rest of the nation.

(e) A somewhat similar pattern appears within cities and large urban regions. New investment is concentrated in particular quarters (the suburban fringe and the central commercial areas) while others decay. Some quarters attract wealthier households while others suffer a continuing loss of their more successful residents. The distribution of some public services (e.g. new schools and good teachers) may reinforce these trends. The results might be described as *down-town poverty*—though they may not be confined to inner areas of the city and a better term is needed to describe them.

(f) A combination of financial hardship, squalid environment, family structure and personal capacities and relationships may produce a pattern of adaption, characterized by particular time orientations and value systems, which some have described as *the culture of poverty*. Within this culture, patterns of behaviour that are rational and comprehensible, at least in the short term, tend to bar individuals and their families from escaping to more successful or comfortable styles of life.

As the Panel recognized, this typology (or indeed any other) cannot do justice to the complexities. It distinguishes between conditions that are not clearly distinguishable in practice. Nevertheless, it is useful for analytical purposes even though the concepts vary in clarity. (The Panel commented that, in the last category, the term 'culture' covers a wide range of factors which need to be separately identified: the concept of a culture of poverty 'is as likely to mislead as to enlighten'.) The objective of any such analysis will be to point to social strategies that can effectively meet the different problems that are labelled 'poverty'.

Crisis poverty is most effectively dealt with by income-maintenance policies. Whether these should be based on an insurance principle is of less importance (however significant it may be in political terms) than that income security should be readily available, that its availability is well known, and that it should be provided in a humane and dignified way. At the same time, however, assistance may be required in many other ways, e.g. the care of dependants, retraining for a new job, or moving to a more suitable house. In terms of strategy (as distinct from relief) it is self-evidently desirable to attempt to reduce the incidence of crises, for example, by removing causes (such as cyclical unemployment and industrial accidents), by providing remedies (such as new jobs and retraining schemes in connection with structural unemployment), and by providing efficient services (such as job-placing). In even broader terms, well-developed systems of curative and preventive medicine can assist in the reduction of crisis poverty (though they may have the effect of increasing long-term dependencies). The arguments here are couched in social terms but there is an obvious economic aspect. The inefficiency of maintaining workers (and their families) in enforced idleness needs no demonstration. Further, in Beveridge's words, 'it is a logical corollary to the payment of high benefits in disability that determined efforts should be made by the State to reduce the number of cases for which benefit is needed'.[33]

Long-term dependencies involve similar issues but, by definition, longer-term support is needed. Economic opportunities for potential workers (whether labelled 'unemployed' or 'disabled') depend to a significant extent on the general state of the economy. It needed a war and the labour shortages to which this gave rise to demonstrate the employability of groups—such as the blind—who had previously been considered to be incapable of making an economic contribution to the common wealth.[34]

Knowledge about the extent and character of long-term dependencies is sadly deficient and thus policy is faltering. It was not until the Chronically Sick and Disabled Persons Act of 1970 that local authorities had a duty 'to secure that they are adequately informed of the numbers and needs of substantially and permanently handicapped persons'.[35] Whether this Act will, in fact, constitute 'a charter for the disabled' (as was hoped at the time of its passing) remains to be seen. The first stage in the elaboration of policies is provided by the official survey of the 'handicapped and impaired' in Great Britain, published in 1971.[36] This revealed that there were some $4\frac{1}{4}$ million people aged sixteen and over living in private households who had some form of physical handicap.

There are many other forms of social and mental handicap which create acute problems,[37] such as general ill-health, mental ill-health, death of the chief wage earner, old age and chronic sickness. On some of these—old age for instance—extensive research has indicated the lines along which policy should develop. Others have been relatively ignored—particularly the mentally ill [38] and the chronically sick.

Life-cycle poverty is perhaps the clearest and best-documented type of poverty.[39] The provision of sufficient income to support dependent children is a major issue here. Since this cannot be achieved

30

by the wage system, family allowances must form a major plank of policy (as must pensions for the elderly). Unfortunately, while increased and extended pensions are publicly acceptable the same is not the case with family allowances,[40] in spite of the overwhelming case for them.

A very large number of issues are relevant to life cycle poverty. In addition to those already mentioned are family planning,[41] working mothers,[42] nursery provision [43] and housing.[44]

When we come to depressed area poverty, down-town poverty and cultures of poverty even broader and more complex issues arise. The characteristic feature here is the concentration and inter-relationship of problems in specific areas. This characteristic renders ineffective policies directed to specific problems. Indeed, 'successes' on a narrow front may exacerbate the wider problems. Improved educational opportunities for example may deprive already deprived areas of their ablest members thus decreasing the potential for community improvement.

Depressed area poverty is basically a problem of inadequate economic activity, frequently (though not always) a legacy of the industrial revolution. Massive assistance in the form of incentives to industrialists and investment in physical superstructure may be needed before such areas can reach the position of having an adequate base for a sustained economic 'take-off'.

Down town poverty and the so-called *culture of poverty* are even more intractable, largely because of our lack of understanding. Tentative steps of a very untraditional character are being taken with the Community Development Programme and the Urban Aid Programme. Though preceded, in line with British conventions, by the deliberations of Committees of Inquiry,[45] these are essentially American imports. The American Economic Opportunity Act of 1964 provided for 'a programme which mobilizes and utilizes in an attack on poverty, public and private resources of any urban or rural . . . area . . . to give promise of progress towards an elimination of poverty through developing employment opportunities, improving human performance, motivation and productivity and bettering the conditions under which people live, learn and work'. The agonizing period of introspection which preceded this Act has no British counterpart, nor was any apparent regard had to its failures—what Daniel Moynihan has labelled 'maximum feasible misunderstanding', in place of the 'maximum feasible participation' with which the anti-poverty programme was to be carried out.[46]

THE URBAN PROGRAMME

The British programmes (which are discussed further in Chapter 5) are modest. They provide aid for 'urban areas of special social need'. These are not defined in the legislation, but administrative circulars have 'advised' local authorities of 'the kind of area envisaged':

They are districts which bear the marks of multiple deprivation, which may show itself, for example, by way of notable deficiencies in the physical environment, particularly in housing; overcrowding of houses; family sizes above the average; persistent unemployment; a high proportion of children in trouble or in need of care; or a combination of these. A substantial degree of immigrant settlement would also be an important factor, though not the only factor, in determining the existence of special social need.[47]

In the first phase of the programme, resources (totalling £3½ million) were concentrated on the expansion and improvement of nursery schools and classes, day nurseries and children's homes. Phase two (1969–70) was wider in scope and resources. Though the main emphasis continued to be on the education and care of young children, the 450 projects approved (for 89 local authorities) also included community centres, family advice centres, hostels for the homeless, a day centre for the elderly, language classes for immigrants, rehabilitation of the mentally disordered, a centre for unattached youngsters, and an experimental project for the rehabilitation of methylated-spirit drinkers.

The total provision for the Urban Programme in England and Wales over the period 1968 to 1972 was £20–25 million. In May 1970, a further £35–40 million was allocated for the four years 1972 to 1976.

Under the third phase of the Programme announced in January 1971, expenditure amounting to £4·8 million was approved for projects both of a capital and a non-capital nature. The kind of work undertaken in this round was more diverse than before, and extended to Housing Aid Centres and extra facilities for General Improvement Areas. Increasing emphasis was given to aid for voluntary organizations.

In August 1971 £450,000 was approved for non-capital schemes providing a wide range of community-oriented facilities, such as play provision, family welfare and housing advice. Aid to voluntary bodies again figured prominently in the allocation.

An additional £6·1 million was made available for capital projects in intermediate and development areas in July 1971, as part of the

Government's infrastructure programme of public works. The types of schemes subsequently approved included such things as community centres, care of the aged and provision for children aged 0–5.

Urban Programme funds are also used to finance the Community Development Project. This is a neighbourhood-based action research experiment, carried out in twelve selected urban localities, with a central research team directed by Professor Greve. It is aimed at 'finding new ways of meeting the needs of people living in areas of high social deprivation, by bringing together the work of all the social services under the leadership of a special project team, and also by tapping resources of self-help and mutual aid which may exist among the people themselves'. The project teams work within a local authority framework and each is supported by a research team appointed by a university.

Unfortunately—in marked contrast to the American situation—there is incredibly little documentation available on the scope, objectives or operation of the British programmes. Though a significant number of academic research workers are associated with them (and monitoring and evaluation is an important explicit element), there is an almost complete absence of writing on the programmes. Little by way of independent comment is, therefore, possible.[48]

This lack of information is characteristic of much of British government, a matter to which we return in the final chapter. Its importance lies not in the difficulties it presents to writers of social commentaries, but in the obstacles it places in the way of informed public debate and public acceptance and support. The development of adequate social policies is dependent upon this support. Without it, crucially important measures may fail—as has happened with family allowances [49] and (in a very different field) with policies aimed at solving the problems of compensation and betterment.[50] It is not without good reason that two eloquent testaments to the inadequacy of social policies should both include the term 'forgotten' in their titles—*The Forgotten People* [51] and *Poverty: The Forgotten Englishmen*.[52] Forgetfulness, ignorance and avoidance may be temporarily comfortable, but in the long run they are incompatible with responsible democratic government.

This rapid review demonstrates the enormously wide range of issues that are relevant to the causes and cures of poverty. Marc Fried has written:

Poverty is an empirical category, not a conceptual entity, and it represents congeries of unrelated problems, unemployment and

33

under-employment, the condition of the aged, the situation of the Negro, the consequences of physical illness, inadequacies in welfare policy and migration, inadequate preparation for the urban environment, changes in agriculture, and the deterioration of rural areas. The problems posed by poverty are not readily accessible for study or resolution in the name of poverty. Like psychiatric disorder, poverty is a social fact that requires explanation. It can serve as an entry into a set of issues which may be examined and changed.[53]

This is precisely the function of this chapter: to serve as an introduction to selected specific issues which are discussed at length in the following chapters. This discussion will underline what experience has clearly demonstrated: that generalist policies aimed at providing equality of opportunity for all are not enough. Increasingly, attention is being focused on methods of 'positive discrimination' in favour of geographical areas of multiple deprivation, thus implicitly accepting the view that 'territorial justice is a prerequisite for social justice'.[54] To this theme we return in the chapter on Social Planning. First, however, we embark on an extended discussion of housing, slum clearance and improvement, and race.[55]

References and Further Reading

1. See P. Townsend, 'Measures and Explorations of Poverty in High Income and Low Income Countries: The Problems of Operationalizing the Concepts of Development Class and Poverty', in *The Concept of Poverty: Working Papers on Methods of Investigation and Life-Styles of the Poor in Different Countries*, edited by P. Townsend, Heinemann, 1970.

2. 'The United States Social Security Administration measure of poverty is of greater purchasing value than the United Kingdom "national assistance" standard but has an approximately similar relationship to average wage levels. Both standards represent very much higher living standards than those experienced by the mass of populations of the poorest developing countries. When measures of poverty are devised for the populations of these countries they are sometimes found to represent higher standards of living than can be secured by *average* wage rates. For example, Professor E. Batson, Director of the School of Social Science and Social Administration, University of Cape Town, devised a Poverty Datum Line which furnished "the barest minimum upon which subsistence and health can theoretically be achieved". When applied at the time to Kenya and Tanganyika it was found to be higher than average wages.' Townsend comments on this as an example of 'the misapplication of Western standards of need to the deprived nations: there are few reliable studies of the components of living standards. Standards of need tend to be unrealistic and lack a consistent theoretical perspective. They are not worked out in relation to the nations to which they are

applied. Rarely in agricultural societies are non-monetary resources adequately investigated and assessed. We must conclude that two standards of poverty are required, "national-relational" and "world-relational" . . .' (ibid., p. 13). Townsend thus distinguishes between the poverty of deprived nations and the poverty within nations. But note: 'A wealthy society which deprives a poor country of resources may simultaneously deprive its own poor classes through maldistribution of those additional resources' (ibid., p. 42).

3. P. Townsend, 'The Meaning of Poverty', *British Journal of Sociology*, September 1962, p. 225.

4. Alvin L. Schorr, *Poor Kids*, Basic Books, 1966, pp. 89–90.

5. The phrase is from Lee Rainwater, *Behind Ghetto Walls*, Allen Lane The Penguin Press, 1971, p. 400.

6. See R. M. Titmuss, 'Universal and Selective Social Services' in *Commitment to Welfare*, Allen & Unwin, 1968, Chapter 10.

7. It was one of the three assumptions which Beveridge declared as being essential to a satisfactory scheme of social security. The three were:

(a) Children's allowances for children up to the age of 15 or if in full time education up to the age of 16;

(b) Comprehensive health and rehabilitation services for prevention and cure of disease and restoration of capacity for work, available to all members of the community;

(c) Maintenance of employment, that is to say avoidance of mass unemployment.

Social Insurance and Allied Services: Report by Sir William Beveridge, Cmd. 6404, HMSO, 1942, p. 120.

8. See Volume I, Chapter 2.

9. Cf. H. Gans, *People and Plans*, Basic Books, 1968, p. 281: 'Ultimately, then, most of the problems of the poor can be traced to unemployment and underemployment, and these in turn are largely responsible for bringing about the crisis of the city.'

10. But see T. Gould and J. Kenyon, *Stories from the Dole Queue*, Maurice Temple Smith, 1972.

11. See, for example, H. Gans, loc. cit.; E. Liebow, *Tally's Corner* (English Edition), Routledge, 1967, especially Chapter 2; W. R. Thompson, *A Preface to Urban Economics*, Johns Hopkins, 1965, especially Chapter 6; etc. No British author could say that 'the analysis of poverty in the cities always begins with the study of the cities' employment characteristics', as does Oscar Ornati, 'Poverty in the Cities' in H. S. Perloff and L. Wingo, *Issues in Urban Economics*, Johns Hopkins Press, 1968, p. 349; see also O. Ornati, *Poverty Amid Affluence*, Twentieth Century Fund, 1966.

12. The phrase is from Daniel Moynihan, 'Poverty in Cities' in L. Loewenstein, *Urban Studies*, Free Press, 1971, p. 193.

13. Ibid., p. 194.

14. T. Gladwin, *Poverty U.S.A.*, Little, Brown & Co., 1967, pp. 138–139.

15. O. Ornati, 'Poverty in the Cities', in *Issues in Urban Economics*, 1968, p. 351.

16. See B. Abel-Smith and P. Townsend, *The Poor and the Poorest*, Bell, 1965.

17. National Board for Prices and Incomes, Report No. 169, *General Problems of Low Pay*, Cmnd. 4648, HMSO, 1971, p. 21. (The quotation continues: 'though there is some evidence that workers in certain low-paid industries have been faring less well than others very recently, despite pay increases which have been high by past standards'.)

18. See particularly: Report No. 166, *Pay and Conditions of Service of Ancillary Workers in the National Health Service*, Cmnd. 4644, HMSO, 1971; Report No. 167, *The Pay and Conditions of Workers in the Laundry and Dry Cleaning Industry*, Cmnd. 4647, HMSO, 1971; Report No. 168, *Pay and Conditions in the Contract Cleaning Trade*, Cmnd. 4637, HMSO, 1971; Report No. 169, *General Problems of Low Pay*, Cmnd. 4648, HMSO, 1971.

19. Department of Employment and Productivity, *A National Minimum Wage: An Enquiry*, HMSO, 1969.

20. *General Problems of Low Pay*, op. cit., p. 43.

21. See T. Lynes, 'The Failure of Selectivity' in D. Bull (ed.), *Family Poverty*, Duckworth, 1971.

22. *Family Income Supplement Bill, 1970, Financial Memorandum*, HMSO, 1970.

23. See Chapter 2.

24. See D. Barker, 'The Family Income Supplement' in D. Bull (ed.), *Family Poverty*, op. cit.

25. In truth, little is known of the disincentive effects of equalizing policies: see C. V. Brown, 'Negative Income Tax and the Incentive to Work', *New Society*, 1 June 1972, pp. 461–463.

26. A. Christopher and others, *Policy for Poverty: A Study of the Urgency of Reform in Social Benefits and of the Advantages and Limitations of a Reverse Income Tax in Replacement of the Existing Structure of State Benefits*, IEA, 1970. For a general discussion on schemes involving some kind of reverse income tax see D. Barker, 'Negative Income Tax' in D. Bull, *Family Poverty*, op. cit.

27. See White Paper, *National Superannuation and Social Insurance*, Cmnd. 3883, HMSO, 1969, and R. M. Titmuss, 'Universal and Selective Social Services' in *Commitment to Welfare*, Allen & Unwin, 1968, pp. 113–123.

28. United States Department of Labor, *Manpower Report of the President 1971*, U.S. Government Printing Office, 1971, p. 91.

29. T. Gladwin, *Poverty U.S.A.*, Little, Brown & Co., 1967, pp. 76–77.

30. See D. P. Moynihan, *Maximum Feasible Misunderstanding*, Free Press, 1969 (Chapter 8), and L. Rainwater and W. Yancey, *The Moynihan Report and the Politics of Controversy*, MIT Press, 1967.

31. L. Rainwater, *Behind Ghetto Walls*, Allen Lane The Penguin Press, 1970, p. 403.

32. Social Science Research Council, *Research on Poverty*, Heinemann, 1968. The chairman of this Panel was D. V. Donnison. The present author was a member. For a different type of categorization see A. Sinfield, 'Poverty Rediscovered', *Race*, Vol. X, No. 2, October 1968, pp. 202–209, reproduced with amendments as Chapter 7 of Volume III of this series.

33. *Social Insurance and Allied Services*, op. cit., p. 158.

34. *Report of the Inter-Department Committee on the Rehabilitation and Resettlement of Disabled Persons* (Tomlinson Report), Cmd. 6415, HMSO, 1943. See also *Report of the Committee of Inquiry on the Rehabilitation, Training and Resettlement of Disabled Persons* (Piercy Report), Cmd. 9883, HMSO, 1956; and Department of Employment, *Services for the Disabled*, HMSO, 1971.

35. It is illustrative of the problems of organizing effective programmes that the official circular to local authorities on this Act was issued jointly by four Ministries: *The Chronically Sick and Disabled Persons Act, 1970*, Department of Health and Social Security Circular 12/70, Department of Education and Science Circular 13/70, Ministry of Housing and Local Government Circular 65/70, Ministry of Transport Circular Roads No. 20/70, HMSO, 1970.

THE DIMENSIONS OF POVERTY

36. Office of Population Censuses and Surveys, Social Survey Division: A. I. Harris, *Handicapped and Impaired in Great Britain* (Part I); and J. R. Buckle, *Work and Housing of Impaired Persons in Great Britain* (Part II), HMSO, 2 vols., 1971.

37. See, for example, A. F. Philp, *Family Failure*, Faber, 1963; H. Wilson, *Delinquency and Child Neglect*, Allen & Unwin, 1962; D. Marsden, *Mothers Alone: Poverty and the Fatherless Family*, Allen Lane The Penguin Press, 1969; M. Wynn, *Fatherless Families*, Michael Joseph, 1964.

38. See, D.H.S.S., *Better Services for the Mentally Handicapped*, Cmnd. 4683, HMSO, 1971.

39. For a recent restatement in relation to family poverty see M. Wynn, *Family Policy*, Michael Joseph, 1970. See also H. Land, *Large Families in London*, Bell, 1970.

40. For an interesting discussion on the 'failure of political communication' on this issue, see J. Walley, 'Children's Allowances: An Economic and Social Necessity' in D. Bull, *Family Poverty*, Duckworth, 1971.

41. See, for example, F. Lafitte, *Family Planning in the Sixties* (Report of the Family Planning Association Working Party), FPA, 1963.

42. See V. Klein, *Britain's Married Women Workers*, Routledge 1965; C. E. Arregger (editor), *Graduate Women at Work*, Oriel, 1966.

43. See S. Yudkin, *A Report on the Care of Pre-School Children*, National Society of Children's Nurseries, 1967.

44. See Chapter 2.

45. Particularly the Plowden Report: see Chapter 5 below.

46. D. P. Moynihan, *Maximum Feasible Misunderstanding*, Free Press, 1969. See also P. Morris and M. Rein, *Dilemmas of Social Reform*, Routledge, 1968.

47. Joint Circular from the Home Office (Circular 225/68), Department of Education and Science (Circular 19/68) and Ministry of Health (Circular 35/68), *Urban Programme*, 4 October 1968.

48. Apart from some mimeographed documents of the Home Office, a number of circulars and a scanty reference in the Annual Reports of the Department of Health and Social Security, there is an unpublished paper by A. H. Halsey (presented to the Social Administration Conference in 1969) and a critical review by Robert Holman in his 'Combating Social Deprivation' (R. Holman *et al.*, *Socially Deprived Families in Britain*, Bedford Square Press, 1970, p. 174 *et seq.*) Such traditional modesty seems peculiarly inappropriate to programmes of this kind.

49. See note 40.

50. See Chapter 5 of Volume I.

51. N. S. Power, *The Forgotten People: A Challenge to a Caring Community*, Arthur James, 1965.

52. K. Coates and R. Silburn, *Poverty: The Forgotten Englishmen*, Penguin Books, 1970.

53. M. Fried, 'Social Differences in Mental Health, in J. Kosa, A. Antonovsky and I. K. Zola, *Poverty and Health: A Sociological Analysis*, Harvard U.P., 1969, p. 149.

54. M. J. Hill and R. M. Issacharoff, *Community Action and Race Relations*, Oxford University Press, 1971, p. 289.

55. Since this chapter was written a valuable book of readings has been published in the Penguin Modern Sociology Readings series: J. L. Roach and J. K. Roach, *Poverty*, Penguin Books, 1972.

Chapter 2

Housing

The distinguishing feature of social policy is that the distribution of the goods and services to which it relates is determined on the basis of an assessment of social need, rather than as a result of market forces. There may be income-related rules of eligibility and charges based on politically determined judgements of 'ability to pay'. In practice, these can introduce an important market element. Nevertheless, in principle, social services are essentially social responses to 'need' as distinct from market responses to 'demand'.

However, in many fields in which social services are provided, a 'private' sector operates. It may be small, as with health and education, or it may be large, as with pensions and housing. Where it is large, policies in relation to the public sector involve, at the least, assumptions about the activities of the private sector. More typically, they involve explicit policies to stimulate, restrain or control the private sector. With private pension schemes, for example, tax reliefs act as a stimulant, while statutory rules relating to the preservation of pension rights act as a control. In this case, current policy is to bring about 'a clear separation of functions. There will be a basic scheme run by the State and of which all employees will be members. On top of this, additional pension provision will come primarily from occupational schemes but there will be a State reserve scheme, separately financed, for the minority without adequate cover.'[1]

By contrast, where the private sector is small, social policy aims at providing a 'comprehensive' public service, as with health and education. Here, policies in relation to the private sector may be non-existent or insignificant: even tax reliefs may be refused.

In practice, simple classifications of this type are subject to numerous qualifications,[2] but the broad distinction is clear. It is also clear that housing is very different from either. Almost a third of the total stock of housing in Britain (and over a half in Scotland) is owned and managed by public authorities. This accommodation is available to all 'in need' (in accordance with the priorities laid down

38

and the rules of eligibility operated by 1,500 separate housing authorities). It is not reserved (unlike the position in the United States) for those with low incomes. To a significant extent public authority housing is an *alternative* to private housing, and households may move from one sector to the other according to their need or aspirations or because of local housing market factors.

Public provision is thus neither comprehensive nor insignificant (though in particular localities 'extreme' cases of both may be found). It follows that policies in relation to the public sector can have important implications for the private sector—and vice versa. For example, a policy aimed at relating rents more closely to the 'needs' of individual tenants may imply not only lower rents for poorer households but higher rents for richer households. Such differentials in rent may encourage better-off tenants to purchase their own houses, thus reducing the demand for public housing and increasing it for private housing. This may, indeed, be an intended consequence. It should be noted, however, that the same consequences could follow from a policy designed to raise standards (and thus costs) in the public sector while leaving the private sector to determine its own standards at the market level. In both cases, nevertheless, the amount of financial benefit received by a given household could increase on moving to an owner-occupied house if tax reliefs are more generous than direct subsidies.

This inter-relationship between different sectors is very marked in housing. It is further complicated by the large number of issues which are relevant to housing policy and to housing market behaviour. Subsidies, tax-reliefs, statutory minimum standards, systems of amortization, deposits, eligibility rules for mortgages and for council houses, improvement grants, property taxes (rates), rent rebates and allowances, rent controls, security of tenure, slum clearance procedures, building trade practices, land controls, restraint of urban growth, regional development: a complete list of relevant issues would be very long. Some of them may not normally be regarded as being appropriately labelled 'housing' issues, but this does not lessen their significance. (As a contrary point, some housing policies may, in fact, be a function of other policies: it may be politically easier for a government to avoid direct controls over land prices by increasing housing subsidies. Similarly it may seek to restrain wage increases by the same 'housing policy'.)

In no field more than housing is there such a multiplicity of possible objectives and such a wide range of techniques available for meeting them. One important implication of this is that the potential for conflict between different housing policies is large—much to the embarrassment of successive governments. Professor Donnison has deftly illustrated this:

> A policy of housing those in most urgent need may conflict with a policy of replacing the worst houses, and both may conflict with a policy for stimulating demand through subsidies directed to those who are most likely to be persuaded by such help to build or buy homes for themselves: different people will benefit from the pursuit of each of these objectives. An attempt to keep pace with the housing needs of expanding industrial centres may conflict with an attempt to revive poverty stricken regions. A policy designed to improve productivity in the building industry may not be best suited for eliminating unemployment in the building trades. A policy designed to eliminate rent controls and create a 'free market' in housing may conflict with the need to avoid inflation of living costs and wages. Every country's housing policies contain the seeds of several such conflicts, for housing is so central a feature of the economy and the way of life it supports that many of the competing aspirations at work in society gain some expression in this field.[3]

In stressing the centrality of housing to such a wide range of issues, however, sight should not be lost of some fundamental characteristics of housing which make it of intrinsic importance for social policy.

THE SPECIAL CHARACTERISTICS OF HOUSING [4]

Three major features characterize housing: its high cost, its durability and its immobility.

Compared with other goods, housing is extremely costly. The current capital cost of a new (three bedroom semi-detached) house in Britain fluctuates around three times the median annual income.[5] As a result, financial mechanisms are necessary to allow this cost to be spread over a long period. This involves an intermediary institution between the producers and consumers of housing. There is a large number of possibilities here, but essentially the intermediary fulfils the function of paying the producer the capital costs and carrying this cost in return for the payment of interest. Two major types of finance are possible. As with television sets, a house can be made available either on simple hire (renting from a landlord) or on hire purchase (buying with a loan from a building society). Given free market conditions, investment in rental housing is dependent upon a rate of return which is competitive with other investments. Demand for rental housing is dependent in part upon the relative cost of buying and the ease with which loans for purchase can be obtained.

Many institutional factors are of crucial importance: for example, taxes and tax reliefs, subsidies (overt and hidden), rent controls and the imposition of minimum standards. Typically, they operate differently in relation to the two sectors. Rent control (at the least) undermines confidence in the private rental market. Tax reliefs on mortgage interest without equivalent reliefs for renters tend to increase the attractiveness of house purchase, as does (less obviously) a system of taxation which ignores the 'income' derived by a house owner by virtue of his ownership. (A person who invests money in buying his own home pays no tax on the imputed income, but if he rents a house and invests his money in shares he gets no tax allowance for his rent payments and pays tax on the dividends he receives on the shares.) Inflation also adds to the attractions of home ownership and (since rents are 'sticky' even if there are no rent controls) reduces the attraction of investment in rental housing. Direct subsidies, of course, have an impact closely related to the form in which they are given. If they are granted only to certain types of owner (e.g. public authorities and non-profit organizations) they will obviously favour the production of dwellings by these owners. If, on the other hand, they are given to households, they may be 'neutral' in this respect. As will be shown later, the British system is highly complex: a result of history rather than design.

Part of the high cost of housing is due to the minimum standards which are imposed by the State. The justification for these is partly social and partly economic. Rising standards of health and convenience have the effect of raising the minimum standard which is socially acceptable. The extreme durability of houses is also highly relevant. Though the life of houses may differ according to standards of construction, design, maintenance, the tempo of economic and social change, and a host of other factors [6] they are generally regarded, in Europe at least, as items of capital investment destined to last for several generations. (Attempts to design short-life houses at low cost have not proved successful: costs have typically been high and lives much longer than envisaged.)

As a result, the standard of new housing (and the standard of up-keep of old housing) is of concern to future generations as well as the one for which the houses are initially provided. What is regarded currently as a socially acceptable housing standard or a market standard may well be considered inadequate for future needs. This line of thought should not be pressed too far: the future can be under- as well as over-discounted. Nevertheless, it is here that another peculiar feature of housing assumes particular importance: the fact that houses are (generally) located in a fixed position on land. In other words, a house cannot be considered in the same way as most economic goods since it is immobile in itself and (until it is demolished) determines the physical use of the land on which it is situated. Thus, when assessing future needs, the question is not merely whether new houses are of an adequate construction (which can be decided on the basis of a broad estimate of life), but also whether they provide sufficient space both within and outside for future demands. Future space needs within a house are difficult to predict in spite of the common assumption that houses will need to be bigger to accommodate the increasing numbers of possessions future households may be expected to have. (Relevant factors here are the future size distribution of households, the rate at which the very young and the elderly form separate households, the amount of residential mobility, the growth of secondary dwellings, and so forth.) Future space needs outside a house can (on current indications) be expected to increase as private car ownership increases.[7] Thus a significant aspect of policy (even if termed 'planning' rather than 'housing' policy) which can affect the supply and cost of housing is the insistence on a level of density or a type of layout which will accommodate an expected future increase in the ownership and use of cars. Some English local planning authorities are currently insisting that all new dwellings shall have at least one car space: since these authorities are generally situated in the more affluent areas of the country, where car-ownership is comparatively high but where land costs are likewise high, the effect can be a significant increase in the cost of new housing.

The question of future needs and standards is complex, but clearly it is one which, given the long life of houses, falls within the scope of government responsibility. Politically, it may be difficult to impose standards based on future needs if these are very markedly different from the standard of existing housing. Added point is given to this when the new standards involve financial costs which have the effect of further increasing the proportion of households who are unable to meet the full economic cost of housing. A balance has to be struck between the standards required for future needs and those which can currently be afforded. If the standards are set only slightly above the existing level the houses will become obsolete rapidly, but if the standard is set too high the gap between costs and rent-paying capacity may be unbridgeable. Basically, however, the issue is the same as that which was raised when minimum standards of sanitation were introduced in the nineteenth century. If the State imposes standards which involve costs greater than can be borne by lower-income groups it must accept the further responsibility for ensuring that these costs are met in some other way.

Similar issues arise where, for 'non-housing' reasons, a particular costly type of housing development is required, for example in national parks, in remote areas, or on sites of high land cost. Again, a policy of restraining the growth of large cities will, in the absence of an equally effective policy restraining demand, have the effect of increasing housing costs, possibly to the level where lower income groups are forced to occupy—and over-occupy—houses at a standard well below that which is socially acceptable, or even be driven into institutional accommodation for the homeless.

As these illustrations show, government policies aimed at particular problems can create further problems, thus involving an extension of the area over which State responsibility is necessary. Nevertheless, State responsibility does not necessarily involve direct State provision. Indeed, even a cursory study of policies in Western Europe and the United States is sufficient to demonstrate that the techniques of direction, control, persuasion and encouragement are multitudinous.[8] While Britain has opted (to a significant extent because of historical factors) for a large publicly owned and managed housing sector, other countries have operated through 'voluntary' agencies or by way of incentives to providers and subsidies to households.

HOUSING TENURE

Great reliance has been placed in British housing policy on the direct provision of housing by public authorities—in the main, the local housing authorities, but also New Town Development Corporations and the Scottish Special Housing Association. At the end of 1970 some 5·7 million dwellings in Britain were publicly owned: forming 28 per cent of the total in England and Wales and 51 per cent in Scotland (an overall national average of 31 per cent). In 1971, new building was divided roughly 45 per cent public and 55 per cent private. Scotland differs markedly from England and Wales: in 1971, over 70 per cent of new building was in the public sector (the proportion in 1970 was over 80 per cent).

With this high rate of public authority building, the proportion which it constitutes of the total stock is steadily increasing: in England and Wales, from 12 per cent in 1947 to 25 per cent in 1961 and 28 per cent in 1970.

It follows, of course, that there has been a decline (at least in proportion) elsewhere. In fact, the decline has been confined to the privately rented sector and has been on a very large scale: from 61 per cent of the total (England and Wales) in 1947 to 31 per cent in 1961 and 15 per cent in 1970.

The stimulation of the public sector (by subsidies, exhortation and programmes) has been accompanied by a virtual neglect of the privately rented sector. The latter has been subject to stringent rent control and taxation policies. There has been virtually no private building for letting since the last war. Important implications flow from this, but before discussing these, the position in relation to the remaining sectors can be summarized.

The third main tenure sector is owner-occupied. This has increased from about a quarter just after the war to a half in 1970. This sector has been aided by easily available mortgage facilities and tax reliefs on mortgage repayments. Moreover, as living standards have risen (and as inflation in house prices has increased the advantages of owner-occupation) aspirations for home-ownership have increased. Another factor of significance here is that, despite the large growth in the public rented sector, the decline in the privately rented sector has been so great that the total proportion of dwellings for renting has declined.

Other sectors are statistically insignificant. Some 240,000 dwellings in England and Wales ($1\frac{1}{2}$ per cent) are in the ownership of housing associations and societies.[9] The contribution of this 'voluntary' housing movement has increased markedly in recent years, and *could* become significant in the future.

Furnished dwellings are frequently not separately identified statistically, but are included with the privately rented unfurnished dwellings. Again, numbers are small (around 200,000 dwellings—but over 500,000 households—in England and Wales). Nevertheless, this sector is of considerable importance in the housing market and is subject to much stress in the inner areas of the larger cities.[10]

The dwellings in these different sectors, and the households who live in them differ in some significant ways,[11] largely as a result of history. Public authority dwellings are of the highest 'standard'—as measured by plumbing facilities, 'fitness' and repairs needed, though owner-occupied dwellings tend to be larger. Privately rented dwellings are of the lowest amenity. History has again played a major role here: long periods of rent control have led to inadequate maintenance and improvement.

Public authority dwellings contain a fairly representative cross-section of the population except for an under-representation of those with the lowest and the highest incomes and a big proportion of large households. The privately rented sector contains a relatively high proportion of the elderly and the poorest households, while the owner-occupied sector is the most diverse—in part as a result of the large-scale transfer of previously rented dwellings to owner-occupiers.

PUBLIC SECTOR POLICIES

These are, of course, broad generalizations applying to the national average situation, and the position varies greatly between different areas. Nevertheless, there are certain general implications that warrant comment. Above all, the large growth in the public sector and the huge decline in the privately rented sector implies that the alternatives to a council house for those who are not able to buy a house are declining rapidly. Thus 'local authorities must take a wider responsibility for people who at one time would have been housed in the private sector'.[12]

The role of the public sector is thus changing, and its position is likely to change further as a result of the Housing Finance Bills currently (Winter 1971/72) passing through Parliament. Apart from recasting the form in which subsidies are provided for public authority housing, this legislation introduces mandatory rent rebates for local authority tenants and (much more innovatory) rent allowances for private tenants. This is a major change in the housing scene, though it is impossible to predict what its effects will be.

This change has been brought about by a desire to replace 'indiscriminate' subsidies by a system of subsidies directed towards relieving specific needs. At the same time, it attempts to bring about a greater rationality not only in the distribution of subsidies but also in the pattern of rents. Much of the debate is couched in terms of equity: the White Paper is entitled *Fair Deal for Housing*.[13] The language of the debate is interesting. The 'fair deal' is elaborated in terms of fairness for the public sector, fairness for the privately rented sector and 'a fairer choice between owning a house and renting one'. Whatever criticisms there may be of the policy, the vocabulary is superb.

The image presented by the White Paper and the Bills is of a comprehensive and rational approach to housing policy. Comprehensiveness, rationality and equity are the *leit-motifs*. Nevertheless, the furnished sector (acknowledged to be the most important arena for stress and injustice) and the owner-occupied sector (where tax reliefs are given on a principle quite contrary to that embodied in the rent rebate and rent allowance schemes) are totally absent from the new 'comprehensive' plan.

Of course, there is a limit to the extent to which the history of housing policies can be overturned at one fell swoop. Moreover— and this is a much more general point to which we shall return in the final chapter—governments like to impress their electorates (and to persuade themselves) that they are masters of the ship of state: in fact, they never are. Policy is essentially 'hope'—hope that the stated objectives will be achieved without any disastrous side effects. Yet, side effects there always are, even if they do not become apparent during the lifetime of a government; and later policies must deal with a situation in which these side effects *are* apparent.

British housing policy was conceived in the context of 'the health of towns' problem of the nineteenth century.[14] Minimum standards of housing were laid down as a means of safeguarding public health. As these became effective the gap between what working-class families could afford and the price of the new minimum-standard housing widened. As already indicated, this had to lead to subsidies: but how were subsidies to be allocated, and what would be their effect on market operations? No politically acceptable answers could be found to these questions until 1919 when, in the euphoric aftermath of the first war, they were carefully designed to give most help where it was needed.[15] The policy rested essentially on the proposition that if houses were built for heroes, they had to be provided at rents which the heroes could afford.[16] This proved unexpectedly costly and the particular subsidy scheme was abandoned; but once committed to the principle of attempting to ensure that housing was provided at a cost which people could afford, there was no going back. Subsidies in some form or other were here to stay. The objectives of subsidy policy have changed from time to time,[17] but they have become a permanent feature of the housing scene, and no comprehensive housing policy is possible which does not take into account both their current scale and the impact they have had over the last half-century.

The side effects have, of course, been very great. Nowhere are they more apparent than in Scotland where fifty years of housing subsidies have had the effect (along with other policies—or the absence of policies—in relation to private housing) of so widening the gap between the cost to the consumer of public and private housing that there is now a huge dependence on the public sector. As a result, other agencies—whether private or voluntary—are quite unable to assist in the provision of rented housing of a tolerable standard.

Scotland is an extreme case, but similar side effects are clearly to be seen in England and Wales. The policy of assisting families to move from the congested conurbations to new and expanding towns, for instance, has been made difficult to operate because of the side effects of rent policies. A major factor influencing rents in any particular area is the relative proportion of older public authority houses built at low historical cost. By 'pooling' the rents of these houses with those of newer ones, the general rent level may be considerably reduced. New and expanding towns typically have few older houses and thus their rents reflect high current costs. As a consequence a family moving to a new area is faced with a rent significantly higher than that charged by the local authority of the area from which they move.[18]

Similarly, voluntary housing associations (except in the case of the long-established bodies such as the Peabody, Sutton, Lewis and Guinness Trusts) seldom have a stock of older houses. Though they are eligible for the same Exchequer subsidies as local authorities, their rents have to cover current costs without the benefit of a low-cost 'pool'. As a consequence their rents are much higher than those of local authorities and they have great difficulty in providing dwellings at rents which lower-income families can afford.[19]

The new legislation is intended to resolve some of these conflicts. How far it will do so is problematic, since the complexities and inter-relationships in the housing system are not readily embraced in a single piece of legislation. Moreover, the research effort which preceded the formulation of the policy was puny. The legislation owes more to 'common sense' interpretations of the needs of the situation than to a thorough assessment of the dynamics of housing market behaviour. In this it follows a strong British tradition.

MANAGEMENT OF 'COMPREHENSIVE' POLICIES

There is much contemporary debate—and effort—on making policies 'comprehensive'. This can be seen in relation to water, pollution, the health services, the social work services, and so on. Attention is focused on providing a framework that will facilitate this. Noteworthy is the absence of discussion on how the new 'comprehensive' policies will work in practice. This is essentially a matter of management, on which we can usefully refer to the 1969 Central Housing Advisory Committee Report on *Council Housing: Purposes, Procedures and Priorities.*

This Report laid great stress on identifying local needs and ensuring that these were met—by some agency or other, not just the local authority. It was thus a far cry from the 1938 Report [20] which was so concerned with the prevention of bed-bugs and assisting necessitous tenants to obtain furniture—'the bare necessities of comfort at a price within their means'. Though this 1938 Report rejected the argument that council tenants would use their baths for storing coal, it held that good management involved a form of social education and should aim at 'teaching a new and inexperienced community to be housing minded'.

The emphasis in the 1969 Report on assessing local needs was a reflection of the fact that there is no longer a *national* housing shortage: instead there is a multiplicity of very different local and regional problems. The solution to these problems—even when they appear similar—can be worked out only on the basis of a thorough assessment of what the problems are and what local resources, skills and agencies are available.

Housing authorities have tended to operate like most British social services. They have 'set up shop' and sat behind the counter waiting for clients to come to them for help. They have then arranged their clients on a 'waiting list'. As a family's 'turn' comes up, their needs are catered for. But no account is taken of those who do not come to the counter, or what might be done for those who are 'waiting'. Indeed, certain important needs are sometimes explicitly rejected—single men, owner-occupiers and newcomers to the area, for example.

On this, the Report argued that the responsibilities of local housing authorities should extend far beyond providing for the needs of those who are actually to be housed by them: they should be looking for hidden needs, for needs which are not being met elsewhere and for needs which may arise in the future.

Had local authorities done this in the past, it is likely that we would not have the acute shortage which now exists of dwellings suitable for elderly households—who increased in number by more than $\frac{1}{2}$ million between 1961 and 1966 and now form about a quarter of all households.

Curiously, the attention which is currently being given to the needs of the elderly has been stimulated by the 'non-problem' of 'under-occupation'. This is worth a brief discussion [21] only because it is frequently viewed as a problem and because it is often thought that, if this could be 'solved', other needs could be met at the same time. Thus, it is argued that if those under-occupying large dwellings would change places with those overcrowding small dwellings, both groups would have their 'needs' met without the necessity for new building.

Such arguments, however, take no account of such factors as quality, price or location. More important, they ignore the fact that (accepting some arbitrary standard of the number of rooms 'needed' by households of different sizes) there is a major shortage of small dwellings. For example, while there were 7·8 million households in Britain in 1966 of one and two persons, there were less than $1\frac{1}{2}$ million dwellings with three or less rooms. The fact of the matter is that household size has changed dramatically in recent decades while dwelling size has not. As Hole and Pountney have put it: 'Despite a consistent trend towards a higher proportion of one and two person households since 1911, the housing stock over the same period has become increasingly concentrated on the five-room dwelling; smaller and larger dwellings are predominantly older and often obsolete. There is, thus, an increasing disjunction between household size and house size, and it is evident that market forces do not of themselves produce a suitable dwelling mix.'[22]

It could be argued that it should be one of the functions of local housing authorities to correct such market imbalances. In fact, however, the overwhelming preoccupation of local authorities with 'housing need' has involved them in adding to the imbalance. Elderly and single people have typically had a low priority for council housing, since their 'problem'—of too much space—has not been considered as urgent as the needs of those who have too little space.

Nevertheless, 'under-occupation' is considerably less in the public sector than it is in the private sectors: while the average number of persons per room in 1966 was 0·70 for council tenants, it was 0·52 for owner-occupiers, and 0·53 for tenants of privately rented unfurnished accommodation.

The objective of policy in this field should be to provide small dwellings in sufficient numbers to enable those who *wish* to move to them to do so: at present this device is simply not available on any significant scale. The increasing emphasis on providing for the elderly [23] (and, more recently, the single 'non-elderly')[24] is a reflection of this.

THE FUNCTION OF COUNCIL HOUSING

Despite its numerical importance, the function which council housing serves—or should serve—is by no means clear. Obviously, with over a quarter of the population living in council housing, its actual function is different today from what it was in the inter-war years. Indeed, the very scale of council housing makes it more difficult to identify or determine its functions:

In a very real sense the question of the priority to be attached to particularly needy groups of people has been confused by the very extensive role now played by local authorities in the total provision of housing. In the evidence we received from local authorities, attention was focused on their wide range of responsibilities and the categorization of housing need. Little thought was given to vulnerable groups living in the private sector on the implicit grounds that their problems received fair priority within general policies directed towards meeting housing needs.[25]

49

The enormous change in the overall tenure pattern of British housing was a major reason why the CHAC report maintained that local authorities should take a wider responsibility for people who at one time would have been housed in the private sector. This applies both to 'general' needs and to rehousing from clearance areas. Increasingly, provision has to be made for 'non-traditional' needs such as those of single people, students, young mobile workers, unmarried professionals, and all those who traditionally have lived in bed-sitter land. At the same time, more traditional needs must not be overlooked—particularly those of the large family, the low-income family and the homeless.

The CHAC Committee strongly supported the Seebohm recommendation that local authorities should 'take increased responsibility for housing the most vulnerable families'. In assessing need, they stated that account should be taken of two factors: the housing conditions in which a household was living and, secondly, the ability of the particular household to cope with those conditions.

> If priorities were based on such a system, a high priority for public rehousing would be for households in bad conditions with which they are unable to cope, and where the potential ability to improve their own situation is low. Households in bad conditions, but able to help themselves can be allocated council housing in turn or helped and advised on how to help themselves if there is likely to be a long wait for council housing due to local shortage.[26]

No recommendation of the Committee has been more widely misinterpreted than this. It has even been suggested that the logical end-result would be council estates forming ghettos of the poor and inadequate. This is nonsense. Indeed, another section of the Report states:

> We are not suggesting that more affluent council tenants should be evicted or that council housing should be reserved for the poor. There are social advantages in having a broad spectrum of social classes living in a community and we certainly would not wish to see an official encouragement to a policy of income segregation. Our point is simply that in allocating council houses local authorities should give particular attention to those with incomes which are low in relation to their needs.[27]

With over $5\frac{1}{2}$ million council houses, the notion of a low-income ghetto is ridiculous. (It could, of course, happen on particular estates but that is a very different issue, to which we return later.)[28]

On this line of argument, local housing authorities have a very particular responsibility in relation to the poor. This function of council housing has tended to be submerged in the totality of its large-scale operations. Unfortunately, the truth of the matter is that local housing authorities, like sound business enterprises, tend to reject 'poor risk' applicants: and, incredibly, social work departments often acquiesce in this. A quotation from Glastonbury's study of homelessness in South Wales and the West of England is illustrative. He reports a Children's Officer as saying:

I wouldn't expect the housing manager to find houses for unsatisfactory tenants just because they had been requested by the Welfare or Children's Department. It all depends on the causes of homelessness and who is to blame. You can't let these people jump the queue ahead of deserving tenants. Public opinion wouldn't stand for it. It's the length of time people have been on the waiting list and the standard of their previous tenancies that matters.[29]

Glastonbury entitles his book *Homeless Near a Thousand Homes* and he suggests that in many areas 'there were a few difficulties over the shortage of tenancies and a great many difficulties resulting from the attitudes of housing managers'.

Clearly the distinction between the deserving poor and the undeserving poor is still with us. However, the reference to public opinion is a valid one. Public opinion can be relied upon to support discrimination against the loafers, the dirty, the unmarried mother, the newcomer and the coloured. But it is the task of a public authority to lead public opinion on these matters—not to follow it. On the other hand, the leaders cannot get too far ahead of public opinion: they will lose their seats at the next election if they do.

It would, however, be a gross error to equate 'problem' families with the 'housing poor'. The latter are simply those in poor housing conditions who face difficulties in improving their situation. In pressure areas (above all in Inner London) this can give rise to homelessness: 'It is the lack of adequate and secure accommodation at rents that can be paid out of average and below-average earnings that renders most people homeless.'[30] However, the housing situation varies so significantly between different areas that generalizations are neither easy nor useful. What is clear is that local authorities need to know and understand the housing position of their areas if they are to devise intelligent and appropriate policies. It follows that whatever may be the function of council housing it is complementary to the functions of other housing providers in the same area, and that the responsibilities of local authorities extend well beyond the council house sector.

51

If local authorities are to have responsibility for the totality of the housing needs of their areas they will be concerned with far more than the provision of council houses: they will be ensuring that the demand is met for houses for purchase, for housing association accommodation, for furnished accommodation. Much of this provision can be made by agencies other than local authorities, and even where the actual house building is best undertaken by local authorities, ownership and management can often with benefit be transferred to others.

The reader will note a clear political judgement here, and it is appropriate to make it explicit: there are areas of the country where the scale of public ownership of housing is so large that questions must arise as to whether undesirable consequences follow. Quite apart from the important issue of the concentration of power (to which we return in the final chapter) there is the question of the effect of a very large public sector on private initiative. The position in Scotland is illustrative.

At present 50 per cent of the Scottish housing stock is publicly owned. In Clydeside the proportion is 61 per cent. On current trends, the Clydeside figure will rise to 75 per cent: in Glasgow it will top 80 per cent. Whatever problems have been solved by this scale of public activity (and the achievements are great) an unintended consequence has been the eclipse of private enterprise. As a result, public authorities have been compelled to do more and more in response to the huge and increasing dependence on them for the provision of decent housing.

The small scale of the owner-occupied sector implies a restricted market—one which is restricted even further by the differences in the price to the occupier of public authority and owner-occupied housing. Those moving into public authority housing in Clydeside pay on average substantially less than half those moving into owner-occupied housing. As more older housing is demolished this gap is likely to widen. Those who wish to buy will need to have an income sufficient for the purchase of a modern house and the filtering process will be stemmed. Filtering is a very important (though inadequately documented) feature of the housing market. A large proportion of recent house purchasers have moved from owner-occupied houses: by selling their existing house they are able to improve their housing standards. At the same time the houses which they vacate are made available for other households who are 'behind' them in the filtering process.

If the cheaper houses are demolished the scope for filtering is restricted. Yet, in Clydeside, a large proportion of these cheaper houses probably need to be demolished anyway: thus, it is not easy to see how the situation can be improved, at least in the short run. What is needed is an increase in the supply of cheap satisfactory houses for owner-occupation. One way of achieving this is by the sale of older public authority houses. Another alternative is the purchase and improvement of improvable old rented tenements, followed by sale to owner-occupiers.

'GRADING' OF COUNCIL TENANTS

The situation in Clydeside is perhaps an extreme one, but the general issue of the power of local housing authorities is not. In particular, the widespread practice of 'grading' tenants according to their suitability for particular standards of housing gives cause for concern. This was expressed (in appropriately diplomatic language) in the CHAC Report. The Committee had a 'feeling that there is a danger that applicants are graded according to an interpretation of their desert; some housing authorities took up a moralistic attitude towards applicants: the underlying philosophy seemed to be that council tenancies were to be given only to those who "deserved" them, and that the "most deserving" should get the best houses. Thus, unmarried mothers, cohabitees, "dirty" families and "transients" tended to be grouped together as "undesirable". Moral rectitude, social conformity, clean living and a "clean" rent book on occasion seemed to be essential qualifications for eligibility—at least for new houses.'[31]

As the Committee's work progressed, they were increasingly led to the view that grading was more related to the stock of housing than the stock of applicants:

We have found considerable variation not only in the extent to which local authorities 'grade' their tenants, but also in the reasons why grading is thought to be necessary. On a very limited scale the justification for grading is that some tenants will not take care of a new house: at the extreme they may wreck it. It would not be sound policy to allocate a high standard house to such an 'unsatisfactory tenant'. But such families are very few in number, though they pose problems for the local authority out of all proportion to their numbers. It is a far cry from allocating specially selected houses to 'unsatisfactory tenants' to grading all according to their 'fitness' for particular types of houses. We were struck by the simple fact that the approach of a number of local authorities to this seemed to vary according to the range of house types they had available. A local authority with a small range (e.g. all post-war houses) see no need for careful grading. On the other hand, a local authority with a great range tend to see a necessity for fine grading.[32]

What all this amounts to is that the bureaucracy of local housing administration has developed procedures for distributing the housing which it controls, and has tended to lose sight of its major objective: to provide for local housing needs. Fortunately, this attitude is beginning to crumble in the face of increasing consumer resistance— or what is known in housing circles (significantly) as the increasing 'choosiness' of council applicants. The implication is that local authorities need to review their housing stock and modernize (or even demolish) some of their 'less desirable' estates. However, the greater is the proportion of a local housing stock which is owned and managed by a local authority, the less sensitive they may be to such an approach. Instead (as can be seen in the 'harder line' being taken by a number of authorities) rules may be elaborated to provide less choice: 'Applicants who refuse to accept a dwelling on perimeter estates shall forego their priority and be relegated to a lower place on the list.'

The choice of housing should be the applicant's, not the local authority's; and the choice ought ideally to be one between houses of different standards and different rents. This is not a novel approach. Circular 41/67 of the Ministry of Housing and Local Government was based on this very principle: 'No family should be denied accommodation suited to its needs because of limited means, *but* tenants should so far as possible be offered a choice of accommodation at varying rent levels.'

The CHAC Committee agreed and went further, but rapidly got into very deep water, and lamely beat a retreat, leaving the issue with the excuse that it took them beyond their terms of reference.[33] The truth of the matter is that there is a very difficult problem of reconciling a policy of giving real choice with a policy of giving the maximum financial assistance for housing. The dilemma is underlined by an extreme example. If housing were provided 'free', there would be a big demand for the best, and allocation would have to be essentially a matter of 'housing management'. At the other extreme, if housing were to be entirely a matter of market economics, the best would be the most expensive and the quality of a family's housing would depend upon their income and the way they were willing and able to spend it.

Britain has a mixed system. The new Housing Finance Bills introduce a greater market element, but they retain a major social policy element. For example, a married couple with one child, with an income of £20 a week, would pay only £1·12 for a dwelling having a rent of £3·00 a week. If they move to a better dwelling the rent they pay goes up by only 40 per cent of the 'fair' rent (in Scotland, the 'standard' rent)—until the ceiling rebate of £6·50 is reached. This is certainly the right principle (whatever reservations there may be about the detailed way in which it is being operated).

Part of the problem of housing management arises from what might be called the 'waiting list philosophy'. This has two very serious shortcomings. First, it implies that the local housing authority is concerned only with those who want, apply for and are considered eligible for council housing. Those who want other types of housing (or housing which the council does not provide); those who do not apply (perhaps because they think it is 'a waste of time' to do so); and those who are rejected as ineligible are ignored. The local authority thus has little or no idea how far they are meeting the needs of their area and, even less, how far the needs of their area are being met by other agencies of housing provision. Secondly, it implies that the role of the local authority is to actively meet the needs only of those at the 'top' of their list: the rest must wait.

All this stems from the way in which public authority housing has developed in Britain. Rather than being responsible for surveying the total needs of their areas and for ensuring that sufficient provision is made by all the appropraite agencies, local authorities have been predominantly concerned with the building and management of houses for those whose needs they recognize. The CHAC Report highlights an alternative approach and the 'fair deal for housing' provides the beginning of a basis for this to be implemented. On previous experience it can be said with some degree of assurance that further changes will rapidly follow.

OWNER OCCUPATION

The three main 'private' sectors serve very differing functions, though since each encompasses a wide range of housing qualities any generalization needs qualification. The largest of these sectors is owner-occupied—comprising (at the end of 1970) some 9¼ million houses, or half of the total stock of houses in Britain. Over half of current house building is for owner-occupiers, though a significant proportion of owner-occupied housing is old and lacking 'amenities': for instance, around a million have no internal lavatory. Most of these older houses were formerly owned by private landlords. As owner-occupiers take over this legacy of a previous age, the tendency is for major improvements to be undertaken, particularly where the purchasers are young households. Improvement grants have been of significance here: between 1965 and 1971 over 450,000 owner-occupied houses were approved for such grants.

The increasing popularity of owner-occupation does not seem to have been checked by the inflation of house prices. This has been dramatic: the overall average purchase price of mortgaged properties in Britain rose from £3,175 in 1966 to £6,051 in the fourth quarter of 1971.[34] In the third quarter of 1971, the average mortgagor had an income of £2,228 and paid 2½ times this income for his house, with an average mortgage of £4,187 (representing 72·5 per cent of the average price of £5,772).

Most mortgages are taken out for a period of twenty to twenty-five years though, given the rate of movement of owner-occupiers, the average mortgage lasts only ten to fifteen years.

The attractions of owner-occupation are clear and, particularly in a period of inflation, tangible. House purchasers buy at current market prices: with inflation, values increase while repayments remain at an 'historical' level. Indeed, continued inflation has greatly facilitated the 'filtering-up' process: house owners have been able to sell their existing houses at the inflated price level and purchase better houses by using the monetary 'profit' to provide the required deposit. How long this can continue is uncertain. It could be that the inflation of house prices is considerably stimulated by the easy availability of loans. If this is, in fact, true, there could be a sudden halt to increasing prices. Certainly, any objective assessment of current demand is difficult to square with the apparent demand as reflected in increasing house prices.[35]

Some of the demand may be due to the increasing apprehension among council tenants about the likely effects of the Housing Finance legislation. Council house rents in England and Wales doubled between 1962 and 1971 [36] and, even if the fears expressed about a further doubling in the near future are exaggerated, there is no doubt that major increases can be anticipated in some areas, at least for the better-off tenants. Indeed, the movement of such tenants out of the council sector is one of the explicit political objectives of the new legislation. To assist this, new powers are provided to enable local authorities to pay legal expenses incurred by council tenants who purchase a house for owner-occupation.

Other pressures on house prices follow from large-scale slum clearance and redevelopment programmes (including the road programmes) which, while they 'abolish slums' also reduce the supply of low-cost houses for purchase. Also relevant are the generous grants available for house improvements (discussed in a later section) which, at least in some areas, have the effect of transferring low-cost houses to a much higher-cost market.

Again, restrictions of land supply are of significance, though how far the 69 per cent increase in the cost of private sector housing land between 1966 and 1971 [37] is due to these is difficult to assess.

Indeed, it must be admitted that housing economics is a poorly developed art, and that forces may be at work that are not currently understood. On some aspects (second dwellings for instance) there is little data available; on many, the paucity of data gives enormous scope for conjecture. Until more adequate information is available and subjected to rigorous analysis, little definite can be said in explanation of current trends.

Nevertheless, it is clear that (whatever the reasons) aspirations to house ownership are increasing. A quarter of a century ago an American author wrote:

The enjoyments that follow from being able to call a thing 'one's very own' are as tenuous and hard to detect as they are real. This clear plus-value placed on property ownership derives from such cultural heritages as our rural property traditions, our idealized doctrine of natural rights in which 'property right' stands forth in bold type, our great stress on privacy in family matters, and our middle-class emphasis on property as an index of status. Together they precipitate in the minds of many home-buying families an unquestioning attitude towards home ownership.[38]

More succinctly, an English White Paper of 1953 gave the official view of owner-occupation: 'Of all forms of saving this is one of the best. Of all forms of ownership this is one of the most satisfying to the individual and the most beneficial to the nation.'[39] In 1953 this was an overtly political view: it is no longer so. The 1971 White Paper, *Fair Deal for Housing*, waxed lyrically on the benefits of owner-occupation:

Home ownership is the most rewarding form of housing tenure. It satisfies a deep and natural desire on the part of the householder to have independent control of the home that shelters him and his family. It gives him the greatest possible security against price changes that threaten his ability to keep it. If the householder buys his house on mortgage, he builds up by steady saving, a capital asset for himself and his dependants. In this country the existence of a strong building society movement helps him to realize these advantages.

Evidence from numerous surveys confirms this. Tax reliefs, the option-mortgage scheme and the easy availability of mortgages has brought home ownership into the realm of possibility for increasing numbers of middle-income households. But, on the other hand, the inflation of house prices has worked in the opposite direction. Certainly this has made owner-occupation [40] an impossibility for lower-income families in places as diverse as London and Glasgow. There is a world of difference between the situation in these areas and in places like Nelson and Rawtenstall.[41]

Tax reliefs on mortgage interest payments may or may not be considered as 'subsidy': this is entirely a matter of definition. Nevertheless, they definitely reduce the cost of buying a house (and, for those who can afford it—the cost of buying a second house). Recognition of this came late, but it was clearly recognized when, under the option-mortgage scheme, house purchasers who were not eligible for tax reliefs were given benefits as if they were. All house purchasers are now eligible for a financial benefit irrespective of their income—though, in the nature of things, the more expensive the house the greater the benefit. Indeed, the astute have noted that it is of considerable financial benefit *not* to pay off a mortgage: a nice illustration of the unintended consequences of a policy.

When inflation is brought into account, an owner-occupier may find himself buying his house for nothing. His annual tax-relieved repayments can be less than the increase in the value of his property. It is unlikely, however, that this will affect the stereotyped view on the vast subsidies going to affluent council tenants, in spite of the fact that council rents increase year by year and that council tenants can never benefit from the increased value of their house when they move.

The abolition of Schedule A tax also brought great benefits to the owner-occupier. This highly popular measure constituted a severe penalty to renters. A man who rents his house and invests in shares is, of course, liable for tax on his dividends and receives no 'relief' on his rent payments; but, if he invests in his home, he escapes tax.

The financial encouragement to, and the financial advantages of, owner-occupation are thus very great—for those who can afford to buy and who pass the eligibility tests of the Building Societies.

The cost of these housing tax benefits is considerably greater than the cost of housing subsidies—though it is by no means easy to define cost in a useful or acceptable way.[42] Should the cost of the subsidies received by council tenants be the figure which appears in the National Accounts—or should it be the difference between their total rent payments and what their rent would be if it were at a market level, or a 'fair' level? There is no scientific answer to such questions:

like much else in this field the answers—and, indeed, the questions—
are very much a matter of politics.

Each of these financial aids to housing has developed separately.
The option-mortgage scheme was an attempt to bring some rationality into the aid given to owner-occupiers. How much further it will
be politically and administratively possible to go remains to be seen.
The current Housing Finance Bills studiously avoid reference to
owner-occupation. Their scope is restricted to rented housing (but
excluding the furnished sector). However, this itself represents a
notable change in thinking: the public and private sectors are to be
brought under a system which applies equally to both. It may be that
the next Housing Finance Bill will extend beyond the rented sector
and cover owner-occupiers; but this could be a long while ahead.

PRIVATE LANDLORDISM

Until the 1972 Housing Finance Bills, tenants of private landlords
were not eligible for rent allowances unless they lived in Birmingham
(where the local authority obtained local act powers to provide such
allowances financed from the general rate fund) or were eligible for
'supplementary benefits' (the current name for what was previously
called 'national assistance'). This major gap in housing policy has
made policies in relation to privately rented housing exceptionally
difficult to operate.

The major strand of policy has been an essentially negative one—
rent control. Introduced as a purely temporary measure in 1915, the
original justification was simple: rents were increasing in the abnormal
situation of a war when the economic response of increased supply
was not possible. Once the abnormal situation had passed we could
revert to the more normal market situation which, it was presumed,
had existed before the war; but normality in this sense was never
reached and so rent control became a permanent element of housing
policy.

Nevertheless, it was not viewed as a permanent element and, thus,
it was not designed to achieve any long-term housing objective. It was
simply assumed that when the housing situation reached some form
of normality it could be jettisoned. As a result, rents were kept at a
level too low for the proper maintenance of property, and problems of
accelerated deterioration were added to those facing other housing
policies.

Not until the Crossman Act of 1965 was any attempt made to
design a long-term policy for the private rental sector; and not until
the 1972 Housing Finance Bills was any explicit provision made for

59

assisting tenants who could not afford a 'fair' rent. Even then tenants of furnished dwellings were excluded.*

The opprobrium which attaches to the stereotypes of private landlordism has been a major factor constraining policy in relation to this once major housing sector. Such evidence as there is demonstrates that the stereotypes typically bear little relation to the truth. A study in Lancaster concluded that the typical landlord in the city was an old-age pensioner owning a single house of low value which had been acquired by inheritance.[43] Further studies have suggested that Lancaster is not very different from other areas.[44] Even in London, 60 per cent of landlords let only one dwelling (though these constitute only 14 per cent of lettings).[45] Nevertheless, in particular areas of 'housing stress', abuses of power by a minority of landlords (epitomized by the activities of the late Perec Rachman, which have added the word 'Rachmanism' to the English language) have been sufficiently numerous to force successive governments to increase and tighten controls over private landlordism. Necessary though these measures were to deal with a totally intolerable situation, they have further tarnished the image of the private landlord and have undoubtedly accelerated his decline. In April 1966 there were 3·4 million privately rented dwellings in Great Britain; by the end of 1970 the figure had fallen to 2·8 million.[46]

The implications of this for the public sector have already been discussed. There are, however, two issues which need discussion at this point: the effectiveness of the controls, and their side effects.

Evidence to the Francis Committee [47] and a recent study of homelessness in London [48] point to the ineffectiveness of measures designed to *control*. Current debate is centred on furnished lettings and the desirability of extending security of tenure (and, in a different context, rent allowances).[49] The essential issue, however, is whether private ownership of housing can be tolerated in areas of extreme housing stress. The Francis Committee expressed their belief that it was essential to preserve the stock of privately rented accommodation, since 'there is a limit to what local authorities can do in the stress areas'.[50] For this reason, they argued that further restrictions on landlords in these areas 'are not going to help in the least'. The position was graphically put by one local authority witness to the Milner Holland Committee who, in discussing controls over multi-occupation, said that they were 'creating a battlefield where the local authority cannot provide the ambulance service to take off the wounded'.[51]

---

* The furnished sector is discussed further in Chapter 4, p. 107.

Nevertheless, there is a case for these areas to be designated *areas of special control* where 'some authority might be set up, with responsibility for the whole area and armed with wide powers to control sales and lettings, to acquire property by agreement or compulsorily over the whole area or large parts of it, to demolish and rebuild as necessary, to require improvements to be carried out or undertake such improvements themselves, and to make grants on a more generous and flexible basis than under the existing law'.[52]

The increasing proportion of coloured people in these stress areas led the National Committee for Commonwealth Immigrants to take up this proposal, which they phrased in terms of designated *areas of special housing need.*[53]

No action has been taken on these proposals, though equally draconian powers are available—and widely used—when areas are required for 'clearance' and redevelopment.

It would, however, be misleading to give the impression that the problem of 'abuse' is representative of the privately rented sector. The majority of private tenants appear to be satisfied with their accommodation, its rent and the landlord.[54] Though apparently in irreversible decline, the private landlord still provides accommodation for 15 per cent of households. The dwellings are typically far from Parker Morris standards, but they are let at generally low rents to households whose incomes tend also to be low.[55]

Finally, a brief reference needs to be made to the side-effects of the controls over 'multi-occupation'.[56] A house in multiple occupation is now defined as one 'which is occupied by persons who do not form a single household'. Such houses are subject to a range of controls which are operated with varying degrees of stringency by different local authorities. At the extreme, a local authority can prohibit the sub-letting of rooms to students on the grounds that there are inadequate means of escape from fire, or inadequate separate plumbing facilities. As a result, in some university towns, the existing shortage of accommodation has been significantly exacerbated.

Unfortunately, the department of the local authority which is responsible for controlling multiple occupation is not the same as the one which is responsible for the provision of housing. Thus the former (the public health department) may be increasing a need for additional accommodation which the latter (the housing department) refuses to acknowledge. At the same time, slum clearance, redevelopment and housing improvements all tend to reduce the supply of suitable accommodation.

THE 'VOLUNTARY' SECTOR

'A reasonably safe generalization about British housing is that the range of choice open to a family in Britain seeking a modern house is more limited than is the case almost anywhere else in Europe.'[57] This has come about because of the decline in the privately rented sector, the concentration of policy on public authority housing and the highly developed facilities for owner-occupation. Other countries have operated 'social housing' policies through a variety of different agencies—trade unions, religious bodies and other 'voluntary' organizations,[58] or *ad hoc* semi-public authorities.[59] In Britain, a voluntary housing movement developed in the nineteenth century. Housing trusts proliferated in a number of the major urban areas, typically bearing edifying names such as the Society for the Improvement of the Condition of the Labouring Classes [60] and also producing a steady if modest profit on the capital invested.[61] But this early endeavour was superseded by the development of council housing after the first war and, though it has continued to develop slowly, it has not resulted in any significant contribution to total housing provision. At the end of 1970 only some 240,000 dwellings were owned by the various types of housing association—a mere 1·4 per cent of the total stock in England and Wales.

The main reason for this lack of development has been simply that successive governments have used local authorities as the main instrument of public policy. Though there is a considerable range of functions which housing associations can serve under housing legislation, the operation of these has been largely dependent upon the co-operation of local authorities. Thus associations have been eligible for Exchequer subsidies, but these are normally channelled through local authorities. As a result, the attitude of local authorities has been crucial to the development of local associations.

Many councils have looked upon associations as a 'fifth wheel to the local authority coach' or as an out-of-date and redundant form of housing provision. Or worse, they have been seen as an unnecessary competitor for scarce land or even as a means by which families are rehoused 'ahead of their turn.' Until the establishment of the Housing Corporation in 1964 the predominant source of capital for voluntary housing was the local authorities and thus voluntary bodies were dependent for both their capital and their subsidies on a 'rival' body. However, by no means have all local authorities been unco-operative. Some have been very willing to encourage and assist an 'alternative' form of housing provision. Most, nevertheless, have given assistance

62

only in return for rights of nomination of a certain proportion of (or, indeed, all) tenants.

This statutory and administrative framework has greatly retarded the growth of voluntary housing provision.[62] Further difficulties were created by land shortages and inflation with which an ill-developed movement was unable to cope. (Unlike local authorities, housing associations seldom have the ready capital to purchase land in advance of requirements; neither do they generally have a pool of older housing which can be instrumental—by way of rent increases—in cushioning new dwellings from the full effects of rising costs.)

Until recently, there was little effective pressure for change. The first change came in 1964 when the Housing Corporation was established with the specific task of stimulating (unsubsidized) cost rent and co-ownership developments by housing societies. The political impetus to this was the increasing concern for the needs (once met by the private rental market) which were not being met by the two major housing sectors—council and owner-occupied. A White Paper explained:

> Post-war building has almost all been either for owner-occupation or for letting by public authorities. Hardly any provision has been made for those—the younger salaried people and the higher wage-earners—who may not be able to buy a house on the ordinary mortgage terms, or who may prefer to rent, though neither wanting nor needing a council house. . . . Even allowing for easier mortgage terms, there will still be many people who want to rent a modern house and who are able to pay what it costs, but who are not attracted by ownership. Since the war there has been almost no building to let other than by public authorities. Fear of rent control, and of the problems associated with management, maintenance and repair, has discouraged private investment. The result is a gap in housing provision; and this the Governments intend to see filled.[63]

The aim was thus explicitly to meet effective demand in a limited band of the total housing market. The success was modest: by 31 March 1970, some 13,000 dwellings had been completed in Britain. The reasons for this small achievement are complex but stem essentially from the 'competition' from other forms of tenure which, given the statutory, administrative and financial framework are much better able to meet current demands and needs.

The new-style 'societies' (cost-rent and co-ownership) have not replaced the traditional bodies. These have continued to operate on a somewhat larger but nevertheless very modest scale.

The terminology in this field is confusing in the extreme. All voluntary bodies are loosely referred to as associations, but technically the cost-rent and co-ownership bodies are *societies*. Associations (even when called societies or trusts) have traditionally provided subsidized dwellings; societies operate without the benefit of a subsidy —though co-ownership societies benefit from the option mortgage scheme. All but the latter are forms of rental tenure. A co-ownership scheme is one in which all the 'members' are corporate owners of the whole scheme, with each member having the right to occupy one of the society's dwellings.

These (and many more) technicalities need not concern us here. The whole field was thoroughly reviewed by the Cohen Committee and, though the Committee was not able to bring its work to a successful conclusion, the evidence presented to it was summarized by DOE officials and published as a 'working paper'.[64] The dissension among the members of this Committee (which led to eventual disbandment) was not only the result of clashes of personality; it reflected a basic disagreement over whether or not the voluntary housing movement had a useful role to play.

So far there has been equivocal governmental reaction. The 1972 Housing Finance Bills provide for rent allowances to tenants of both traditional associations and cost-rent societies (but not for co-ownerships since they receive tax-reliefs under the option mortgage scheme). Associations will also receive the benefit of subsidies similar to those granted to local authorities.* Nevertheless, there has been little serious discussion (certainly at a political level) of the role which the voluntary housing movement might play. The White Paper of 1971 [65] merely states that: 'The voluntary housing movement holds a special place in the Government's housing policies. It makes a distinctive contribution to meeting people's housing needs. It can rely on the Government's continued encouragement and support.' No indication is given of what this 'special place' is. Yet, there is (at least in the opinion of the author) a clear case for a 'third arm' of housing provision.

To put the matter at its least, a housing market predominantly and increasingly divided into only two tenures presents little in the way of choice—particularly to those who fail, for one reason or another, to pass the eligibility tests of the managers of council houses and the managers of building societies. Though these two sectors can very

---

* The Bills are before Parliament at the time of writing (Winter 1971–72). Some very substantial amendments have been proposed by the Government which could significantly increase the future viability of the voluntary housing movement.

satisfactorily meet the needs of large sections of the population their position of power in a duopolistic market is unhealthy.

Moreover, there are needs which neither sector can easily meet, such as those of students, elderly people who wish to move to a retirement area or to the area in which their married children live, mobile young professionals and executives, ex-prisoners, migrant workers, and the family wanting temporary accommodation in a new area before deciding on a house to buy. Then again, there is a wide range of improvements, conversions and, on a wider scale, area re-habilitation to meet the needs of the present inhabitants (rather than the economic demand of higher-income families wishing to purchase older property for 'modernization' and 'gentrification').

There is also a potential (regarded with scepticism by many) for the development of co-operatives which could effectively 'combine the advantages of owner-occupation and tenancy, both in new housing and in existing property'.[67] In this connection, more studies assessing the successes (and failures) of existing co-ownership schemes are needed,[68] and further thought requires to be given to the ideas of Greve [69] and Nevitt [70] for the involvement of tenants in democratic management. Hopefully, these would lead towards the development of new forms of tenure which would not fit neatly into the current British classification.

It is a sad commentary on the British housing situation that the highly articulated debate on council tenancy *versus* owner-occupation claims virtually all the attention of politicians, and that it is held that a strong case has to be made out for any other alternatives.

References and Further Reading

1. See K. M. Slack, 'Social Administration Digest, 1 April to 31 August 1971', *Journal of Social Policy*, Vol. 1, No. 1, January 1972, p. 75.

2. There is a large literature on this but see in particular R. M. Titmuss, 'The Social Division of Welfare', in *Essays on The Welfare State*, Allen & Unwin, 1958.

3. D. V. Donnison, *The Government of Housing*, Penguin Books, 1967, p. 86.

4. This section is based on the discussion in Chapter XIII of the author's *Housing and Local Government*, Allen & Unwin, 1966.

5. The 1970 median weekly earnings of all full-time male workers in Great Britain was £29·80 (DEP New Earnings Survey, 1971, *DEP Gazette*, January 1972, p. 39). The average price of a new three-bedroom semi-detached house purchased on mortgage in England and Wales in 1970 was £4,300 (*Housing Statistics*, No. 23, November 1971, p. 71).

Since 1970 house prices have risen more rapidly than earnings. (For figures on house prices see Nationwide Building Society, *Occasional Bulletin 107*, February 1972.)

6. See Economic Commission for Europe, *Cost, Repetition and Maintenance: Related Aspects of Building Prices*, United Nations, 1963.

7. See Colin Buchanan & Partners, *The Prospect for Housing*, Nationwide Building Society, 1971.

8. See particularly D. V. Donnison, *The Government of Housing*, Penguin Books, 1967; also Economic Commission for Europe, *Financing of Housing in Europe*, United Nations, 1958; Economic Commission for Europe, *Major Long-Term Problems of Government Housing and Related Policies*, United Nations, 1966; and E. G. Howes, *Housing in Britain, France and Western Germany*, Planning Broadsheet, No. 490, PEP, 1965.

9. DOE, *Housing Associations: A Working Paper of the Central Housing Advisory Committee*, HMSO, 1971, p. 119.

10. See *Report of the Committee on Housing in Greater London* (Milner Holland Report), Cmnd. 2605, HMSO, 1965 and *Report of the Committee on the Rent Acts* (Francis Report), Cmnd. 4609, HMSO, 1971.

11. See J. B. Cullingworth, *English Housing Trends*, Bell, 1965; M. Woolf, *The Housing Survey in England and Wales*, Government Social Survey, 1967, and statistics from the House Condition Survey, England and Wales, 1967 in *Economic Trends*, No. 175, May 1968 and in the White Paper, *Old Houses into New Homes*, Cmnd. 3602, HMSO, 1968.

For Scotland, see J. B. Cullingworth, *Scottish Housing in 1965*, Government Social Survey 1967, and J. B. Cullingworth and C. J. Watson, *Housing in Clydeside 1970*, HMSO, 1971.

12. CHAC, *Council Housing: Purposes, Procedures and Priorities*, HMSO, 1969, para. 14.

13. Cmnd. 4728, HMSO, 1971. The Scottish White Paper is entitled *The Reform of Housing Finance in Scotland* (Cmnd. 4727, HMSO, 1971).

14. See W. Ashworth, *The Genesis of Modern British Town Planning*, Routledge, 1954.

15. See M. Bowley, *Housing and the State 1919–1944*, Allen & Unwin, 1945.

16. For a discussion of the attempts to introduce subsidies before the first war see P. Wilding, 'Towards Exchequer Subsidies for Housing 1906–1914', *Social and Economic Administration*, Vol. 6, No. 1, January 1972, pp. 3–18.

17. See M. Bowley, op. cit., and D. V. Donnison, *Housing Policy Since The War*, Occasional Papers on Social Administration, No. 1, Codicote Press, Welwyn, 1960.

18. See J. B. Cullingworth and V. A. Karn, *The Ownership and Management of Housing in the New Towns*, HMSO, 1968. For a discussion of council house rents see R. A. Parker, *The Rents of Council Houses*, Occasional Papers on Social Administration, No. 22, Bell, 1967.

19. For further discussion see DOE, *Housing Associations: A Working Paper of the Central Housing Advisory Committee*, HMSO, 1971.

20. CHAC, *The Management of Municipal Housing Estates*, HMSO, 1938.

21. For further discussion see W. V. Hole and M. T. Pountney, *Trends in Population, Housing and Occupancy Rates 1861–1961*, HMSO, 1971 and CHAC, *Council Housing: Purposes, Procedures and Priorities*, HMSO, 1969, pp. 6–11.

22. W. V. Hole and M. T. Pountney, ibid., p. 36.

23. Though care must be taken not to think of the 9 million 'elderly' as if they were a homogeneous group: see CHAC, op. cit., pp. 95–103.

24. See DOE, *Housing Single People*, Design Bulletin 23, HMSO, 1971.

25. CHAC, *Council Housing: Purposes, Procedures and Priorities*, HMSO, 1969, para. 53.

26. Ibid., para. 118.

27. Ibid., para. 56.

28. See Chapter 5.

29. B. Glastonbury, *Homeless Near A Thousand Homes: A Study of Homeless Families In South Wales and the West of England*, Allen & Unwin, 1971, p. 155.

30. J. Greve, D. Page and S. Greve, *Homelessness in London*, Scottish Academic Press, 1971, p. 247.

31. *Council Housing: Purposes, Procedures and Priorities*, op. cit., para. 96.

32. Ibid., para. 90.

33. Ibid., paras 92–95.

34. *Housing Statistics*, No. 24, February 1972, Table 50. Unless otherwise indicated all figures are taken from recent issues of this quarterly statistical publication.

35. A useful review is to be found in G. R. Vale, *Is The Housing Problem Solved? A Review of Recent Estimates*, Housing Centre Trust, 1971. See also, in particular, A. E. Holmans, 'A Forecast of Effective Demand for Housing in Great Britain in the 1970's', *Social Trends*, No. 1, 1970, HMSO, 1970.

36. *Housing Statistics*, No. 23, November 1971, p. 78.

37. Ibid., p. 75.

38. J. P. Dean, *Home Ownership: Is It Sound?*, Harper, 1945, p. 13.

39. *Houses—The Next Step*, Cmd. 8996, HMSO, 1953.

40. The reference is to owner-occupation of good quality housing. Significant numbers of 'recent buyers' in Clydeside paid less than £1,000 for their dwellings, but these were typically poor-quality tenemental properties; see J. B. Cullingworth and C. J. Watson, *Housing in Clydeside 1970*, HMSO, 1971, p. 25.

41. See DOE, *New Life in Old Towns*, HMSO, 1971.

42. See, for example, C. Crouch and M. Wolf, 'Inequality in Housing' in P. Townsend and N. Bosanquet, *Labour and Inequality*, Fabian Society, 1972.

43. J. B. Cullingworth, *Housing in Transition: A Case Study in the City of Lancaster 1958–1962*, Heinemann, 1963.

44. See MHLG, *The Deeplish Study*, HMSO, 1966, pp. 34–37; and J. Greve, *Private Landlords in England*, Occasional Papers on Social Administration No. 16, Bell, 1965.

45. *Report of the Committee on Housing in Greater London* (Milner Holland Report), Cmnd. 2605, HMSO, 1965, pp. 147–161 and Appendix V.

46. *Housing Statistics*, No. 21, May 1971, p. 70.

47. *Report of the Committee on the Rents Acts*, Cmnd. 4609, HMSO, 1971.

48. J. Greve, D. Page and S. Greve, *Homelessness in London*, Scottish Academic Press, 1971.

49. See, for example, M. Wicks, *Rent Allowances: The Exclusion of Furnished Tenancies*, Child Poverty Action Group, Housing Finance Bill, Discussion Paper 2, and D. Bebb, *Rent Rebates and the Furnished Tenant*, Shelter, 1972.

50. *Report of the Committee on the Rent Acts*, 1971, p. 212.

51. *Report of the Committee on Housing in Greater London*, 1965, p. 96.

52. Ibid., pp. 122–123. The Milner Holland Committee did not press the idea, but said that they 'favoured' it and thought 'it should be carefully examined' (see p. 228).

53. National Committee for Commonwealth Immigrants, *Areas of Special Housing Need*, 1967.

54. See *Report on the Tenants Survey, 1970*, published as an Appendix to the *Report of the Committee on the Rent Acts*, 1971, especially p. 293.

55. In 1969 the median annual household income in Great Britain was

£2,017 for owner-occupiers with a mortgage, £1,407 for local authority tenants, and £1,189 for tenants of privately rented unfurnished dwellings (*Housing Statistics*, No. 22, August 1971, p. 82). Unfortunately, statistics on rents are so deficient as to make it impossible to give meaningful averages. However, as a corrective to the impression created by constant references to London rents, the following figures, relating to privately rented unfurnished dwellings, taken from recent Conurbation Housing Surveys are illustrative:

West Midlands Conurbation, 1966, average annual *gross* rent—£110·00

West Yorkshire Conurbation, 1969, average annual *gross* rent—£77·00

Clydeside Conurbation, 1970, average annual rent: *gross*—£67·00; *net* £34·00.

56. For an outline of these see MHLG Circular 67/69, *Housing Act 1969: Houses in Multiple Occupation*, HMSO, 1969.

57. L. E. Waddilove, *Housing Associations*, PEP, 1962.

58. See, for example, J. Greve, *Voluntary Housing in Scandinavia: A Study of Denmark, Norway and Sweden*, Centre for Urban and Regional Studies, University of Birmingham, Occasional Paper No. 21, 1971.

59. See, for example, C. J. Watson, *Social Housing Policy in Belgium*, Centre for Urban and Regional Studies, University of Birmingham, Occasional Paper No. 19, 1971.

60. See J. Simon, *English Sanitary Institutions*, London, 1890.

61. See the discussion in W. Ashworth, *The Genesis of Modern British Town Planning*, Routledge, 1954, pp. 82–97, and D. Owen, *English Philanthropy 1660–1960*, Oxford University Press, 1965, Chapter 14, 'Philanthropy and Five Per Cent'.

62. See U. J. Stack, *The Development of a Housing Association*, Centre for Urban and Regional Studies, University of Birmingham, Occasional Paper No. 1, 1968.

63. White Paper, *Housing*, Cmnd. 2050, HMSO, 1963, p. 7.

64. DOE, *Housing Associations*, HMSO, 1971. See also National Federation of Housing Societies, *Housing to Let by Non-Profit Organisations: Planning for Tomorrow*, NFHS, 1971.

65. *Fair Deal for Housing*, Cmnd. 4728, HMSO, 1971, p. 16.

66. See Housing Centre, Report on the Conference on 'Housing's Third Arm', *Housing Review*, Vol. XI, May–June 1962, pp. 77–93.

67. D. V. Donnison, 'Housing Policy: What of the Future?', *Housing Review*, Vol. 14, No. 6, Nov.–Dec. 1965.

68. See D. Page (ed.), *Housing Associations: Three Surveys*, Centre for Urban and Regional Studies, University of Birmingham, Research Memorandum No. 7, 1971; and P. Bagot, *A Comparative Study of Three Forms of Housing Tenure*, Architectural Research Unit, University of Edinburgh, 1971.

69. J. Greve, *Voluntary Housing in Scandinavia*, op. cit., p. 85.

70. A. A. Nevitt, *Fair Deal for Householders*, Fabian Society, 1971.

Chapter 3

Slum Clearance and Improvement

PUBLIC POLICIES [1]

The assessment of housing conditions may better be undertaken by the novelist than by the statistician. The statistician can only manipulate figures of 'objective' indices such as persons per room, the absence of sanitary fittings and (less successfully) certain structural defects. He cannot measure the stresses and strains which families experience by living in inadequate housing. It has even been proved impossible to relate housing conditions convincingly to health.[2] Housing is only one element in the physical and social environment and it is unrealistic to try to isolate its influence.

Indeed, it may well be that traditional measures reflect middle-class attitudes of what 'decent' housing should be.[3] Nevertheless, policy is determined on the basis of available statistics and, though these may be inadequate in important ways, they are by no means without value.

In 1966, some $2\frac{1}{2}$ million households in Great Britain lacked exclusive use of a fixed bath, and 3·9 million were without exclusive use of an inside w.c.—the latter representing well over a fifth (22·8 per cent) of all households.[4] A 1967 house condition survey in England and Wales showed that a total of 1·8 million dwellings (12 per cent of the total) were statutorily 'unfit for human habitation'.[5] No strictly comparable figures are available for Scotland, but a national housing survey carried out in the same year [6] estimated a total of 151,000 dwellings (9 per cent) which were either unfit or had a life of less than five years. The 1970 Clydeside Survey [7] (using the new Scottish 'tolerable standard') [8] strongly indicates that this was a gross underestimate.

These figures reflect history. Britain (like France and Belgium) has a long history of industrialization. Most of the inadequate houses date from the period of nineteenth century urban growth. Virtually all the 'unfit' houses, for example, were built before 1919 (though unfitness should not be equated with age: 70 per cent of pre-1919 dwellings are not unfit). The contrast with Scandinavian countries, whose industrial revolutions came at a later stage when wealth was greater and standards higher, is marked.

69

As a result, British policies in relation to clearance and redevelopment are of long standing. Over a third of a million houses were demolished in the slum clearance programme of the thirties; by 1938 demolitions were running at the rate of 90,000 a year. Had it not been for the war, over a million older houses would (at this rate of progress) have been demolished by 1951. The war, however, not only delayed clearance programmes: it resulted in enforced neglect and deterioration. War damage, shortage of building resources and (of increasing importance in the period of post-war inflation) rent control increased the problem of old and inadequate housing.

It was not until the mid-fifties that clearance could generally be resumed: the absolute quantitative shortage was too great. Some 100,000 houses were cleared by the end of 1954. Since then (1955–71) 1¼ million houses have been demolished—a million in England and Wales and 250,000 in Scotland.

This represents a major achievement, though it has not been without its critics, particularly in relation to the large clearance schemes in the major cities. Della Nevitt, for instance, has complained:

Few people have any understanding of the chaos which has been caused in the London housing market by the 1957–72 slum clearance programmes . . . The operation has been carried out in a thoroughly haphazard and unco-ordinated manner, and the social pressures created culminated in angry campaigns of squatting. In the next decade it is essential that slum clearance should be fully co-ordinated with transport, employment and private house building plans. Every delay in co-ordinated development is automatically reflected in further pressures upon the very limited stock of conveniently sited existing houses, and appears automatically in rising house prices.[9]

There is a number of issues here which are frequently overlooked or given inadequate attention in the concentration of effort on the clearance of physically inadequate dwellings. One is the adequacy or otherwise of the new 'peripheral' developments which are needed to rehouse the 'overspill' from clearance areas: this is discussed in Chapter 5. Another is the impact on the housing market: a matter which has been of no apparent concern to local authorities who have acted on the assumption that the dwellings which they provide effectively 'replace' those which they demolish. Reference has already been made (in the previous chapter) to the necessity for local authorities to 'take a wider responsibility for people who at one time would have been housed in the private sector'. As clearance programmes continue to deplete this sector, this becomes increasingly important.

But this involves a very much greater understanding of the housing market and sensitivity in policy than has so far been evidenced. Moreover, it is questionable to what extent an increasing trend towards the municipalization of the housing provision in central and inner cities is desirable. However sensitive and liberal a local authority tries to be, it is unlikely to be able to meet all the categories of 'need' that are catered for in areas designated for clearance—even if the people concerned wish to become council tenants.

This is more than a plea for other agencies. (That is a separate issue.) It is a question of housing economics. Clearance and redevelopment involve not only the replacement of old houses by new ones: they also involve the substitution of expensive houses for cheap houses. The rapid erosion of the low-price housing market has ramifications throughout the whole housing market. The fact that little study of this has been undertaken is the result of a lack of interest on the part of academic economists and (a connected but less excusable reason) the lack of economic skills in government. (Until very recently the central department responsible for housing had *no* housing economists on its staff.)

Of course, not all clearance areas consist of 'low-price housing'. In the districts of inner London, for example, where housing pressures are intense, housing which (on any assessment) is of slum quality can be of very high price. Yet, in part at least, this can be the result of clearance in nearby areas. Furthermore, the inner London situation is not typical. (It is unfortunate that central policy is determined and legislation drafted in the area which is so untypical of the rest of the country.) [10]

Few studies of the effects of clearance have been undertaken and those that have are almost inevitably deficient in that they relate only to those who are rehoused; those who are not are difficult to trace. Thus even intense satisfaction on the part of those rehoused is no guide to the overall success of a redevelopment scheme. The Ministry's studies of redevelopment in St Mary's, Oldham provide a nice case in point. The first of these [11] showed that the majority of residents in St Mary's had an extremely strong attachment to the area: 'Some would have preferred to go on living in their slum houses if moving to better accommodation meant leaving St Mary's.' The area was decayed physically, but it still attracted young people in search of cheap housing and, though most of the residents were dissatisfied with their housing conditions, 'improvements to the houses in the form of comforts and decorations were preferred to major (and more expensive) amenities such as baths and water heaters'.

A study carried out following redevelopment [12] noted that 'the

71

technical requirements of the Council's demolition and building programme' made it impossible to rehouse the majority in the area which they preferred (*viz*. the same area) and 'the majority accepted the Council's offer of resettlement in existing houses and flats on out-lying Oldham Council estates'. Most of these liked their new houses and the new area (but so did the smaller number of households who rehoused themselves in conditions as bad as those they had left).

But two questions remain unanswered. First, what of those who re-housed themselves and were untraceable? Secondly, what was the effect of the clearance and redevelopment programme on the total housing market? Only when these questions are satisfactorily answered can a firm socio-economic justification be provided for wholesale clearance.

It is, of course, easy to criticize public programmes in this way. Rarely is it possible for a public authority (or even a research team) to assemble all the relevant data and to prepare a clear, unequivocal analysis in advance of the making of decisions. Moreover, the function which an area serves and the satisfactions which it provides for its inhabitants are not only difficult to assess in themselves; they typically have to be weighed against other considerations, such as the need for new roads, schools and open space. Again, a public authority must be more forward-looking than any individual needs to be; an area may be satisfactory to elderly residents but quite intolerable to younger people. In this connection it is interesting to note the not uncommon finding of social surveys that it is the elderly who are the most satisfied with 'inadequate housing'.[13] Yet the very fact that younger people are likely to 'move out' means that change will in any case take place around the elderly who remain.

There is, however, a danger of falling into the trap of indiscriminate generalization. It is nonsensical to generalize about the needs, attitudes and wishes of 'the elderly', 'the young' or 'the family in inadequate housing'. To abstract one element, such as their age or their plumbing facilities as a basis for general comment is to deny the complexities of reality.

Unfortunately, the state of social science is such that arguments and counter-arguments are based on the evidence of 132 families living in an Oldham slum,[14] 88 families rehoused on a Scottish housing estate,[15] or 264 families moving to an overspill scheme.[16] To date, social research in this field (as in most others) has provided useful insights, but it has not yet been able to identify the crucial variables. It is thus far from the point of development at which it can provide clear guide-lines for policy.

THE PROCESS OF CLEARANCE

Nevertheless, accumulated research on the *process* of clearance and rehousing provides more than sufficient cause for concern—as well as some indications of the ways in which improvement can be brought about.[17] The redevelopment of areas of old housing involves a very lengthy and complex series of steps.[18] At each of these, problems, conflicts and delays can arise. The sophisticated planner who is involved in the process understands the complications (or at least some of them), but the affected citizen does not. He is likely to be uninformed, bewildered or even frightened or bellicose.

In connection with this, the common plea is for more information. The latest Central Housing Advisory Committee report made the issue appear a straightforward one: 'Those to be affected by a scheme for clearance must be informed from the earliest moment (and kept informed) of what is to happen to them, what choices will be open to them, and what their rights and obligations are. Above all, people will want to know when and where they are moving.'[19] In fact, the problems can be very difficult, particularly in large schemes, since uncertainty enters into virtually every stage of the redevelopment process. 'Large scale development involves planning, acquiring, rehousing, clearing, designing, building and letting. At all stages there are elements of uncertainty. Can the site be acquired? When will purchase be completed? By when can people be rehoused? How long will redevelopment take?'[20] Periods of intense activity alternate with long time-lags while decisions are taken and statutory procedures completed.

The lengthy nature of the whole process results from the inherent complexities, the multiplicity of departments involved, the time taken for objections to be made by owners and for these to be considered by the local authority and (if agreement cannot be reached by negotiation) the time taken in arranging, holding and deciding upon a public inquiry.[21] These procedures result from the democratic concern for property rights. It can be argued that the emphasis is wrong: 'The history of housing law dealing with housing problems represents a concentration on property to the exclusion of consideration for persons. Similar to society today, damage to property holds greater penalties than damage to people . . . For example, the Public Health Inspector is required by law to inspect premises and not people.'[22]

The emphasis is, however, shifting—as is evidenced by the procedures for public participation statutorily required by the new Planning Act, and the publication of the Skeffington Report.[23]

73

Muchnick's study of redevelopment in Liverpool, however, shows the great extent to which change is required: 'The interplay of organizational needs and preferences among the multiplicity of Corporation actors overrides the establishment of a human renewal programme. There is little awareness of and no commitment to the resolution of social problems attendant to physical redevelopment.'[24]

The crucial issue is whether greater public participation, more concern for 'social issues' in redevelopment, and a much larger degree of community involvement is compatible with the current policy emphasis on major programmes of large-scale physical redevelopment. The reaction may well be that of a Newcastle citizen who summed up the operation of a joint committee of councillors, officials and citizens (concerned with the Rye Hill scheme): 'It's like going home and your wife says, "Would you like bacon and eggs for tea?," and you say, "No, I'd like steak and chips," and you end up with bacon and eggs—she listens to what you have to say, but it's still bacon and eggs.'[25]

There are some major issues here to which we return in later chapters, but the immediately relevant issue is the *scale* of redevelopment. The social, economic, administrative, financial, political and physical problems involved in large-scale redevelopment are so great that adequate attention can rarely be given to all of them. Since British policies (despite avowedly social aims) have stemmed largely from physical considerations, are operated within the framework of legislation expressed mainly in physical terms, and are administered predominantly by 'physical planners', a low priority has been accorded to social considerations. If these are now to have a higher priority other issues must be radically affected. A good illustration is provided by the studies of urban renewal in Nelson and Rawtenstall which are discussed in a later section. Here the starting point was not how best to redevelop older areas, but how best to deal with older areas—by any of a number of means, of which redevelopment was only one.

Before examining these other means, however, it is useful to discuss the role of the private sector in redevelopment.

PRIVATE REDEVELOPMENT

Though private enterprise plays a major role in the provision of new suburban housing, slum clearance and residential redevelopment is almost entirely a public sector activity in Britain. Private enterprise is predominantly confined to commercial, office and shop redevelopment. The reason for this is simple: the latter is profitable; redevelopment for housing is not. Again, history has played a large part in this: subsidies for clearance and residential redevelopment have been restricted to public authorities.

Two studies undertaken in the early sixties (one in London and one in a northern industrial town) demonstrated that private residential redevelopment was not economically feasible.[26] In Fulham house prices were buoyant, and redevelopment could be justified on commercial grounds only if there was a change to a more valuable use or a very substantial increase in density. The level of prices in Bolton was much lower but, by the same token, so would have been the rate of return on investment in the redevelopment of the area. In neither case was it possible to design an acceptable scheme which would provide for the rehousing of those already living in the area.

Similarly, studies undertaken for the Milner Holland Committee on *Housing in Greater London* showed that private redevelopment resulted in 'a complete change in the kinds of people occupying the accommodation'.[27] This was true for both redevelopment and rehabilitation. Furthermore, whether the action embraced a whole district or individual houses, common consequences could be clearly seen: 'One is the remarkable rise in prices; another is the progressive transfer of housing stock from renting to owner-occupancy; a third is the reduction in net occupancy rate and density as individual households replace multiple occupation; and a fourth is the alteration in socio-economic structure as the population changes from mainly working class to mainly upper middle class.'

In short, private residential renewal is economically feasible only in areas where there is a significant middle-class demand, and it is socially acceptable only in areas where a change in socio-economic character is desirable.

DEMAND FOR INNER CITY PRIVATE HOUSING

In conditions of acute shortage it is possible to market virtually any type of housing, irrespective of price and condition. Only exceptionally high-priced accommodation is likely to remain vacant. As the housing situation improves, those seeking accommodation become more and more descriminating, while suppliers (whether private or public) have to become more and more responsive to this discriminating demand. (Indeed, housing provided in a period of acute shortage may rapidly become unwanted in a succeeding period of abundance.)

The price of housing in a private market is determined by the interaction of demand and supply. New housing can be provided only at a price which is sufficient to cover the cost of providing it (including a profit margin). If the cost of supply is higher than the market will bear, the housing will not be provided unless a subsidy is given to bring the price down to the required level.

In general, new housing in suburban locations can be provided more cheaply than in inner cities, since land prices are cheaper and no redevelopment is required. Private redevelopment takes place only when the price which can be obtained for the new dwellings is sufficient to cover not only the cost of building these dwellings but also the cost of purchasing and clearing the structures existing on the site. In economic terms this is not a typical situation. Other factors, however, add considerable complications. Land has to be assembled, existing tenants have to be rehoused, planning restrictions tend to be more onerous than in suburban locations, and site preparation costs are frequently higher.

Further, demand is less certain. The demand for inner-city housing is affected by the supply of outer-city or suburban housing, the relative quality of environments and services, the transport network and the cost of the journey to work, the location of employment and a host of similar factors. Perhaps the most important of these factors is the quality of the environment: it is not easy to provide an inner-city environment which is accepted as being as good, in physical and social terms, as a suburban environment. It is difficult enough for a public authority; for a private developer it presents exceptional problems. And finally, why should the private sector enter this problem-laden field while suburban developments are booming? It is perhaps significant that private sector interest in residential rehabilitation has been stimulated by forecasts of the decline in the demand for additional housing (based largely on demographic changes) and the prediction that future housing requirements will be much more dependent upon slum clearance.

Before examining these issues further it needs to be stressed that London, as always, has to be considered separately. Its sheer size, its attractions and the functions which it serves, puts it in a class entirely of its own. Here the high market prices paid for new and rehabilitated housing evidence the demand which exists for inner-city residential location. Nevertheless, the market for *new* private housing in London would seem to be restricted to a small luxury sector: the major demand appears to be for rehabilitated dwellings—or, probably even more significant, old dwellings which can (with the aid of improvement grants) be rehabilitated by individual owner-occupiers. It must, however, be admitted that, except to a limited extent in London, there is little hard evidence on the potential demand for new private inner-urban housing.

A survey commissioned by the Economic Development Committee for Building throws some light on the attitudes of suburban owner-occupiers to the purchase of new housing in redevelopment areas.[28] The survey covered two groups of owner-occupiers in the fifteen largest towns (outside London) in England and Wales [29]: owner-occupiers of 'new' homes (built between 1967 and 1969) and owner-occupiers of 'older' houses (built between 1930 and 1959).

Only about 4 to 5 per cent of those who were likely to move within five years were attracted by the idea of buying a new house in a redeveloped urban area. The report concluded that 'given the inherent inaccuracies of predictive data, the evidence discourages much reliance on these sectors of house owners as a market for the proposed new housing'—though, if the sample was representative, the number of owner-occupiers of post-1930 houses who might be interested could be between 16,000 and 20,000 annually.

Of greater interest, however, are the reported attitudes to environment. Great importance is clearly attached to a 'semi-rural' environment: the fresh air and cleanliness which was provided by the estates on which these owner-occupiers lived. In striking contrast is the dirty, noisy and unpleasant image of the inner urban areas. Descriptions of the environmental improvements which would form part of a redevelopment scheme did not dispel this image. This general attitude was not over-ridden by the perceived advantages of an inner area: better transport, shopping, indoor entertainment, job opportunities for women, and facilities for teenagers. Shopping and transport were the most important of these: both were also a source of dissatisfaction with suburban estates.

Younger house owners (under the age of 35) and those with children showed the greatest interest in the idea of moving to a redeveloped area. Attitudes hardened with age, though the length of time spent in the suburbs did not appear to be important: 'Once the move to the suburbs has been made, the pressures to stay there are clearly very great.'

The evidence of the survey underlines the disfavour with which maisonettes, flats, terraced houses and patio-type developments are regarded (at least in the provinces): the great majority wanted a house with its own garden. However, there was no marked preference between owning a new house and an older one.

The survey did not include households living in inner urban areas but there is a presumption (and scattered evidence) that they would be more attracted by the idea of buying in a redeveloped area.

77

However, there is little evidence to show what prices they would be prepared to pay for new houses: this is the crux of the issue.

Two other aspects are also clearly of great importance: the general environment and the type of houses that are provided.

The inner urban environment is surely more than a question of 'image': it is a very big issue of urban quality which 'skilful land-scaping' will not fundamentally change. More easily changeable is density. Private suburban development is typically at a density of ten to twelve dwellings to the acre. Public authority development in new and expanding towns is generally around sixteen dwellings to the acre, while redevelopment is rarely less than twenty, and can rise to 100 in schemes with tower blocks. The evidence from the private sector (outside London) suggests that lower densities are necessary if private sales are to be achieved.

This, however, raises several major issues. Given present land prices, lower densities would lead to higher dwelling costs (probably above the level at which they could be sold). Yet, if this is a reflection of demand, why are land prices so high? And, why is it that there is an apparently large demand for public authority housing in inner cities. Indeed, why can public authorities do what the private sector cannot?

There are no certain answers to these questions, but a number of points can be made. First, it seems clear that public authority re-development is 'uneconomic' in the sense that a private developer could not undertake it at a commercially acceptable return on the capital employed. In other words the dwellings would not sell (or let) at a profit on the open market. The NEDC Working Party [30] produced figures which illustrate this. They obtained the actual costs of a number of recently completed local authority redevelopment schemes which were considered to be 'not too dissimilar from the kind of development a private builder might carry out'. (Unfortunately, no details are given.) These costs were updated (to 1969 prices) and compared with valuations which were made of the dwellings for vacant freehold possession and for letting at fair market rent. The comparison is set out in the Table opposite.

In only one case is the valuation higher than the costs. The figure, however, under-estimated the size of the gap between costs and value since the former excludes land while the latter includes it. This was done explicitly since land costs 'are generally so high in redevelop-ment areas that it would be unrealistic to expect the whole costs to be recovered in the sale price (or rental income) on the open market'. Nevertheless, as was recognized (and presumably ignored because of the difficulty of determining the figure), the market value of the land

78

Costs and Value of Selected Local Authority Redevelopment Schemes

Scheme	Approximate area of site	Average density	Approximate total costs (excluding land) at 1969 prices	Valuation for vacant possession freehold (including land)	Difference (5)–(4)	Valuation for fair market rent (including land)	Net Return (7) on (4)
	Acres	*Dwellings per acre*	£000	£000	£000	£000 p.a.	% p.a.
(1)	(2)	(3)	(4)	(5)	(6)	(7)	(8)
A (London)	12	45·5	3,492	2,437	−1,055	152	4·4
B (London)	13	40	2,066	2,830	+ 764	207	9·9
C (London)	24·5	44	6,718	4,917	−1,801	355	5·3
D (Midlands)	6	36	728	684	− 44	54	7·7
E (Midlands)	8	60	1,977	1,070	− 907	107	5·4
F (North)	16	32·5	2,390	1,800	− 590	109	4·5

for the new use should have been included. It is clear that had this been done none of the schemes would have been shown to be commercially viable.

The Working Party ascribed the difference between costs and value to the high density of the redevelopment. Yet, for a local authority high density is desirable both to meet (their assessment of) the local demand and to minimize the land cost per dwelling unit. To some extent the latter is a function of the subsidy system while the former is not unrelated to the rents at which local authority dwellings are provided. It is an exaggeration to say that the land prices are 'artificially' raised by local authority action and that the demand exists only because of the heavily subsidized rent. Nevertheless, there is a sufficient element of truth in this to make further discussion appropriate.[31]

Local authority redevelopment is not, of course, undertaken because it is 'economic'. Indeed, it is precisely because it is not that public action is necessary. The cost of land acquisition may be higher than it would be if local authorities were not 'in the market', but this is not a relevant point since they are and must be if slums are to be cleared and new roads, schools and other public services provided. Neither is it valid to argue that local authorities should hold back until values fall to a level at which redevelopment becomes economic. This is appropriate for commercial redevelopment, but if slum clearance were held back until the value of the properties fell to a level which made redevelopment profitable, very little clearance would ever take place. In fact, the properties in clearance areas typically do have very low values (except where there is multiple occupation) and houses which are statutorily 'unfit for human habitation' are acquired at site value (though this harsh rule has been considerably modified, particularly for owner-occupiers). However, clearance areas typically are densely developed and, as a result, the site values (which are assessed for individual ownerships) are consequently higher than is the case with undeveloped land. Further, areas of slum housing are frequently peppered with commercial and industrial premises which have considerably higher values but whose clearance is necessary if a satisfactory redevelopment scheme is to be achieved. This can very significantly increase the cost of acquisition. In inner London, while areas consisting solely of housing may cost £34,000 an acre, those containing mixed uses may cost double this amount.[32] In the provinces, costs of acquiring central slum clearance sites can work out at £30,000 to £40,000 an acre. By contrast, peripheral sites are only £3,000 to £5,000 an acre.

There is also the cost of the clearance itself which can amount, in areas of terraced housing at forty to the acre, to £4,000 an acre. Demolition costs do not, of course, bear any relation to the value of the property and they are, therefore, more important when values are low. Further additional costs are involved on account of the length of time taken by clearance and redevelopment (democratic processes are necessarily time-consuming), of site preparation and of construction itself: all these tend to be higher in redevelopment schemes than on virgin sites.

Redevelopment is thus inevitably costly. A commercial 'return' could be anticipated only if the new use were highly profitable. But those who are displaced by clearance require to be rehoused, and local authorities (rightly) have a statutory responsibility in this connection. Occupiers of dwellings in redevelopment areas are not numbered among the most affluent. The gap between their rent paying ability and current 'cost rents' is a large one which has to be met by subsidies.

Until recently, these subsidies were available only in connection with local authority redevelopment. The cost of land acquisition and clearance was grant-aided through housing subsidies to local authorities. Under the Housing Finance Bills of 1972, subsidies for slum clearance are provided separately from those for new house building. The new slum clearance subsidy (payable for at least fifteen years) meets 75 per cent of the difference between the cost and the value of cleared land. This 'value' will be determined by the use to which the land is put.

The point immediately relevant to the current discussion is that the new subsidy will allow land to be sold to private builders at a price which reflects its value (not the cost of acquisition and clearance); thus residential redevelopment need no longer be restricted to local authorities. How far there will be a demand for new owner-occupied houses in clearance areas remains to be seen, but at least such demand as there is (or could be) will not be thwarted by the imposition on the private builder of the costs of the non-market operation of slum clearance.

As with all changes in particular parts of the intricate web of housing policies, the implications of this are not easy to forecast. New conflicts may arise—for instance, between the desire to meet the needs of people displaced from an area and the desire to provide a wider range of choice and to attract professional workers to the inner city.

IMPROVEMENT

Articulate professionals and even politicians tend to lay an undue emphasis on the contribution which new housing makes to the solution of housing problems. Yet new building adds less than 2 per cent to the housing stock each year. A sensible housing policy will, therefore, be heavily concerned with existing housing. To put the matter at its lowest, if existing houses are allowed to deteriorate into slums, they will need to be demolished and replaced at public expense. Moreover, 'blight' is contagious and can spread rapidly to adjacent properties and whole areas of older housing.

A formidable battery of powers exists to compel owners to keep their properties in a 'fit' state. These stem from nineteenth-century public health considerations, as do the powers of slum clearance. These approaches are, however, decreasingly relevant to the current British situation (though this is not to deny the continued existence of totally unfit housing in a number of areas). A study of the housing conditions in Lancaster shows how the situation is changing:

> The problem of old housing in Lancaster is not one of slums. The majority of the remaining old houses in the city are basically sound, and with adequate maintenance and improvement could usefully provide for local needs for at least another generation. Two-thirds of these houses were owner-occupied in 1960 and the proportion has undoubtedly increased since then. In this situation the nineteenth-century concept of slum clearance is becoming increasingly outmoded. The problem is no longer one of old insanitary courts, of back-to-back houses, of dangers to the public health, or of abject poverty. Rather it is one of sound old houses needing improvement and continued maintenance. The political problem is also changing: in the phraseology of stereotypes, the unpitying and unpitied landlord is being replaced by the upstanding owner-occupier. Dispossession of owner-occupiers for the sake of redevelopment is quite a different matter from the dispossession of landlords in the interests of public health . . . The problem is now one of raising the quality of housing in the city. This calls for a policy of improvement, rehabilitation and conservation—of the neighbourhood as well as of individual houses.[33]

It was to meet this type of situation that improvement grants (originally introduced in 1926 for agricultural dwellings) have increasingly been made a major plank of housing policy since the mid-fifties. Furthermore, the emphasis has gradually shifted from individual house improvements, first to the improvement of streets or areas of inadequate housing, and later to the improvement of the total environment.

Initially it was assumed that houses could be neatly divided into two groups: those which were unfit for human habitation, and those which were 'essentially sound'.[34] (This is, incidentally, a nice illustration of the way in which legislation can define problems.) However, as experience was gained, the 'improvement philosophy' gradually broadened. It came to be realized that there was a very wide range of housing situations related not only to the presence or otherwise of plumbing facilities and the state of repair of individual houses, but also to the varying socio-economic character of different areas. A house 'lacking amenities' in Chelsea was, in important ways, very different from an identical house in Rochdale. The 'appropriate action' was similarly different. Later, it was understood that 'appropriate action' defined in housing market terms was not necessarily equally appropriate in social policy terms. A middle-class 'invasion' might restore the physical fabric and raise the quality (and 'tone') of a neighbourhood, but the social costs of this were borne by displaced lower-income families. The problem thus became re-defined.

Growing concern for the environment also led to an increased awareness of the importance of the factors *causing* deterioration. It is clear that these are more numerous (and infinitely more complex) than housing legislation recognizes. Through traffic and inadequate parking provision were quickly recognized as being of physical importance. The answer—in physical terms—was the re-routing of traffic, the closure of streets, the provision of parking spaces (together with cobbled areas and the planting of trees). More serious causes of physical blight such as obnoxious industries (and the almost traditional factory chimney and gasometer) were obviously more difficult to deal with.

Beyond this, understanding is limited, but there is an increasing appreciation of the fact that in addition to 'simple' physical factors, more complex socio-economic forces are at work in deteriorating (and improving) areas. There is more than a growing suspicion that the quality of an area is related much more to its socio-economic character (and changes in this) than to physical features.

Even more important, improvement has come to be seen as an *alternative* to redevelopment. The improvement versus redevelopment issue has now been translated from the confines of academic debate to the arena of practical politics. Initially the question was conceived in economic terms: is it cheaper to improve or to redevelop?[35] More recent research, however, has been concerned with a more wide-ranging assessment. The most recent (at the time of writing) is notable in this respect: the study carried out by Robert Matthew, Johnson-Marshall and Partners in Nelson and Rawtenstall.[36] These two towns are not, of course, representative—except possibly, of similar towns in similar regions. But this is the point: the 'most appropriate' action can be determined only in the context of the local situation—not by reference to general principles or economic formulae.

In these towns the housing problem, both currently and in the foreseeable future, is not one of shortage, but of obsolescence. In this context, the relevant choice is not between redevelopment and improvement: it is between improvement and continuing neglect.

The posing of the relevant questions is perhaps the most difficult issue for policy-makers and politicians (as it similarly is for research workers). Much of the debate on improvement *versus* redevelopment has been posed in 'comprehensive' terms: the choice has been seen as one between 'full' improvement (including provision for at least one car space per dwelling) and 'complete' redevelopment. The Nelson-Rawtenstall Study did not accept such constraints. Instead it posed the questions: 'What are the problems of the study areas?' and 'How can these most satisfactorily be met?'

By careful social study of the areas, the researchers found that 'any preconceptions we had about how the areas should be physically improved were not in line with what was needed or wanted'. Visual improvement, for example, was of limited relevance 'because the demolition of houses necessary to secure it could not be justified in the light of the ascertained needs and because the residents themselves would not derive a commensurate benefit from such things as more open space and man-made landscape'.

The study areas fulfilled the role of providing cheap and convenient homes for small, mainly elderly households. 'In these predominantly adult areas the success of changes made in the environment will not be measured by how near they come to bringing particular standards into parity with those of new housing estates . . . (but) . . . by how much more convenient and pleasing they make the areas for a population of similar age structure and social composition to that which now inhabits them.'

Improvements were needed to arrest deterioration, and to make selected areas attractive in a declining housing market situation. It was thought that the inner areas were most appropriate for this. The study concluded:

Where there are concentrations of old houses in inner urban areas there are also likely to be concentrations of people who by virtue of their economic situation and social status are adversely influenced by the effects of poor living conditions. Improving the quality of life for the inhabitants of such an area is thus not simply a matter of visual change or of physical amenity: to be successful the improvement needs to be based on an understanding of the social circumstances, and should include measures aimed directly at the social as well as the physical rehabilitation of the area.

These extracts do not (and are not intended to) do full justice to the study. They have been selected to demonstrate the approach adopted by the study team. It is a far cry from the 'idealistic' and 'thorough-going' approach of those who see older areas as mean and nasty streets of obsolete houses which should be demolished to make way for an environment of 'modern standards'.

Of course, Nelson and Rawtenstall are different in significant ways from, for example, Southwark or Barnsbury or Sparkbrook or Rye Hill or St Ann's.[37] These areas need equally sensitive studies if the 'most appropriate' help is to be given to the people who live there.

Perhaps in no field do planning policies more clearly deny that 'the best is the enemy of the good'. Both professionals and elected members are hesitant to commit themselves to 'planning solutions' which appear to them as being second-best. They may be second-best in relation to the ideal environment to which middle-class people aspire, but this is irrelevant: what is relevant are the attitudes and aspirations of those who are affected by housing and planning policies. These cannot be established by reference to an Act of Parliament.

Questions of improvement policy highlight a wider issue: what should be the role of public authorities? The British tradition has been for the local authorities to do all or nothing. Areas selected for 'action' get the full treatment: the others await their turn. This is clearly inadequate, and it is highly insensitive to social and economic trends and their impact on different areas.

So far as improvement policy is concerned the essential requirement is for the local authority to provide a framework within which the benefits of improvements made by individual property owners can be made to accrue not only to the occupiers but also to the whole neighbourhood. This involves a positive role for the local authority: a role in which it attempts to activate local interest and in which it plays its own part as provider of public and social services. An increasing number of local authorities are adopting this approach— which involves a major reorientation of local policy. Instead of investigating public health 'nuisances' or sanitary 'defects' and issuing 'notices', the local authority has to embark on an intensive publicity campaign, backed up by a technical assistance programme. These are accompanied by a comprehensive survey of the physical and social deficiencies of the area. Owners are encouraged to undertake improvements and are given advice on plans, builders, etc. Apart from the normal improvement grants, loans are made available to cover the balance of the cost. On occasion, the local authority even undertakes to act as the owner's agent. For tenanted property temporary rehousing can be offered.[38]

One major deterrent to the improvement of privately rented dwellings should be removed by the 1972 Housing Finance legislation. This will make private tenants who cannot afford the increased rents which follow improvement eligible for rent allowances. How far this will encourage landlords (particularly the large numbers of elderly owners of one or two dwellings) to undertake improvement, however, remains to be seen.

The main conclusion of this discussion, however, is a social one. Without necessarily subscribing to the view that all old urban areas constitute jolly social communities, it is clear that little attention is generally given to the social functions of older areas. Yet it is essential to know what functions an area serves (and how well it serves them) before a policy can be determined for dealing with that area.[39]

In other words, it is necessary to know *who* we are talking about: the *young* en route for suburbia? The *elderly* trapped by institutional constraints such as the policies of building societies? The *coloured immigrant* seeking a place where he can live without being ostracized? The *settled* who have been overtaken by decay? The *poor* who have no alternative open to them? Or the *mobile* who have no long term interest in the area? And what will be the effect of 'improvement' on the area? Will it change its function: if so how are the displaced needs to be met?

These questions need to be raised not only in relation to particular areas, but also in relation to general housing policies. The improvement of old areas is fundamentally a different problem from the traditional policies of providing houses and clearing slums. In the first case local authorities are dealing with 'applicants'. In the second they are dealing with areas where the wishes of the inhabitants may have to take second place to the need for redevelopment (though not necessarily as low a 'place' as they might, on occasion, do now). In improvement areas, however, the local authority will be essentially concerned with the needs and wishes of the inhabitants. They will, therefore, need to establish what these are, how they can be reconciled (since conflicts might well arise), and how far the needs of the

86

inhabitants can be met within the area or in acceptable alternative locations.

In conclusion, it must be stressed that different areas have very different problems. Housing problems are local problems set in a regional context. Statutory provisions can provide only a framework for the solution of these problems; the effectiveness of their use in any particular locality depends on as full an understanding of the nature of the local problems as can be obtained by all the techniques now available.

References and Further Reading

1. For a discussion of statutory powers, together with a historical sketch, see the author's *Town and Country Planning in Britain*, Allen & Unwin, 4th edition, 1972, Chapter XI, and *Housing and Local Government*, Allen & Unwin, 1966, particularly Chapter VIII.

2. One classic study demonstrated that, in the circumstances of the time, improved housing led to higher death rates: the higher rents of the better housing resulted in less money for food and hence poor nutrition. (G. C. M. M'Gonigle and J. Kirby, *Poverty and Public Health*, Gollancz, 1936.) For a brave (unsuccessful) attempt to measure the effects of housing on morbidity and mental health, see D. M. Wilner *et al.*, *The Housing Environment and Family Life*, Johns Hopkins, 1962.

3. Cf. Alvin Schorr's comment that 'there is a serious issue whether it is middle-class town planners or lower-class slum dwellers who feel strongly about crowding'. (A. L. Schorr, *Slums and Social Insecurity*, Nelson, 1964, p. 11.) At another point (p. 137) Schorr remarks that the Central Housing Advisory Committee provides advice which 'rests on what is known by the well-informed . . . it has no means of evaluating conventional wisdom'. It is difficult to refute this (especially for an author who is a member of the Committee), but see my 'Note of Reservation' to the Denington Committee Report on *Our Older Homes*, HMSO, 1966.

4. 1966 Sample Census figures.

5. Data from the 1967 House Condition Survey are scattered around several publications:
   (i) White Paper, *Old Houses into New Homes*, Cmnd. 3602, 1968, Appendix.
   (ii) *Housing Statistics*, No. 9, April 1968, Supplementary Tables IV–XIX and No. 10, July 1968, Supplementary Tables XI–XIII.
   (iii) *Economic Trends*, No. 175, May 1968, pp. xxiv–xxxvi.

6. J. B. Cullingworth, *Scottish Housing in 1965*, HMSO, 1967.

7. J. B. Cullingworth and C. J. Watson, *Housing in Clydeside 1970*, HMSO, 1971.

8. See J. B. Cullingworth, *Town and Country Planning in Britain*, Allen & Unwin, 4th edition, 1972, pp. 262–263; Scottish Housing Advisory Committee, *Scotland's Older Houses*, HMSO, 1967; and Scottish Development Department, The New Scottish Handbook, Bulletin 2, *Slum Clearance and Improvements*, HMSO, 1969.

9. Della Nevitt, 'Prices in the Housing Market', *The Guardian*, 17 March 1972.

10. Also relevant in this connection is the fact that (because of the severity of its problems) London has had more (and more thorough) studies than other areas. Ministers tend to ignore the fact that these studies may be totally irrelevant to other areas, even when the point is made explicitly—as it was by the Milner Holland Committee (*Housing in Greater London*, Cmnd. 2605, 1965, p. 2).

11. MHLG, *Living in a Slum*, Design Bulletin 19, HMSO, 1970.

12. MHLG, *Moving Out of a Slum*, Design Bulletin 20, HMSO, 1970.

13. For example, the Oldham study found that 'among those from St Mary's who rehoused themselves a larger proportion of the older people said that they were satisfied with their houses, even when they lacked amenities', ibid., p. 24.

14. MHLG, *Living in a Slum*, op. cit.

15. V. Hole, 'Social Effects of Planned Rehousing', *Town Planning Review*, July 1959, pp. 161–173.

16. J. B. Cullingworth, 'Social Implications of Overspill: The Worsley Social Survey', *Sociological Review*, Vol. 8, No. 1, July 1960.

17. See, for example, the Oldham Study, *Moving out of a Slum*; J. Norris, *Human Aspects of Redevelopment*, Midlands New Towns Society, 1960; Southwark Council of Social Service, *From Rumour to Removal*, 1971; C. Ungerson, *Moving House*, Occasional Papers on Social Administration, No. 44, Bell, 1971; H. Jennings, *Societies in the Making*, Routledge, 1962.

18. For a revealing case study see 'High Flats in Finsbury' in D. V. Donnison, V. Chapman and others, *Social Policy and Administration: Studies in the Development of Social Services at the Local Level*, Allen & Unwin, 1965.

19. *Council Housing: Purposes, Procedures and Priorities*, HMSO, 1969, p. 28.

20. Councillor C. Halford (Southwark Borough Council), in *From Rumour to Removal*, op. cit., p. 3.

21. For a discussion of the administrative delays involved in (Scottish) clearance orders and public inquiries see Scottish Housing Advisory Committee, *Scotland's Older Houses*, HMSO, 1967, pp. 62–67.

22. G. I. Lacey, in *From Rumour to Removal*, op. cit., p. 5.

23. Report of the Committee on Public Participation in Planning, *People and Planning*, HMSO, 1969. See further Chapter 6 below.

24. D. M. Muchnick, *Urban Renewal in Liverpool*, Occasional Papers on Social Administration, No. 33, Bell, 1970.

25. J. G. Davies, *The Evangelistic Bureaucrat: A Study of a Planning Exercise in Newcastle-upon-Tyne*, Tavistock, 1972, p. 162.

26. Taylor Woodrow Group, *The Fulham Study*, 1963 and Hallmark Securities, *The Halliwell Report*, 1966. Both studies were published privately and are difficult to obtain, but summaries appear in *New Homes in the Cities: The Role of the Private Developer in Urban Renewal in England and Wales*, NECD, HMSO, 1971.

27. *Report of the Committee on Housing in Greater London* (Milner Holland Report), Cmnd. 2605, HMSO, 1965, Appendix VI 'Redevelopment and Rehabilitation: Three Case Studies'.

28. See, National Economic Development Office, *New Homes in the Cities: The Role of the Private Developer in Urban Renewal in England and Wales*, HMSO, 1971.

29. The 15 towns were: Birmingham, Bradford, Bristol, Cardiff, Coventry, Kingston-upon-Hull, Leeds, Leicester, Liverpool, Manchester, Newcastle-upon-Tyne, Nottingham, Sheffield, Stoke-on-Trent and Wolverhampton.

30. Ibid., pp. 7–9.

31. For further discussion on land prices see Volume I, Chapter 5.

32. Figures in this section are taken from *New Homes in the Cities*, op. cit., p. 19.

33. J. B. Cullingworth, *Housing in Transition: A Case Study in the City of Lancaster, 1958–1962*, Heinemann, 1963, pp. 216–217.

34. See White Paper, *Houses: The Next Step*, Cmd. 8996, HMSO, 1953.

35. See L. Needleman, *The Economics of Housing*, Staples, 1965; E. M. Sigsworth and R. K. Wilkinson, 'Rebuilding or Renovation?', *Urban Studies*, Vol. 4, No. 2, June 1967, pp. 109–121; L. Needleman, 'Rebuild or Renovation? A Reply', *Urban Studies*, Vol. 5, No. 1, February 1968, pp. 86–90; L. Needleman, 'The Comparative Economics of Improvement and New Building', *Urban Studies*, Vol. 6, No. 2, June 1969, pp. 196–209; MHLG Circular No. 65/69, *Area Improvement* (Appendix B: 'Area Improvement: Economic Aspects').

36. DOE, *New Life in Old Towns*, HMSO, 1971.

37. On Southwark see, *From Rumour to Removal*, Southwark Council of Social Service 1971 and C. Ungerson, *Moving Home*, Occasional Papers on Social Administration No. 44, Bell, 1971; on Barnsbury: MHLG, *Barnsbury Environmental Study*, MHLG, 1968; on Sparkbrook: J. Rex and R. Moore, *Race, Community and Conflict: A Study of Sparkbrook*, Oxford University Press, 1967; on Rye Hill: J. G. Davies, *The Evangelistic Bureaucrat: A Study of a Planning Exercise in Newcastle-upon-Tyne*, Tavistock, 1972, and the comments of one of the planners involved: G. E. Cherry, *Town Planning in its Social Context*, Leonard Hill, 1970, pp. 4–6 and 145–146; on St Ann's: K. Coates and R. Silburn, *Poverty —The Forgotten Englishmen*, Penguin Books, 1970.

38. There is an extensive and growing amount of writing on this subject. See, for example, the series of articles in *Official Architecture and Planning*, February 1970; T. L. C. Duncan, R. D. Ballantyne and T. D. Muir, *The Kings Heath Study: Report of an Exploratory Study of Attitudes to House and Neighbourhood Improvement in an Older Part of Birmingham*, University of Birmingham, Centre for Urban and Regional Studies, Research Memorandum No. 6, 1971; J. Fleming, 'The Central Areas of our Towns and Cities: Recondition or Renew?', *Housing*, January 1971, Vol. 6, No. 5, pp. 8–17; P. Graham, 'Priorities for Action in Improvement Areas', *Town Planning Review*, January 1971, Vol. 42, No. 1, pp. 45–60; A. J. Shelton, 'Public Participation in Practice', *Architects' Journal*, 13 October 1971, Vol. 154, No. 41, pp. 805–808.

39. Cf. *Losing Out: A Study on Colville and Tavistock*, Notting Hill People's Association Housing Group, 1972. This is prefaced by the statement: 'Notting Hill, for eighty years notorious for its overcrowded houses, its shifting, restless, persecuted population is finally to be improved; not by bringing peace and dignity to those who have suffered for so long, but by clearing them out to make way for the rich and secure, who are now anxious to live close to the heart of the city.'

Chapter 4

Race and Colour

DISCRIMINATION

Had this book been written twenty years ago it is unlikely that it would have been considered appropriate to devote a chapter to racial problems. Passing reference might have been made to the 150,000 Polish ex-servicemen,[1] the 90,000 European Volunteer Workers,[2] (together with the resettlement policies formulated to assist their resettlement in Britain), or to the long history of immigration from Europe and Ireland,[3] or to the possible role of sponsored immigration in averting a declining population,[4] or even to the 492 West Indians who arrived on the *Empire Windrush* in June 1948 and to the coloured Commonwealth residents who numbered 75,000 at the time of the 1951 Census [5]; but as a 'problem' race was peripheral and highly localized. By the beginning of the sixties, however, the 'problem' loomed so large in political terms that the traditional British *laissez-faire* policy was abandoned in favour of statutorily controlled immigration. Perhaps even more striking was the passing of anti-discriminatory legislation a mere three years afterwards—the first legislation in British history aimed at protecting a specific minority.

The reasons for the major change in the climate of opinion which this reflected have been documented by Deakin and Foot [6]; but in a word the fundamental issue was colour. The deep-seated prejudice against coloured people was fanned into political pressure for 'controls' by the Nottingham and Notting Hill 'riots' of 1958, by the view that coloured immigrants were creating insoluble housing and schooling problems, by organized pressure from such bodies as the Birmingham Immigration Control Association, and (following the increasing debate on controls) by the 'rising tide' of immigrants.

So focused did the debate become that by the mid-sixties the term 'immigrant' popularly meant 'coloured': a confusion encouraged by the curious idea that it was more polite not to refer directly to colour, and by the perceived practical difficulty of counting coloured people except by reference to their (or their parents') birthplace.

Controls over Commonwealth immigration were introduced in

1962, and extended in 1965, 1968 and 1971. Anti-racial discrimination legislation was first passed in 1965 and extended in 1968. These two sets of Acts underline the ambivalent attitude towards colour. The former aim to restrict the inflow of Commonwealth citizens as narrowly as is practicable, while the latter aim to secure equality of treatment for those who are allowed entry to Britain. It is difficult to reconcile explicit policies of discrimination against coloured people who seek to enter with explicit policies of racial equality (and even more so, 'positive' discrimination) for those who are 'accepted'. As Lester and Bindman have put it:

The law, therefore, has two faces. One face confronts the stranger at the gate; the other is turned towards the stranger within. They express the ambivalence of public policies. The hostile expression of our immigration law casts doubt upon the friendly expression of our race relations law ... If our immigration laws are racially discriminatory in their aims and effects, it becomes difficult to persuade employers, workers, property developers and house-owners to treat people on their merit, regardless of race ... With one face, the law embodies and reinforces racial inequality; with the other, it expresses and urges racial equality.[7]

This ambivalence, uncertainty and confusion characterizes British policies towards the coloured minority. It is in striking contrast to the certainty and confidence with which entry to the Common Market is being effected, despite the importance that this has for future immigration policies.[8] The assumption that this will not raise issues of colour highlights the point that it is colour which is basically at issue.

The matter is further complicated by the fears resulting from an awareness (though not an understanding) of the racial strife that besets American cities. The British situation is, however, very different in kind as well as in degree, though there is no guarantee (in spite of differences in the historical background) that it will remain so. For the present, the coloured population of Britain is much smaller (both in absolute and proportionate terms); is less 'concentrated' and has few of the ghetto characteristics of the U.S.A.; does not (at least yet) experience the massive rate of unemployment which is endemic in American cities; and is not subject to anything like the same educational segregation.

Moreover, there are doubts as to how far the facts of racial discrimination make the immigration of coloured people substantively different from that of previous immigrants, and how far the problems which they face in deprived urban areas are different from those of white people living in the same conditions.

On one line of argument, coloured immigrants fill the lower status occupations vacated by the indigenous population in the economically flourishing conurbations. They have formed concentrated settlements in inner urban areas which suffer from physical and social deterioration. The disadvantages of these areas, in particular through inferior schooling and declining employment prospects, are exacerbated by a stereotyped role for and discrimination against coloured people. As a result (the argument concludes) subsequent generations of coloured British citizens will become trapped in a vicious circle of deprivation.

On the other hand, it can be argued that while there is abundant cause for concern about the position of coloured people, they consitute only a minority of those who are deprived. While there are clearly aspects of the coloured person's situation which require special attention (language; understanding of the mechanics of British society; and racial discrimination), a socially just policy must be aimed at deprivation as such. In any case, we are still in a 'first generation' situation—probably more than a third (half a million) of the coloured population currently living in Britain were born here: a half of these are under the age of five and most of the remainder are still at school. It is too soon (so the argument continues) to accept that the coloured population as such are facing the vicious circle. Coloured people are becoming more and more accepted by the host society which was unfamiliar with coloured (as distinct from European) immigrants. While it is true that many coloured immigrants have filled lower status jobs, this is the general case with immigrants. The fact that they are a minority even within these lower status occupations means that we may hope that these are not type cast as 'coloured-only' occupations. Moreover, coloured workers are fairly well distributed across a range of occupations and (since by definition migrants are people of initiative) they may rise occupationally more quickly than the indigenous population who have been caught, through social or personal factors, in the inner city syndrome.

On this line of argument colour discrimination needs to be tackled by effective race relations legislation, combined with positive policies to monitor its success, while deprivation is tackled by co-ordinated policies in relation to housing, education and employment. Governments may not live up to their ideals, but even if they did, the policies could well be seen to be inadequate in terms both of social policy and of the potential explosiveness of the race issue. The need to avoid racial strife is a matter of civil order (not social justice). Policies specifically aimed at combating deprivation among a coloured minority might prevent civil disorder, but they would be socially unjust and might well cause white resentment and even backlash.

Given the alternative interpretations of the situation, it must occasion no surprise that government policies are ambiguous and faltering. But though the future is uncertain, there is no denying the extent of discrimination. The evidence is clearly that in employment, housing and the provision of services, the coloured person suffers racial discrimination 'varying in extent from the massive to the substantial. The experience of white immigrants, such as Hungarians and Cypriots, compared to black or brown immigrants, such as West Indians, leaves no doubt that the major component in the discrimination is colour.'[9] Similarly, there is no doubt about the disadvantage which coloured people suffer by virtue of their concentration in deprived areas.

Coloured immigrants have gone to areas where their labour is needed. Areas of persistently low demand for labour (such as Scotland, North East England and Wales) have attracted only small numbers. Within the areas of high labour demand they have settled in those parts from which the white residents have been moving in large numbers to the better housing conditions of suburbia and beyond. Thus, many coloured people 'have gone to the decreasing urban cores of expanding industrial regions'.[10] These urban cores have been losing population for decades, but they are the traditional 'reception areas' for migrants from abroad and other parts of Britain whose welcome in the labour market is not matched by a similar welcome in the housing market.

As coloured people have settled in these areas, others have joined them, even if the labour demand which was the original attraction slackened in the meantime.

The housing and employment situation of coloured people has been extensively documented, particularly in the publications of the Institute of Race Relations.[11] Unfortunately, the available statistical data is grossly deficient, mainly because few separate records are kept for coloured people (a matter to which we return later in this chapter). Nevertheless, the picture of discrimination in both housing and jobs is consistent. Similarly, educational provision is inferior—largely as a result of the association of areas of bad housing with poor schools. Indeed, there is a triangle of forces: 'Housing for the adult, at the apex, determines education for the child, which determines employment for the adolescent.'[12] This inter-relationship between housing, education and employment is a recurrent theme in the varied issues discussed in this book. Nowhere is it clearer than in relation to the

93

disadvantaged coloured minority. To quote *Colour and Citizenship* again:

> Low income coupled with financial instability are direct corollaries of poor or restricted employment opportunities, and these in turn close many of the avenues of escape from the initial areas of reception for the immigrant with their inadequate housing. These areas are also often those with the poorest educational facilities. Thus, the children of the original immigrants may receive an education which is less than adequate and leaves them ill-fitted for the labour market. If the children of immigrants also find their employment opportunities restricted for reasons not directly related to their education, then the whole vicious circle is repeated and reinforced. But, although a great deal of discussion in political circles and the press has been devoted to the problems of concentration of coloured communities and incipient ghettoes, and those of schools with high proportions of coloured school-children, far less has been said about the restrictions on employment opportunities for coloured workers, which has been one of the main factors responsible for the concentrations in housing and education.... Problems in the field of employment are inextricably bound up with those of education and housing, and problems in these two fields, which have received the lion's share of the attention of politicians, administrators, commentators and the general public, are insoluble without due attention and energy being devoted to the equally important field of employment.[13]

Policies on one front are thus inadequate unless accompanied by policies on other fronts. Good quality education and training are insufficient without full opportunities for entry to appropriate employment. Good employment opportunities cannot be such without concurrent housing opportunities. At every turn, policies can be sabotaged by discrimination on the part of those who control access to employment and housing. In the following sections, employment, education and housing are discussed separately, but it is their inter-relationship that presents the most difficult problem for policy.

EMPLOYMENT

A major reason for immigration is employment opportunity. The post-war period (until recently) has been characterized by a chronic labour shortage and this had led to a substantial immigration. Between 1945 and 1957 there was a net immigration of more than 350,000 European nationals into the United Kingdom.[14] During these years, coloured people made a relatively small contribution to total immigration (though no statistics were kept until 1955, and it was not until the introduction of controls by the Commonwealth Immigrants Act 1962 that the statistics became adequate). David Stephen has argued that the immigration of the period 1948–1968 (which was predominantly to the prosperous areas of Britain) 'took place against a background of unemployment in the development areas because British Governments had consciously or unconsciously rejected internal migration (taking the workers to the jobs) as too costly a way of filling the unfilled vacancies in the Midlands and the South East. Commonwealth immigrants could be brought in at a lower immediate social cost.'[15] Be that as it may, with a very few notable exceptions, no efforts were made to match employment vacancies with the supply of migrant labour before the process of migration got under way.[16] (The exceptions included London Transport, the British Hotels and Restaurants Association and the National Health Service who made direct arrangements with the Barbados Government for the recruitment of skilled labour: these employers were also exceptional in that they undertook some initial responsibility for the housing and welfare of immigrants.) Despite this *laissez-faire* policy, coloured immigration was highly responsive to British labour market conditions, increasing in times of labour shortage and falling when unemployment rose. (Subject to a time-lag of three months, immigration fluctuated with almost mathematical precision in relation to the fluctuation in job vacancies.) It was not until the threat of controls that a major increase in immigration unrelated to the employment situation took place.[17]

Large numbers of coloured immigrants have moved into jobs vacated by English workers who, in conditions of full (and 'overfull') employment, have been upwardly mobile. In other words, they have taken low-status unpopular jobs. This has also encouraged the prejudiced view that coloured people are low class and unskilled— ignoring the fact that they take the jobs they can get. Nevertheless, generalizations about the employment of coloured people need heavy qualification. To consider coloured people in homogeneous terms would be to accept one of the classical stereotypes of racial prejudice: that immigrants are an undifferentiated and low class group. Though there is abundant evidence that discrimination results in difficulties for coloured people in obtaining jobs appropriate to their skills and abilities, the employment situation of the different immigrant groups shows marked variations.[18] There are also striking differences between different areas which cannot be accounted for by the occupational structures of these areas: all immigrant groups for

95

instance have a less favourable occupational achievement in the West Midlands than in London.[19]

Unfortunately, such evidence as there is shows little change between 1961 and 1966 in the concentration of coloured workers in certain occupations and their absence in others. The worry is that occupational class may become hardened by the 'triangle' of employment, housing and educational disadvantages into occupational *caste*.

Discrimination is insidious: it is not touched by pious declarations. Yet much of British policy has been essentially declaratory. It has suffered from what Deakin and Cohen have described as 'the delusion that this is an area in which solutions can be left to time, education and goodwill'.[20] The Race Relations Acts are essentially declaratory: they provide machinery for conciliation but few powers of enforcement—despite the strong evidence of the need for these.[21] Moreover, they only provide machinery for investigating complaints —not a system for ascertaining whether discriminatory situations exist. A policy of 'no discrimination' is not a policy unless measures are taken to implement and enforce it. This involves strenuous efforts, as a case described by Deakin and Cohen clearly demonstrates.[22] This was of a large group of retail stores which evolved a specific policy towards the employment of coloured sales staff.

Though the company had employed coloured workers for a number of years there were very few on the sales staff. As a result of the personal initiative of the Deputy Chairman and Managing Director, attempts were made to rectify this. Repeated circulars to store managers asking them to employ more non-European sales staff did not have the desired effect. Records were then kept—and circulated— of the number of non-European staff in each store. Finally, after further chasing of the laggards (identified by the records), it was declared that if any store managers persisted in disregarding the policy they would be dismissed. Though there were difficulties at lower levels (the female staff of one branch threatened to walk out *en masse* if any coloured staff were employed) these evaporated in response to persistence from the management.

Without positive measures to overcome prejudice, inclinations to avoid embarrassing situations, and sheer inertia, *de facto* discrimination will not be prevented. As we shall see, such an approach is equally important in relation to housing. The fact that local housing authorities are nearly (though not completely) unanimous in declaring that they have a policy of non-discrimination means that, in practice, they have no policy at all.

The retail stores example also shows the importance of monitoring the effects of policy. Without adequate records it is impossible to say whether a policy is working or not.

On a broader front, employment statistics reveal occupations and industries in which there are few coloured people. As with the 'laggard' retail stores, the basic problem lies in those fields of employment where there are few coloured workers, not in those where there are many. In the words of Rose, 'it is in the occupations and industries where the coloured immigrant is rare or absent that the answers to concentration, lack of achievement and frustration are to be found'.[23]

An additional range of problems arises with coloured school-leavers (who possibly average 14,000 a year). Here geographical concentration creates not only problems of education (discussed in the following section) but also problems of restricted opportunity. This restricted opportunity is further limited by the narrow range of jobs for which they apply—itself a function of their perception of the opportunities open to them.

Studies in long-established coloured settlements (*sic*) demonstrate that prejudice, discrimination and disadvantage take their toll over several generations unless positive measures are taken to combat them.[24] 'We see a second and third generation which lives in a quasi-ghetto, is denied the opportunities available to white English-speaking immigrants, is less ambitious, and achieves less than they do . . . they chose to stay in the coloured quarters because it is safer to trust their own kind. Yet no one relishes the prospect of being cut off from the main stream of Cardiff city life; it is accepted as a regrettable and unhappy consequence of the insecurity of being coloured in a white city.'[25] Thus the inter-relationships between employment, education and housing are again illustrated.

EDUCATION

Coloured children face a range of difficulties. If they arrive in Britain at an early age they experience a 'culture shock' which may be even more bewildering for the young than it is for the adult. If they are 'late arrivals' they may be 'two, three or four years behind in comparison with our own children' and find that they are treated as being mentally sub-normal instead of educationally backward.[26] Many immigrant children have a poor command of English. Others have 'unrealistic aspirations',[27] perhaps fostered by their aspiring parents, by their need to strive harder in a racially segregated society than their white counterparts, or simply because of the social status and level of legitimate aspiration which a stratified society assigns to them. These difficulties are compounded when coloured children live —as they frequently do—in deprived areas: 'The sad fact is that, if a child attending school in this country today is coloured, there is a high probability that the child will also fall into the category of educationally under-privileged or deprived children.'[28]

Coloured children can also suffer from inadequate teachers and inadequate teaching. (The ideals of professionalism are always constrained by the attitudes and prejudices of the society of which the professionals are a part.) Lack of understanding and, at times, clear prejudice diminish the potential contribution which the educational system is in a unique position to provide to coloured children.

All these handicaps severely restrict the opportunity of coloured children to obtain and fully benefit from an education appropriate to their 'age, ability and aptitude'. Many white children suffer some of these disadvantages, but the fact of colour adds a particular significance. Coloured people are readily distinguished by their colour: because of this 'they are easily identifiable as a proportionally under-achieving sector of society; they are readily stereotyped as fit only for menial jobs; they tend even themselves to accept this stereotype; and the vicious circle turns upon itself'. Thus the danger arises—as with poverty—of a cycle of deprivation and disadvantage being self-reinforcing.

In education, as in other fields,[29] it is important to highlight the particular problems of West Indians. In many ways these are different from those of Asian and other immigrants.

Large numbers of West Indian children followed their mothers to Britain several years later. Their problems of adjustment are great. They leave the emotional security of the family network in the West Indies for the unfamiliar strains and stresses of British urban society. Learning by rote in very large classes is replaced by the greater permissiveness of the British educational system—though their parents may hold more traditional, even Victorian attitudes.

A high proportion of West Indian mothers go out to work and young children are looked after by (frequently illegal) childminders. Such children have little opportunity to develop verbal and perceptual skills and can arrive in the school system severely handicapped.[30] English may in fact be a second language, with Creolized English or a French patois being the first. When these problems are added to those of inadequate schools and over-large classes, and (hopefully diminishing) lack of understanding and experience on the part of teachers, educational progress can be seriously retarded.

Indian, Pakistani and Cypriot children may suffer similar problems in the schools, but they tend to have stronger family support, and parents are often more likely to have a more positive attitude towards education and advancement.

All such generalizations need qualifying, but there is sufficient evidence to justify them.[31] In particular, the high proportion of West Indian children in ESN schools has become a scandal in certain areas.[32] This is a tragic index of the inadequacy of the educational system to respond effectively to the problems and needs of coloured children. The Inner London Education Authority have drawn attention to the importance of cultural deprivation, educational neglect and emotional instability. Their conclusions are that 'more and better provision for children whose backwardness is due to causes other than limited intelligence' is needed, but 'until suitable provision exists, some retarded and disturbed children will continue to attend special schools: their dual function should therefore be recognised, especially when staffing standards are being considered'.[33]

The reaction of the spokesmen for the coloured, however, is becoming increasingly angry:

> The Black child labours under three crucial handicaps: (1) *Low expectations on his part* about his likely performance in a white-controlled system of education; (2) *Low motivation* to succeed academically because he feels the cards are stacked against him; (3) *Low teacher-expectations* which affect the amount of effort expended on his behalf by the teacher, and also affect his own image of himself and his abilities. If the system is rigged against you and if everyone expects you to fail, the chances are *you will* expect to fail too. If you expect to fail, the chances are, you will.[34]

The quotation comes from a pamphlet written by a West Indian teacher and researcher, Bernard Coard, under the title *How the West Indian Child is made Educationally Sub-Normal in the British School System*. (A reading of this pamphlet should shatter any complacent view that educational problems are purely 'transitional'.) Apart from recommendations relating to reform in the State educational system, he argues that black people 'need to open Black nursery schools and supplementary schools throughout the areas we live in'.

Coloured minorities are beginning to demand and play an increasingly active and independent role. The implications of this for policy have yet to be assessed but, as we shall see, the effects are already becoming apparent (in relation to 'dispersal' for example).

To date, policy has been largely aimed at the removal of the social and physical handicaps of the deprived areas in which so many families live. A major issue which faces policy-makers and administrators here is whether these policies are to be operated with a focus on coloured people or on a broader front with the objective of removing deprivation more generally. In the three fields under consideration the approach has differed. Discrimination and disadvantage in relation to employment is essentially an issue of colour and this has been the focus of policy (though it is officially referred to as 'race' and could well extend in the future, for example to sexual discrimination). Housing and environmental improvement policies have been much more generalized: a result (in part) of the fact that the responsible government department [35] is concerned predominantly with physical matters. In the case of education, however (together with the urban and community development programmes) the position is far less clear.

Initially, apart from advice on teaching English to immigrants,[36] the main plank of policy was the dispersal of immigrant children to prevent the proportion exceeding a third in any school.[37] Julia McNeal has analysed the assumptions underlying this policy: that assimilation was the ultimate goal of policy; that immigrant pupils were a burden on the schools; that they caused a drop in standards which led white parents to withdraw their children; and that the resulting concentration and separation were considered bad for immigrants for several reasons: the immigrant child would not learn English; they would not learn the British way of life; and, perhaps, separation conjured up images of apartheid, or segregation in the United States, and therefore must be wrong in itself for coloured children in Britain.[38]

The policy also implied an assumption that it could be effective in overcoming the effects of residential concentration and that the advantages thus secured would outweight the disadvantages of discriminating against coloured children in this way (there was no suggestion that white children should be 'bussed' to schools from which immigrant children were being dispersed); of separating the dispersed children from their local playmates; of depriving the dispersed children of the specialist provision for language teaching which was available only in the schools from which they were removed. (At this stage it was not appreciated that concentration had the positive advantage of enabling full use to be made of the limited number of specialist teachers who were then available.)

Throughout, it was never clear whether the objective of dispersal was to assist in the teaching of English or in the prevention of the formation of black schools—or both. No satisfactory answer was ever provided to the question posed by the Chief Education Officer of Brent: 'Why shouldn't schools in predominantly immigrant areas be predominantly immigrant?'[39] An acceptance of this in educational terms (the dispersal of *families* from predominantly immigrant areas is a very different matter) might have led to a much greater concern for the provision of appropriate teaching materials, the development of teacher training courses in language teaching for immigrants, and the provision of pre-school play groups and nursery schools in areas of significant immigration.[40]

Above all, it ignored the fact that many coloured children live in areas of concentration; thus measures which might be taken to ameliorate the problems to which this gives rise or even to prevent or reduce it were not considered. But this was not a responsibility of an *education* ministry!

There has been a considerable move away from dispersal as a recommended policy [41] as policy has developed on other fronts: the channelling of additional resources to areas of high immigration, the increased assistance provided by the Local Government Act of 1966, the influence of the Plowden Report, and the initial development of the Urban Programme under the Local Government Grants (Social Need) Act of 1969.

As Julia McNeal has pointed out,[42] the policy began in a piece-meal and undirected way: the 'quota' of qualified teachers, which is fixed annually for each local education authority by the Department of Education and Science, was increased for those with concentrations of non-English speaking immigrant children. By the school year 1970–71 some 3,000 teachers were added to the quotas of 54 local education authorities.[43] Under Section 11 of the Local Government Act 1966 grants were provided for the employment of extra staff (including teachers) required to deal with the difficulties arising from 'differences of language and customs'. Originally at the rate of 50 per cent, these grants were increased in 1969 to 75 per cent.

After the publication of the Plowden Report these measures were followed by the Government's Urban Programme. This was announced in 1968 as a programme of expenditure 'designed to raise the level of social service in areas of acute social need, and thus help to provide an equal opportunity for all citizens'. Under the Local Government Grants (Social Need) Act 1969, a specific grant is paid for approved projects undertaken by local authorities having 'urban areas of special social need'.*

There is regrettably little published information on the Urban Programme and it is not easy to assess its effectiveness.[44] In the present context two points can be made. First, a policy which began with a focus on education has developed into a broad concern for

* See Chapter 5, p. 140.

'social need'. Secondly, the policy has been to provide direct help to those in need (which *includes* immigrants) rather than specifically to immigrants. (There has been considerable confusion on this point, stemming in part from the popular conception of the programme as an 'answer to Powellism', and the fact that the co-ordinating department is the Home Office—a department which is better known for its role in the control of immigration than for its responsibilities for social policy.)

There has thus been a rejection of the concept of a policy of 'positive discrimination' for coloured people. This represents an acceptance of the view that in education the problems of the coloured child are to a large extent shared by the uncoloured child living in the same neighbourhood. The qualifications that need to be made to this (e.g. in relation to language) become decreasingly important as fewer and fewer of the coloured school population have a non-British birthplace,[45] (though more subtle problems, e.g. of white teacher-black pupil relationships are not so easily disposed of). The declining emphasis on bussing also reflects the increased recognition of the importance of the neighbourhood and the neighbourhood school. The focus thus shifts to the deficiencies of the neighbourhood. The problem is not 'near-black schools' but the underlying causes of these. To the extent that they are a result of discrimination and lack of opportunity in housing they can be tackled only by housing policies; and similarly with employment.

HOUSING [46]

The bad housing conditions in which so many coloured people live has been extensively documented.[47] So has the discrimination to which they are subject in the housing market.[48] Coloured immigrants—like uncoloured immigrants from abroad and from other parts of the British Isles—have concentrated in areas where (at least initially) their labour is required and where there is the most ready access to accommodation. The fact that these are often areas of bad housing is a result that could be expected to follow from the fact that typically no specific housing provision was made (unlike the situation in a number of European countries where a major aim has been to co-ordinate labour market and housing policies).[49] Had there been no colour discrimination in employment and housing it could have been anticipated that coloured immigrants would have followed the dispersal pattern of previous generations of immigrants: obtaining better jobs and better houses over (and beyond) the whole geographical area of the cities. However, discrimination on a large scale in employment and in both the private and the public housing sectors (overt and 'incidental') has barred coloured people from many better housing areas. As a result the majority of coloured people have been confined to the inner cities and seedier suburbs.

Major changes in the overall structure of the housing market (which are discussed more fully in Chapter 2) have considerably exacerbated the problems. In particular, the declining supply of privately rented accommodation has meant increasing competition for what remains, and increasing dependence on the public sector for good quality rented housing.

Traditionally, the poorer sections of the community have improved their housing conditions by moving out of cities: they have done this either by buying or renting. Purchase of good quality housing (in good quality areas) can be difficult for coloured people because of cost (which of course affects uncoloured people also), or because the cheaper good houses are in areas where there is little employment opportunity for them, or because of racial discrimination. 'House purchase, in fact, is a prime example of a situation in which a coloured person in Britain may be at a disadvantage as an immigrant, as a low wage-earner, or as a person in a low-status job, and specifically on the grounds of his race. In the first instance, as a newcomer, perhaps with poor English, he is open to all kinds of exploitation. His general ignorance of the market may limit his own awareness of what is available, and it may be natural to him to look first in the run-down locality where he has already been living in lodgings and has formed some connections, rather than seeking straight away the newer suburban housing to which is attached better finance and value for money.'[50] It is this which underlines the fact that a high proportion of coloured immigrants* (particularly in the West Midlands where older type housing is so much cheaper than in London) are owner-occupiers.

If a coloured person thus has difficulty in 'moving out' to an owner-occupied house he is reliant on the rented sectors; but since there is (for reasons explained in Chapter 2) virtually no new privately rented housing, he becomes dependent on the public sector. Yet the proportion of coloured immigrants who are council tenants is low. In practice, though nearly all local housing authorities maintain that they do not discriminate against coloured people as such, the effect of selection procedures is unquestionably discriminatory.

* Here, as elsewhere, the term 'immigrant' is used in its proper sense and not as a 'euphimism'. Most statistics relate to coloured immigrants, not to the total population of coloured people.

Consequently, coloured immigrants are thrown back on to the poor quality private sectors.

COUNCIL HOUSING

An examination of the operation of the public authority housing sector demonstrates the validity of Elizabeth Burney's view that 'in housing above all, immigrants expose the reluctance of Britain's social, economic and political institutions to serve the demands of the weak, the unfortunate and the unorthodox'.[51] Even more than in other fields, the experience of the coloured immigrant in relation to public authority housing highlights basic inadequacies which have for long prejudiced the position of needy groups.

Indicative of the approach of local housing authorities is the strong plea made to the Cullingworth Committee* 'not to make an issue of colour'. The argument here (which is characteristic of most of the British approach to its coloured minority) is that as long as local authorities follow strictly fair practices in allocation and rehousing, coloured applicants would receive the same treatment as others in like circumstances. This is simply not true. Discrimination takes place at the office level, in the selection, assessment and grading of individual families. (In this, local housing authorities are no different from other organizations: much outright discrimination takes place on the shop-floor, in local offices and generally at the lower levels of management.) Moreover, discrimination is frequently straightforward prejudice which is not seen as such.[52] A nice illustration of this is provided by the housing manager who explained that his authority 'made no discrimination: coloured families are integrated with the other tenants'. Precisely what this meant was not clear, but the manager's views were: 'Immigrants are happier housed together in colonies so that they can pursue their own way of life without causing a nuisance or annoyance to the indigenous population who wish to continue leading their own way of life.' Clearly, whatever the official policy, those who operate it have views and attitudes which must affect the way in which they treat coloured people.

Yet even if it were true that coloured applicants received 'the same treatment as others in like circumstances', the question is begged as to whether this treatment is right and fair. It may not infringe the Race Relations Acts, but it may still be highly undesirable.

* The personal description is used, with slight embarrassment, as an alternative to the lengthy and inelegant full description: the Housing Management Sub-Committee of the Central Housing Advisory Committee. Its report, *Council Housing: Purposes, Procedures and Priorities*, was published by HMSO in 1969.

It is important to stress that in one sense local authority housing policies must be discriminatory. Having a 'policy' in relation to the distribution of housing benefits *means* giving priority to some needs over others. Decisions have to be taken about who is to be eligible and—since houses vary in size, quality, location, etc.—about who is to be eligible for particular houses.

Approached in this way, the question is not whether there is discrimination against coloured people, but whether the rules of eligibility and the management procedures have the effect of treating coloured people unfairly. In this context, treatment can be unfair in two senses. First, the coloured can be treated unfairly in comparison with the uncoloured; secondly, they—along with the uncoloured— can be treated unfairly in relation to broader issues of equality. For instance, a rule which requires applicants who are 'non-native' to wait for two years before they can be considered for rehousing, while requiring 'natives' to wait for only one year is clearly unfair in the first sense. If all applicants had to wait for two years, this unfairness would be removed, but the unfairness of a rule which requires any- one to 'wait' remains. (It should be added—in fairness!—that this view is by no means unanimously accepted: local authorities have very strong views on 'residential qualifications' which are being weakened only in response to a marked decline in the demand for council houses.)

The Cullingworth Committee considered three areas in which (in their view) policies and practices had a discriminatory effect. These they labelled eligibility, assessment and access. Of the eligibility rules, the residential qualification was the most serious. This naturally has the effect of discriminating against the coloured newcomer to an area since its object is to discriminate against all newcomers. As coloured people increasingly meet the residential qualification, they auto- matically become eligible for consideration provided that they are not rendered ineligible by other rules which exclude, for example, owner-occupiers, single men and 'cohabitees'—or simply because they have more members in their family than can be accommodated in the size of dwelling which is available. Eligibility rules may also exclude furnished tenants, sub-tenants and lodgers who live in slum areas which are redeveloped by the local authority.

Assessment (which is considered further in Chapter 2) is a technique of management designed to select the most appropriate dwelling for individual applicants. Even when undertaken with the utmost care by fully trained and skilled staff, the scope for unconscious bias against families who do not necessarily subscribe to (or, living in appalling conditions, cannot meet) the housekeeping norms of middle-class behaviour is self-evident. In fact, many of those responsible for assessment—or 'grading' as it is more accurately termed—are far from being fully trained and skilled. As a result there are good grounds for fearing the validity of Elizabeth Burney's harsh words: 'The principle is simple: a clean person gets a clean house and a dirty person gets a dirty house. In between are all kinds of subtle gradings which are the everyday material of housing management ... Those of a lower standard both economically and socially are, therefore, segregated in public-sector housing in much the same way as they would be on the private market.'[53] Even more telling—indeed frightening—is the comment of one housing manager that 'I wouldn't put coloured people on a new estate mixed up with all the young couples. It's got to go slowly. Better to start them off among the older people who are more tolerant.'[54]

Access is a more subtle concept: essentially it means understanding 'the system'. As the Cullingworth Committee noted, this is difficult enough for the sophisticated: 'We ourselves, who are not unfamiliar with the system, found many perplexing issues which took much unravelling and, on occasion, gave rise to conflicting interpretations from expert advisers.' Not without good reason did they conclude that the system may be totally incomprehensible and shrouded in mystery to a relative newcomer.

The tragedy of the situation is that the public sector may well, in its good intentioned but small-minded way, be exacerbating the very problems which it is in a unique position to alleviate. Above all, it can provide the means by which coloured people can move to the opportunities of the more advantaged areas beyond the inner cities. Housing is one part of the 'track' to wider opportunity: the other part of the tract being employment. This implies that local authorities should operate a policy of 'dispersal'. The Cullingworth Committee stressed the desirability of this, though they stressed that it should not become 'the overriding preoccupation of policy':

We are convinced that any policy of dispersal in the field of housing must be implemented with great sensitivity, with no element of compulsion or direction, and can proceed only at the pace of the needs and wishes of the people involved. It must not be assumed that coloured people wish to disperse themselves rapidly among the white community, but at the same time the opposite must not be assumed. The evidence we have received makes us very conscious of the fact that it is very easy for local authorities to conclude that coloured people wish to live in concentrations. Limited employment opportunities can conspire to reinforce this. Thus, though the policy of dispersal must be implemented with sensitivity, it must be a *policy*. Dispersal is a laudable aim of policy, but this policy needs pursuing with full respect for the wishes of the people concerned. Dispersal of immigrant concentrations should be regarded as a desirable consequence, but not the overriding purpose, of housing individual immigrant families on council estates. The criterion of full, informed, individual choice comes first.

This emphasis on the elimination of obstacles to choice characterizes the approach which has been adopted by Government over the last decade or so. Increasing doubts, however, are being felt on its adequacy and even its relevance. But before discussing this further it is necessary to examine the private housing sectors—within which the majority of coloured people live.

PRIVATELY RENTED HOUSING

The decline of the privately rented sector has already been commented upon. Within this sector, however, it is important to distinguish between the unfurnished and furnished parts. The distinction is crucial, not because furniture in itself is of particular relevance, but because different legal codes apply according to whether or not a tenancy is furnished. An unfurnished tenancy is subject to rent restriction and security of tenure for life [55] (and, under the new Housing Finance legislation comes within the scope of the rent allowance scheme). In relation to furnished tenancies, though a 'reasonable' rent can be determined by a Rent Tribunal, only a limited security of tenure can be granted. (Furnished tenants are also excluded from the rent allowance scheme.)

These are the legal differences, but the *de facto* differences are larger. The security of the furnished tenant is minimal and, thus, the rent restriction provisions are largely irrelevant. This is one reason why, in parts of London at least, furnished dwellings actually increased between 1961 and 1966, both as a proportion of the total (declining) number of privately rented dwellings and, more strikingly, in absolute terms.[56] 'Increasingly, landlords turn to the furnished sector where returns are higher and control laxer than in the unfurnished sector.'[57] This was a market response which was quite predictable.

Though the statistics are scanty, the evidence shows that coloured people are heavily over-represented in the furnished sectors of the areas in which they live, rising to 52 per cent in the 'stress areas' studied by the Francis Committee. They also figure largely among applicants to Rent Tribunals. The Francis Committee reported that

107

'nearly half the applicants in London were coloured—a third from the West Indies'. In some Boroughs much higher proportions were reported: 'These figures undoubtedly reflect the difficulties facing immigrants, especially coloured immigrants, in finding alternative accommodation.'[58]

It is particularly in the furnished sector that 'abuses' are prevalent. These affect white people as well as those who are coloured, but the coloured suffer the additional handicap of racial discrimination. The more overt form of this ('sorry, no coloured') have been banished by the Race Relations legislation, but less overt forms remain and are difficult, if not impossible, to be dealt with by the crude machinery of the law.[59]

The exigencies of the housing market have led to the growth of coloured landlordism (though there are other causes, particularly among Asians—as is indicated in the following section on owner-occupation). Purchase of large houses and the letting of individual floors or rooms has enabled a specifically coloured housing market to develop. This has provided protection against racial discrimination, but does nothing to abate the abuses to which private landlordism (particularly in multi-occupied property) can give rise. The bad landlord—like the bad tenant—is not restricted to any one colour, creed or ethnic origin. More charitably, the stresses and strains of multi-occupation affect all who are subject to them, irrespective of colour. Furthermore, the complex law relating to this leads to a constant battle between the local authorities (attempting to prevent 'the creation of more slums') and the landlords (meeting—however inadequately—a housing need which could not be met elsewhere).[60] The fact that landlords may have purchased their houses with the aid of short-term loans (sometimes at high rates of interest)[61] further increases their problems: they must exact a high rent income from their property if they are to meet their loan repayments.

At worst, the pressures on this small but highly vulnerable part of the housing market can lead to homelessness. Since recognition of homelessness is very much a matter of administrative reaction, it is more of a statistical artifact than a truly measured problem. But the figures, for what they are worth, show a major increase (in London) in the proportion of coloured immigrants among a rising number of homeless families.[62] Moreover, a relatively very high proportion of homeless coloured families in London become homeless because their landlord requires the accommodation for his own use (possibly including the use by newly arrived members of his family) or because he has defaulted on his mortgage and is being dispossessed.[63] Housing market pressures are clearly seen here.

Evidence from areas other than London is hard to come by, but in Birmingham a 1964 Council Report noted that 'action by the Health and other Committees on schemes for the improvement of housing conditions in Sparkbrook and other multi-occupation areas has led to an increase in the number of homeless families requiring assistance'.[64]

To add insult to injury, coloured people become not only 'associated' with poor housing conditions but also are blamed for creating these very conditions—into which housing market and social pressures have forced them.

OWNER-OCCUPATION

Large numbers of coloured people have become owner-occupiers, particularly in those parts of the country where older, cheaper houses have been available for purchase. In the West Midlands Conurbation, for example, while 42 per cent of English households in 1966 were owner-occupiers, the proportion among coloured immigrants was 60 per cent.[65] The reasons for this are varied,[66] and no doubt differ between different areas of the country. Difficulty of obtaining council housing is obviously one factor (particularly where harsh residential qualification rules apply), but it is by no means the only one. In some areas, the relative cheapness of mortgage repayments on low cost terraced houses compared with rents makes owner-occupation a financial attraction. Indians and Pakistanis frequently show a marked preference for owning.[67] One Asian in Newcastle-upon-Tyne typifies this: 'I don't want a Council house. Why pay rent? Only Englishmen do that—I like my own place.'[68]

Discrimination in the private rental market may be more important in other areas. Certainly, there is a marked difference between the situation in Birmingham described by Rex and Moore and that in Newcastle-upon-Tyne described by Davies. The differences relate not only to the intensity of local shortages (though this is important) but also to the character of the housing stock. While cheap terraced houses can be purchased in some areas, in others only large, socially obsolete houses are easily available. These lend themselves to multi-occupation which, in any case, may be necessary to enable the purchaser to pay off his mortgage. Availability of mortgages is another factor of importance: here a number of local authorities have used their powers to assist coloured people to buy in areas which building societies may regard as a 'poor risk'.[69]

The 'real' demand for owner-occupation by coloured people is impossible to assess, as indeed it is with the non-coloured. Difficulties

109

of access to other forms of tenure undoubtedly play their part, as probably does the fact that discrimination in the owner-occupied market is now constrained by the Race Relations legislation. The increasingly generous improvement grants on older property, together with the 'improvement area' policies could be of considerable value in raising the standards of the poorer quality housing and environments in which many of these owner-occupiers live.

DISPERSAL

Evidence of the way in which coloured people are (or are not) 'filtering up' in the housing market is non-existent. Current housing market conditions (characterized by increasing prices in all tenures) could be a serious constraint here.

But, as already mentioned, increasing doubts are being expressed about the validity of policies of dispersal. A Report by the Housing Panel of the Birmingham Community Relations Committee typifies the mounting emphasis which is being placed on the more positive aspects of concentration:

> Dispersal of immigrants is not a solution to the problems of areas like Handsworth and Sparkbrook . . . The difficulties of these areas will not be solved by moving sections of the population but only by concentrated action within the areas themselves. There appears to be no great support from immigrants for the policy of dispersal and neither is there any substantial wish by the indigenous residents to leave. Both wish to see improvements within the districts and given these improvements wish to remain . . . What is needed is the injection of more interest, more effort and more money into the areas of decay and neglect.[70]

This, however, is to polarize the issue. Policies of dispersal are not intended simply to redistribute coloured people geographically: they are intended to remove the barriers to voluntary movement. They are not an *alternative* to area improvement. There is, of course, a danger that they might be viewed as such and, to the extent that this is so, arguments such as those put forward by the Birmingham Community Relations Committee can be of value. But they can also lead to the acceptance of the view that coloured people do not wish to move to suburban areas. This view is already prevalent, for instance, among the housing management staffs of local authorities. It can easily become a self-fulfilling prophecy.

It must be stressed that dispersal of immigrant concentrations (at least in the view of the author) 'should be regarded as a desirable consequence, but not the overriding purpose'[71] of providing full, informed and real opportunity for coloured people to move from inner urban areas.

Indeed, for all we know, dispersal may be taking place on a substantial scale, even in the council house sector. Only adequate 'records' could show how far this is so.

'RECORDS' OF COLOURED PEOPLE

The keeping of separate records of coloured people—their employment, health, education and housing—is morally repugnant to many. Indeed, some argue that it is in itself discriminatory. Curiously, there seems relatively little objection in the field of health—where there is a long tradition of keeping records of 'relevant' groups. At the other extreme is housing, where records (e.g. in terms of who applies and who does not apply for public sector housing, and of who gets what) are rare. To argue the case for keeping records of colour involves a prior argument on keeping any records at all.[72]

All inquiries on the position of coloured people in British society have concluded that the keeping of records is necessary. Without them, it is impossible to assess what the true position is and whether policies are working in the way desired.

There is much confusion on this issue. To maintain that colour is irrelevant is to treat a moral axiom as if it were a fact: what *is* can be very different from what *should be*. In contemporary British society, colour of skin is not irrelevant. The very fact that discrimination is so frequently unintentional strongly supports the case for keeping records. They enable a local authority to satisfy itself that they are not following policies or practices which lead to the very discrimination they wish to avoid. This is not, however, the only reason for keeping records: a local authority needs to know whether coloured people are being helped as they should be, that (in relation to housing) those who should be on the housing list are, that coloured people are not unintentionally being allocated disproportionate numbers of poorer-quality houses, and that maximum dispersal which is compatible with the wishes of coloured citizens is taking place. All this goes further than the need to avoid charges of discrimination under the Race Relations legislation.

This leaves open the question of what form records should take. Since it is colour which is the crucial issue, logic dictates that this is what should be recorded, but visions of clerks dealing with the public using 'colour charts' to determine whether a person was 'fully' coloured

111

have diverted attention to less tendentious and less embarrassing proxies. The Cullingworth Committee, not very convincingly, stated that:

> In considering this issue we have assumed as an act of faith that records will be needed only for a limited period. We may be proved wrong in this, but we look forward to the day when policies have achieved their objective, and colour is as irrelevant in practice as it is in principle. The implication is that we are concerned with a system of recording which has current operational value. It will need review at regular intervals.

On this approach, the Committee maintained that the simplest concept was that of birthplace: 'Though this will become increasingly irrelevant, the fact remains that it is relevant at the present time. A rather better alternative, however, might be "country of origin". Though both these concepts have shortcomings we think they are better than any others. Whatever concept is used, we think it should be used openly and with full explanation.'[73]

In fact, neither of these is sufficient as a proxy for either race or colour. If records are accepted as being necessary, surely they should relate to the matter which is at issue—colour.

POSITIVE POLICIES

One of the main motifs in this chapter has been the insidious nature of discrimination. If this is accepted, then records will not 'speak for themselves'. Already, one hears the argument that the reason why so few coloured people are in council houses is because 'they don't want council houses'. As increasing numbers become eligible for council housing, the argument is shifting to 'coloured people don't want to move out of the inner city'.

This may be true in a narrow sense, since employment opportunities outside the inner city may be restricted or simply unknown. But clearly it is only a partial truth and points to the need for relating housing opportunities with employment opportunities.

On any analysis it is the inter-relationship between housing, employment and education which is fundamental. Given a standard of achievement which is restricted by the educational situation of a deprived area, employment and housing opportunities in more advantaged areas may be closed to the coloured worker. As Hill and Issacharoff have succinctly put it, 'discrimination cannot be proved in the case of under-achievement'.[74]

Without denying the importance of individual policies directed towards reducing overt colour discrimination, of increasing the educational, employment and housing opportunities for coloured people, and of improving the environments in which they live, a major objective must be to co-ordinate policies in such a way that they recognize and take account of the inter-relationships between housing, employment and education.

This is easier said than done when policies in relation to each of these are the separate responsibilities of different central ministries and local authority departments. Yet the range of issues with which local and central government have to deal is so great that any hope of organizing all relevant functions in a single department is forlorn, though this does not imply that the present distribution of functions is the best that can be devised. This applies particularly to central government organisation, where the position of the Home Office (with a major role in regulation and a minor role in social policy) is both ambiguous and—in relation to local government—ineffective.

Nevertheless, too much should not be expected of organisational change. A major difficulty in this field is that, to each Government Department or Division of a Department, the problems of coloured people are marginal. These margins add up to a formidable total. Though the Home Office has 'responsibilities' in relation to the 'total', it has very little power save that of exhortation. Its role, in fact, is that of maintaining pressure—behind the scenes—on other Departments. Its problem is that this role is ill-defined and is not supported by effective powers. This may be much more important than the 'regulatory' image which the Home Office bears.

In short, since the problems of coloured people raise a wide range of issues for which central government responsibility is (inevitably) straddled over several departments, effective action implies, not merely co-ordination, but power over these several departments. The Home Office lacks this power: but mere transfer of responsibility to another Department would, of itself, achieve nothing. An 'Office of the Prime Minister' (such as has been suggested for population policy)[75] might be more effective, but only if it were given adequate powers.

There is, however, an argument against a distinctive 'office' devoted to issues of colour. In essence this stems from the doubt as to how far coloured people constitute, or should be treated as having, problems which are separate from those of the larger problems of disadvantage and deprivation in British society. There is a real fear—certainly on the part of politicians—that an overt concentration on deprivation among a coloured minority could cause resentment and even a white backlash. Pressures from black militants are viewed with alarm, not

113

solely because they threaten the mainstay of current policy (which is directed to issues of general deprivation, with specifically racial issues being dealt with by race relations legislation), but because they may lead to open conflict and civil disorder.

Government is essentially the art of maintaining a balance of forces. The problems raised by a coloured minority show how inequitable this balance is. Policy is aimed at reducing the inequities, but the political constraints are such that progress is slow, if not minimal. Participation is in vogue but, from the viewpoint of central government, the limits to this are defined. Yet participation is not readily controlled and can easily lead to an imbalance of forces.

From a different viewpoint, 'the system' is seen as requiring such fundamental changes that militancy is essential: only this can bring about the fundamental changes which are needed to secure greater equality.

Deep divisions of opinion are to be discerned on these issues: they are reflected not only in the lack of surefootedness on the part of Government, but also in academic publications and—at the time of writing—in the dissension which is threatening the continued existence of the Institute of Race Relations.

Within this context, the establishment of new machinery for dealing with the problems faced by the coloured population (in addition to the existing statutory and voluntary organizations) would be seen as an acknowledgement of both the severity of the problem and the political power of black militancy. Even if this is an invalid (or inadequate) diagnosis, there can be no doubt that Government is fearful of the disruptive potential of the race issue. The problem is thus not only one of equality and justice, but also of civil order. The rantings of an Enoch Powell, the intransigence of the Irish question, the uncertainties in Rhodesia, etc. make the issue one on which Government is hesitant and fearful.

These are very broad questions which cannot be pursued here. The question of 'adequate powers' for the implementation of current policies must, however, be discussed further. Essentially, these should require Departments to undertake specific tasks, to collect relevant statistics and to ensure that their local offices or (where appropriate) local authorities meet certain 'performance standards'. For example, levels of grant to local authorities could be dependent upon satisfactory standards being met in relation to education or housing.

A recent decision on a very different issue illustrates the point: in February 1972 the Minister for Transport Industries announced that he had withdrawn from 135 local authorities their exemption from the county road safety rate 'since their road safety arrangements were considered unsatisfactory'. This was stated to be 'part of a general drive by the Department of the Environment to raise the standard of local road safety work'.[76]

Road safety, of course, is a less politically delicate issue than race, but the example clearly illustrates the type of action which Government can take when it is sure of itself. Though such sureness cannot be expected in relation to racial questions, a major objective of policy currently must be to assist coloured people to break out of areas of bad housing and general deprivation.[77] Central government has a role to play here which it has so far ignored. For instance, despite the very large subsidies provided to local housing authorities, no control (or even machinery) exists to ensure that desirable or even acceptable policies are followed. The Department of the Environment contents itself with the issuing of general guidance. No steps are taken to ensure that this is followed or even to establish how far it is followed. No statistics are required on who gets council houses, still less who gets council houses of different qualities.[78]

This is a field in which central government has been very sensitive to the feelings of local authorities, as is nicely illustrated by their answers to the Select Committee's questions on the action taken on the Cullingworth Report.[79] It is no argument to say that 'the Secretary of State has no power to intervene in the way in which local authorities allocate their houses to individuals'[80]; the question is not one of allocation to individuals, but of general policies and standards of performance.

The Department of the Environment exercises detailed (in fact *too* detailed) controls over the design of dwellings, and new legislation introduces stringent controls over rents—so much so that it can be argued that, so far as rent policy is concerned, local authorities are being downgraded to 'merely agents for the central government'.[81] The issue is thus clearly identified as one of the importance which central government attaches to allocation policies.

This is not to suggest that central government has a monopoly of wisdom: there is abundant evidence to disprove this. But by making the matter one which is of clear importance to central government and focusing greater attention on it, local authority policies would be formulated within a more adequate framework. Moreover, this is a matter on which local authorities may in fact (whatever they may say) welcome more initiative from central government. It is easier for local politicians to justify a policy in relation to the housing of coloured people by reference to central government directives than by reference to principles of justice. There is a nice parallel here with the Race Relations Acts which enable landlords to defend the letting of accommodation to coloured people against the criticism of prejudiced neighbours on the grounds that the law prohibits discrimination. Such a 'defence' may be of particular relevance to smaller authorities where local prejudices can have a greater political impact than in a big city.[82] The Race Relations Acts themselves are ill suited to the promoting of positive policies in the public sector. Greater central government involvement is necessary.

At the local government level, machinery can be established for co-ordinating separate areas of responsibility. New approaches to the related issues of housing, employment and training are needed. Some experience has been gained in this respect in relation to the administration of overspill and, above all, in the new towns—though little has yet been achieved in relation to coloured people, mainly because this has not been seen as an issue which is relevant to the new and expanding towns policy. Further, the training element has been largely ignored. The revival of interest in this, stimulated by rising levels of unemployment, provides an opportunity for a new effort.[83] There is some hope, too, in the gradual movement in local government towards greater acceptance of community development as a proper activity for local authorities to support, and also towards greater acceptance of the concept of corporate community planning.

Many of the issues which fall to be considered under the heading of 'colour' highlight wider issues of social injustice and deprivation. Problems of unequal opportunity, of underachievement, of bad housing, poor schools and multiple deprivation are problems of long standing. The coloured suffer more because they are so visible in a white society, because there is colour discrimination, and because it is so easy for the ignorant to blame them for the problems of the decaying parts of inner cities (the fact that the same problems of decay afflict cities which do not have significant numbers of coloured immigrants being conveniently ignored). These 'colour problems' (which, it will be observed, are basically deficiencies in the response of the white majority) exacerbate problems which are shared by a disadvantaged white minority. Fortunately, there is evidence that the majority of the British population are tolerantly inclined, that there is proportionately more tolerance among those who live near coloured people, and that those who are aged under 35 (and especially those who have had contact with coloured people at work) are the most tolerant.[84]

This gives hope that the British situation will not degenerate as it has in the United States (where, in any case, history is different). Yet there is no ground for complacency, and time is by no means the great healer. The very fact that so many problems faced by the

116

coloured are experienced by much larger numbers of the uncoloured points to the basic social inequities which are involved.

Elizabeth Burney has appropriately referred to the way in which coloured immigrants are 'the barium meal, which, processed through the digestive system of our society, exposes to the X-ray eye the very points of weakness in that system'.[85]

Experience shows that these weaknesses are not easily removed. New directions of policy are being sought as it becomes clear that generalist policies aimed at providing equality of opportunity for all are not enough.

References and Further Reading

1. See J. Zubrzychi, *Polish Immigrants in Britain*, Martinus Nijhoff, 1956.

2. See J. A. Tannahill, *European Volunteer Workers in Britain*, Manchester University Press, 1958.

3. See J. A. Jackson, *The Irish in Britain*, Routledge, 1963.

4. See *Report of the Royal Commission on Population*, Cmd. 7695, HMSO, 1949, p. 124. The Commission saw the possibility of large-scale sponsored immigration as one of the 'undesirable consequences' of a falling population, but 'Immigration on a large scale into a fully established society like ours could only be welcomed without reserve if the immigrants were of good human stock and were not prevented by their religion or race from intermarrying with the host population and becoming merged in it' (paragraph 329). A clearer statement of the 'assimilation' approach to race relations would be difficult to find. For further discussion see S. Patterson, 'Immigrants and Minority Groups in British Society', Chapter 2 of S. Abbott (ed.), *The Prevention of Racial Discrimination in Britain*, Oxford University Press, 1971, p. 26 *et seq.*

5. See E. J. B. Rose and associates, *Colour and Citizenship: A Report on British Race Relations*, Oxford University Press, 1969, pp. 72–73.

6. N. Deakin, 'The Politics of the Commonwealth Immigrants Bill', *Political Quarterly*, Vol. 39, No. 1, January-March, 1968, and P. Foot, *Immigration and Race in British Politics*, Penguin Books, 1965. See also S. Patterson, 'Immigrants and Minority Groups in British Society' in S. Abbott (ed.), *The Prevention of Racial Discrimination in Britain*, Oxford University Press, 1971, pp. 21–26; and E. J. B. Rose, op. cit., Chapter 16.

7. A. Lester and G. Bindman, *Race and Law*, Penguin Books, 1972, pp. 13–14.

8. See W. R. Böhning, *The United Kingdom, the European Community and The Migration of Workers* (in the press).

9. W. W. Daniel, *Racial Discrimination in England*, Penguin Books, 1968, p. 209. See also R. Jowell and P. Prescott-Clarke, 'Racial Discrimination and White Collar Workers in Britain', Chapter 7 of S. Abbott (ed.), *The Prevention of Racial Discrimination in Britain*, Oxford University Press, 1971. For a classic analysis of prejudice see G. W. Allport, *The Nature of Prejudice*, Addison-Wesley, 1954; a short discussion is to be found in the concluding chapter of M. J. Hill and R. M. Issacharoff, *Community Action and Race Relations*, Oxford University Press, 1971, p. 287.

10. G. C. K. Peach, 'Factors Affecting the Distribution of West Indians in

Britain', Institute of British Geographers, *Transactions and Papers, 1966* (No. 36). This applies also to Indian and Pakistani immigrants.

11. See, for example, E. J. B. Rose and associates, op. cit.; S. Abbott, op. cit.; S. Patterson, *Immigrants in Industry*, Oxford University Press, 1968; P. Wright, *The Coloured Worker in British Industry*, Oxford University Press, 1968; and E. Burney, *Housing on Trial*, Oxford University Press, 1967.

12. E. J. B. Rose and associates, op. cit., p. 261.

13. Ibid., pp. 296–297.

14. Ibid., p. 78, quoting A. T. Bouscaron, *International Migrations since 1945*, Praeger, 1963. Nevertheless, total emigration from the United Kingdom exceeded total immigration. See further Chapter 1 of Volume I.

15. D. Stephen, 'The Social Consequences' in D. Evans (ed.), *Destiny or Delusion: Britain and the Common Market*, Gollancz, 1971, Ch. VII. Stephen's argument is a restatement (in unequivocal terms) of Professor Peston's contribution to E. J. B. Rose and associates, op. cit., Chapter 31.

16. E. J. B. Rose and associates, loc. cit., (on which this section leans heavily).

17. See G. C. K. Peach, *West Indian Migration to Britain*, Oxford University Press, 1968.

18. See E. J. B. Rose and associates, op. cit., Chapter 13.

19. Loc. cit. For a technical discussion of *The Economic Impact of Commonwealth Immigration* see the book with this title by K. Jones and D. Smith, Cambridge University Press, 1970.

20. In S. Abbott, op. cit., p. 399.

21. See L. Kushnick, 'British Anti-Discrimination Legislation' in S. Abbott, op. cit., Chapter 9. Hepple has pointed out that 'the pre-occupation of the British industrial relations system with procedural rather than substantive rules of collective bargaining (rules regulating conflict, rather than codified rules about wages and conditions), helps to explain why employers and unions, despite frequent declarations against discrimination, have left discriminatory practices undisturbed for so long. "Peace" has been considered more important than justice for individual victims of discrimination' (Ibid., p. 169). Hepple also points out that the Donovan Report (*Report of the Royal Commission on Trade Unions and Employers' Associations*, Cmnd. 3623, HMSO, 1969) makes only passing references to race or colour; see B. Hepple, 'The Donovan Report and Race Relations', Institute of Race Relations *Newsletter*, October 1968. He poses the question: 'Will it need more dockers marching—and another Royal Commission —to convince those who are called on to implement the Donovan reforms that "racial disputes" are not on the periphery of our industrial situation, but symptomatic of its most central conflicts?'

22. S. Abbott, op. cit., pp. 404–406.

23. E. J. B. Rose and associates, op. cit., p. 181.

24. See A. H. Richmond, *Colour Prejudice in Britain: A Study of West Indian Workers in Liverpool 1942–51*, Routledge 1954; M. Banton, *The Coloured Quarter*, Cape 1955; K. L. Little, *Negroes in Britain: A Study of Racial Relations in English Society*, Routledge 1947; S. Collins, *Coloured Minorities in Britain*, Lutterworth 1957; E. J. B. Rose and associates, op. cit., pp. 487–490; and the (presumably) forthcoming report by L. Bloom on Bute Town, Cardiff.

25. E. J. B. Rose and associates, loc. cit. See also Liverpool Youth Organizations Committee, *Special But Not Separate: A Report on the Situation of Young, Coloured People in Liverpool*, 1968.

26. Select Committee on Race Relations and Immigration, Session 1968–1969, *The Problems of Coloured School Leavers, Report*, p. 19. The Select Committee

quote a case of one child who had been in a remedial class but was now applying for a university place (loc. cit.).

27. Ibid., *Report*, p. 18. The evidence of the Runnymede Trust is of particular interest on this point: ibid *Evidence*, pp. 1151–1152.

28. Ibid., p. 245 (Evidence of the Community Relations Commission).

29. For example, large and increasing numbers of West Indian and half-West Indian children have come into the care of the Children's Service in London. A major reason for this lies in cultural differences: 'As the West Indian family system is characteristically very loosely structured, de-emphasizing the nuclear family and permitting a wide range of unlegalized relationships, many situations arise which, in an English context, would justify reception into care, but which, in a West Indian context are normal and tolerable.' Moreover, West Indian parents take a very different view of institutional care from English parents: 'Having their children in care can help them to fulfil the ambitions which brought them to England.' (K. Fitzherbert, *West Indian Children in London*, Occasional Papers on Social Administration, No. 19, Bell, 1967, p. 107.) The contrast with Asians is striking: see, for example, R. Desai, *Indian Immigrants in Britain*, Oxford University Press, 1963.

30. See *The Illegal Child-Minders: A Report on the Growth of Unregistered Child-Minding and the West Indian Community*, Priority Area Children, Cambridge, 1971.

31. See, for example, Inner London Education Authority, *The Education of Immigrant pupils in Primary Schools* (ILEA Report No. 959).

32. See Inner London Education Authority, *The Education of Immigrant Pupils in Special Schools for Educationally Sub-Normal Children* (ILEA Report No. 657), 1968.

33. Ibid., p. 5.

34. B. Coard, *How the West Indian Child is made Educationally Sub-Normal in the British School System*, published for the Caribbean Education and Community Workers' Association by New Beacon Books, 1971 (italics in the original).

35. Now the Department of the Environment, previously the Ministry of Housing and Local Government.

36. Ministry of Education, *English for Immigrants*, Pamphlet No. 43, HMSO, 1963.

37. For a discussion of this policy see E. J. B. Rose and associates, op. cit., Chapter 18, or S. Abbott, op. cit., Chapter 5. The policy was set out in Circular 7/65 of the Department of Education and Science. (This is reproduced in the evidence to the Select Committee, op. cit., Vol. II, pp. 156–162.) See also the White Paper, *Immigration for the Commonwealth*, Cmnd. 2739, HMSO, 1965. A survey of administrative policies is to be found in J. Power, *Immigrants in School*, Councils and Education Press, 1967.

38. S. Abbott, op. cit., p. 125.

39. Quoted in S. Abbott, op. cit., p. 128.

40. See E. J. B. Rose and associates, op. cit., p. 288.

41. See evidence of the Department of Education and Science to the Select Committee (*The Problems of Coloured School Leavers*), op. cit., and S. Abbott, op. cit., p. 130. The most recent statement on dispersal policy is to be found in *The Education of Immigrants* (DES Survey No. 13, HMSO, 1971): this exhibits a similarly ambiguous movement away from the policy of dispersal.

42. S. Abbott, op. cit., pp. 121–122 and Select Committee, *The Problems of Coloured School Leavers*, op. cit., Evidence of the Department of Education and Science.

43. DES, *Education and Science in 1970*, HMSO, 1971, p. 15.

44. But see R. Holman, 'Combating Social Deprivation' in R. Holman *et al.*, *Socially Deprived Families in Britain*, Bedford Square Press, 1970; S. Abbott, op. cit., pp. 122–123 and 396; and E. J. B. Rose and associates, op. cit., pp. 684–685.

45. A survey in Lambeth showed that while 68 per cent of all coloured people were born abroad, the proportion for those aged 5–11 was 49 per cent while for those under the age of five it was as low as 6 per cent. (Quoted in Central Housing Advisory Committee, *Council Housing: Purposes, Procedures and Priorities*, HMSO, 1969, p. 139.)

46. The fact that the author was the Chairman of the Central Housing Advisory Committee's Sub-Committee on Housing Management will not escape the notice of those who compare this section with Chapter 9 of *Council Housing: Purposes, Procedures and Priorities* (HMSO, 1969).

47. See particularly E. J. B. Rose and associates, op. cit., Chapter 12.

48. See, for example, W. W. Daniel, *Racial Discrimination in Britain*, Penguin Books, 1968; E. Burney, *Housing on Trial: A Study of Immigrants and Local Government*, Oxford University Press, 1967 and the *Annual Reports* of the Race Relations Board (HMSO).

49. See the publications of OECD, for example, R. Descloitres, *The Foreign Worker: Adaptation to Industrial Work and Urban Life*, OECD, 1967; L. C. Hunter and G. L. Reid, *Urban Worker Mobility*, OECD, 1968; and *Final Report of the International Joint Seminar on Geographical and Occupational Mobility of Manpower*, OECD, 1964.

50. E. Burney in S. Abbott, op. cit., p. 103. One of the classic arguments used in relation to coloured people is that their presence depresses house prices. On this see V. A. Karn, 'Property Values Amongst Indians and Pakistanis in a Yorkshire Town', *Race*, Vol. X, No. 3, January 1969, pp. 269–284.

51. E. Burney, *Housing on Trial: A Study of Immigrants and Local Government*, Oxford University Press, 1967, p. 2.

52. This was forcibly impressed on the author by a garage proprietor who said that 'of course' he did not discriminate: he employed several coloured girls, 'but you couldn't expect the white girls to use the same lavatories could you?'

53. E. Burney, op. cit., p. 71.

54. Ibid., p. 75.

55. Only the briefest summary is provided here. A full account is to be found in the *Report of the Committee on the Rent Acts* (Francis Report), Cmnd. 4608, HMSO, 1971.

56. See J. Greve, D. Page and S. Greve, *Homelessness in London*, Scottish Academic Press, 1971, Chapter 2. No later figures are currently available.

57. E. Burney in S. Abbott, op. cit., p. 100.

58. *Report of the Committee on the Rent Acts*, op. cit., p. 134.

59. See Chapter 9 of W. W. Daniel, *Racial Discrimination in England*, Penguin Books, 1968.

60. See J. Rex and R. Moore, *Race, Community and Conflict: A Study of Sparkbrook*, Oxford University Press, 1967, especially Chapters 2 and 5.

61. See Select Committee on Race Relations and Immigration, Session 1970–1971, *Housing, Vol. 1: Report*, H.C. 508–I, HMSO, Chapter 10.

62. J. Greve, *et al.*, op. cit., p. 101.

63. Ibid., p. 91.

64. J. Rex and R. Moore, op. cit., p. 25.

65. E. J. B. Rose and associates, op. cit., pp. 132–138.

66. See the evidence of the author and Miss Valerie Karn to the Select Com-

mittee on Race Relations and Immigration, *Housing* op. cit., Vol. 2, Q. 43–46.

67. See, for example, V. A. Karn, 'Property Values Amongst Indians and Pakistanis in a Yorkshire Town', *Race*, Vol. 10, No. 3, January 1969, pp. 269–284.

68. J. G. Davies, *The Evangelistic Bureaucrat: A Study of a Planning Exercise in Newcastle upon Tyne*, Tavistock, 1972, p. 29.

69. See, for example, S. Jenkins, *Here to Live: A Study of Race Relations in an English Town* (Leamington Spa), Runnymede Trust, 1971; and V. A. Karn, op. cit.

70. 'Dispersal—an Irrelevancy', *Race Today*, Vol. 4, No. 3, March 1972, p. 94.

71. *Council Housing: Purposes, Procedures and Priorities*, op. cit., paragraph 412.

72. See the author's evidence to the Select Committee on Race Relations and Immigration, Session 1970–71, *Housing*, H.C. 508–II, HMSO, p. 15.

73. See also Select Committee on Race Relations and Immigration, Session 1970–71, *Housing, Vol. I: Report*, H.C. 508–I, HMSO, 1971, Chapter 3.

74. M. J. Hill and R. M. Issacharoff, *Community Action and Race Relations*, Oxford University Press, 1971, p. 290.

75. See Chapter 1 of Volume I, p. 23.

76. DOE Press Release, 16 February 1972.

77. This is not to suggest that the policy should be one of wholesale dispersal: see the quotation given earlier from the Cullingworth Report, and E. J. B. Rose and associates, op. cit., pp. 678–683.

78. As Elizabeth Burney suggests, 'a few statistics would concentrate their minds more wonderfully than pages of exhortation' (*Housing on Trial*, op. cit., p. 239).

79. Select Committee on Race Relations and Immigration, Session 1970–71 *Housing: Vol. 2, Evidence*, pp. 22 *et. seq.*

80. Ibid., p. 23.

81. A. A. Nevitt, 'The New Housing Legislation', *Housing Review*, Vol. 21, No. 2, March-April 1972, p. 62.

82. Cf. Elizabeth Burney's comments on the G.L.C., Manchester and Wolverhampton, op. cit., pp. 221–222.

83. See DEP, *Training for the Future*, DEP 1971, and S. Mukherjee, *Changing Manpower Needs*, PEP, 1972.

84. W. W. Daniel, op. cit., and E. J. B. Rose and associates, op. cit., Chapter 28 and p. 675.

85. E. Burney, op. cit., p. 4.

Chapter 5

Social Planning

Planning, despite its avowedly social aims, has been in the main a physical activity. In large part this is due to the relatively advanced state of the art of physical planning and the professionalism that accompanies this. Furthermore, the objectives and achievements of physical planning can be readily measured (at least in quantitative terms)—numbers of houses and mileage of roads built, the acreages redeveloped, the number of dwellings improved or demolished, and so forth. In terms of sheer technological achievement the successes far outweigh the failures. The publicity attending the latter (as when roofs blew off in Hatfield New Town or when the Ronan Point flats and certain box girder bridges collapsed) underlines their rarity.

Social objectives and achievements are a very different matter. Here the objectives are seldom clear or even the subject of common agreement (except when expressed in terms of such extreme generality as to be operationally meaningless). A motorway can be designed to meet a measurable capacity: any failure can be measured and rectified. A bridge can be designed to bear a specific load: if it fails to meet this there is unequivocal evidence. But what is the social counterpart of a crumbled motorway or a collapsed bridge?

The issue is more than one of the functional adequacy of physical structures. This can be assessed and measured by 'user studies'. It is more than the adequacy or popularity of physical provision. This can be measured by the intensity of use and by surveys. Such approaches are not without their difficulties, but at least the objectives are clear. Yet they are limited to restricted 'performance standards'. They may enable a judgement to be formed on physical adequacy or shortcomings, but they are of little utility in measuring social success or failure. A new estate may be a superb technological achievement: it may even be generally accepted as a visual delight; yet this tells us nothing about its social adequacy.

Much of the problem stems from the fact that we have a few 'social measures'. Most statistics and 'standards' relate to physical features (number of units, densities, plumbing) or costs (per dwelling, per

122

person). Of course, social commentary exists in abundance—usually in terms of what is wrong and, at most, with some simplistic ideas of how to correct the errors. But the physical features may be totally irrelevant to social considerations.

The crux of the matter is that there is a world of difference between convenience and social welfare. As Lowry has succinctly put it, 'a private bath and toilet does not seem to cure juvenile delinquency'.[1] Physical planning can increase convenience, but another dimension of planning is required for social welfare. Indeed, identical physical environments (whether good or bad) can have totally different social results.

Early social reformers thought simplistically that good sanitation would result in good behaviour. Later formulations were more elaborate. A classic statement was that of John Burns, the President of the Local Government Board, made in the debates on the first piece of British Planning Legislation—the Housing, Town Planning, Etc. Act of 1909:

> The object of the Bill is to provide a domestic condition for the people in which their physical health, their morals, their character and their whole social condition can be improved by what we hope to secure in this Bill. The Bill aims in broad outline at, and hopes to secure, the home healthy, the house beautiful, the town pleasant, the city dignified and the suburb salubrious.[2]

Whatever the historical justification for such statements, it is abundantly clear that in contemporary society they have little validity. Even in terms of physical health the effects of good housing may be slight and can be outweighed by other factors. As long ago as 1933, a study in Stockton-on-Tees demonstrated that the higher rents which families had to pay on moving from a slum area to a new housing estate led to malnutrition and higher death rates.[3] Numerous studies since then have demonstrated the importance of a wide range of factors—of which the physical environment is only one—to social welfare.[4]

'A good home in a good environment' is a major goal, but stated thus it poses far more questions than it answers. The family needs to be able to afford the good home, to have security against unemployment and ill-health, and to have access to a wide range of social services and community services. The environment needs to be 'good' not only in terms of physical layout and design, but also in terms of social opportunity and satisfaction. This is a matter partly of the provision of services, but also of the social composition of the area and its relationship with other areas.

123

Social welfare is a compound of nutrition, health, shelter, income and income-security, employment and job satisfaction, personal liberty, access to social facilities, opportunity for self-fulfilment and for influencing political processes, and a wide range of similar factors which together make up the quality of life.

Clearly this is a huge field to contemplate, let alone to analyse and formulate policies for. It is small wonder that physical planning policies on the one hand and separated social policies in relation to specific fields on the other hand are the most which have been achievable. Nevertheless, there has been increasing recognition of the need to devise comprehensive approaches. A number of these are discussed in the following pages.

NEW COMMUNITIES

Since the end of the last war, over 200,000 homes have been built in designated new and expanding towns. Far greater numbers have been built in large housing estates on the periphery of the conurbations. The social planning problems of these new communities have attracted considerable attention. They do, however, differ markedly. At one extreme there is the comprehensively planned new town where the objective is to create a 'balanced community', where eligibility for a house is largely dependent upon the securing of a job in the town, and where there is an *ad hoc* development corporation with wide powers 'to do anything necessary or expedient for the purposes of the new town or for the purposes incidental thereto'. At the other extreme, there is the municipal housing estate developed at very rapid speed for families for a big city's housing list, where no provision is made for employment and where no attempt is made to develop a 'balanced community'.

Between these extremes there is a wide range. Some 'peripheral estates' are virtually new towns with their own town centres and industrial areas (as at Wythenshawe, Manchester). New towns range in planned size from 13,000 to 500,000 and while many exist primarily to cater for the 'overspill' from the conurbations, some have wider regional and industrial development objectives. Some have built on the sites of very small communities (e.g. Peterlee and Glenrothes) while others are based on substantial towns (e.g. Hemel Hempstead). The latest new towns are not only relatively huge in target population but are expansions of large towns (e.g. Peterborough and Warrington).

Expanding towns also range from small market towns anxious to arrest their economic decline (e.g. Haverhill) to major town development schemes (as at Basingstoke). Some are in remote locations, while others are on the periphery of conurbations. Typically they are on a small scale and many are characterized by a lack of 'market attraction' to industry and private enterprise.

The most important differences between new towns, peripheral housing estates and expanding towns stem from their statutory foundation. New towns are developed under the New Towns Acts by development corporations established for the purpose. Peripheral estates are developed by a local authority either within its administrative boundaries or beyond. The latter have tended to attract more attention in relation to social planning because of the problems highlighted by the administration of overspill. The 'exporting authority' (i.e. the authority exporting its population to the area of another authority) is normally concerned only with the provision of houses under the normal powers of the Housing Acts while the receiving authorities are responsible for all the social and community services. Expanding towns, though varying in administrative arrangements, are developed by a local authority (usually the 'receiving authority') in co-operation with an exporting authority and the county council, using powers provided by the Town Development Acts.

These are all publicly sponsored new communities. Private developments defy categorization and, in any case, few have been studied.[5]

To complete the picture it is necessary to refer to redevelopment areas. In Britain these are normally entirely municipal undertakings. Their number and scale has increased significantly in recent years. They are not normally considered as 'new communities', but this is to some extent a matter of definition. Be that as it may, since they involve the clearance of existing areas and at least the disturbance (if not the total disruption) of an existing community, it is appropriate to discuss them separately.

The 'problems' of these new communities are generally thought of in terms of social provision (e.g. lack of meeting places, little provision for leisure activities, inadequate schools and social services, all leading to stress, loneliness, 'new town blues' and the like). On this approach, 'social planning' is concerned with the provision of the buildings and services which are lacking. Though this is an important element, social planning is also concerned with more elusive issues of community, of the social structure, and of the quality of life.

The character of a new community is affected by the way in which the families are selected. In most new and expanding towns the selection is predominantly by way of employment. Formal machinery exists (industrial selection schemes) for selecting tenants who are both in housing need and have the skills required for employment in

125

the area.[6] By no means do all families pass through such a scheme, but the majority (at least in the public authority housing sector) must obtain a job in the town before they become eligible for a house. As a result the social character of the new community is to a large extent determined by the employment structure which in turn is determined by the type of industries which are attracted to the area.

Generalization here is difficult, but since new areas tend to attract modern manufacturing industry employing relatively high pro-portions of non-manual and skilled and semi-skilled workers, there tends to be an under-representation of unskilled workers. This is particularly so in the new towns which have been criticized for failing to achieve a representative cross-section of the population.[7] The essence of the matter, however, is that new jobs are not representative of old jobs.[8] But there is some evidence that the new towns assist in social mobility. A report from Harlow New Town, for example, argues that many of those now classified as skilled workers in the town originally came as partly skilled workers from poor housing conditions in London and have subsequently acquired new skills and status through industrial training schemes.[9]

In new communities developed as housing estates without any employment qualification, social character is determined by the housing selection process operated by the responsible authority, the types of dwelling provided, the situation in relation to local employ-ment and commuting possibilities, and the severity of the 'exporting' area's housing problem. The last factor is crucial. The greater is the housing problem the more likely are the families moving to the estate to be those who were previously in acute housing need—both because these will be accorded the highest priority for tenancies by the local authority and because they will be less unwilling to put up with the disadvantages of commuting.[10] Where much of a municipality's housing operations are concerned with slum clearance, the displaced families may have little or no choice other than to move to a big over-spill estate.

These estates are commonly developed in their entirety as council housing estates. Consequently, anyone who does not 'qualify' on the local authority's eligibility rules is excluded and the estates have a marked degree of social homogeneity. The teachers, social workers, doctors and others who man the social services have to live elsewhere. Even if special 'allocations' are made to such people, they may well prefer to live in a different social environment or to become owner-occupiers rather than council tenants. At the extreme, it may prove difficult to find adequate numbers of professional and semi-profes-sional people to staff the services. Issues of the quality of the community leadership and social organization then turn into much more apparent 'problems'.

These features are of particular importance in the huge council estates of the post-war years. Surprisingly little study has been directed to these, but the following quotation from the Report of a Working Party on Community Problems in Glasgow housing schemes is illustrative:

> In each of the new housing areas it is noteworthy that the population is not a representative cross section of the Glasgow community. Few professional people actually live in the areas and, indeed, many would require strong inducement to work there. Doctors, dentists and school-teachers have to travel from other residential areas to their daily work in the community.
>
> In the later areas to be developed and particularly in Easterhouse, a high proportion of the residents were housed there not as a result of their own wish to leave their previous neighbourhoods but because of the demolition of their former homes to permit the redevelopment of older parts of the City. For those involuntarily displaced, the attraction of, and their enthusiasm for, their new homes tends to be weakened when they find in their new neighbourhood few of the customary facilities for community life. It is also unusual to find former neighbours rehoused in the same street in a new housing area.
>
> In addition, it must be realized that it is very exceptional to find more than one generation of a family as householders in a new housing area. The housewife in Drumchapel has a mother in Cowcaddens; the girl who gets married in Easterhouse sets up house in Dennistoun.
>
> In these circumstances it is not surprising that the new housing areas should be subject to strains and stresses unknown to older communities.[11]

This is a striking official indictment of the social character of the large housing estate. It stems from an understandable but—with hindsight—regrettable preoccupation with the physical problems of inadequate housing, redevelopment and 'overspill'. Furthermore, given the speed of the operation and the need to match new building programmes with clearance, the strains on management become very great. Rules of thumb predominate; wider social objectives become secondary to the immediate need to let new houses and empty old ones.

The important point here is that 'social issues' cannot be left to be dealt with following the completion of a development or during the course of development. They need to be planned for in advance. Some problems can, in this way, be entirely avoided; others can be mitigated.

For example, all new communities tend to be characterized by the youthfulness of their populations. The more families are selected from 'the top of the housing list' and the more rapid the speed of development, the more youthful will the population be: hence the larger proportion of young people and children in a peripheral housing estate than in a new town. Of course, young families are more mobile than the middle aged and the elderly.[12] Some imbalance in age structure is thus inevitable, but it can be reduced—and there are good reasons why a positive social planning approach should attempt to reduce it.

In the first place, a major imbalance in population structure gives rise to the problem of 'peaks' and 'troughs'. The immediate need is to meet a peak demand for maternity, child-welfare and nursery services. This is followed by a peaking in the demand for primary schools, then secondary schools, youth services, employment for school-leavers, and finally 'second-generation' housing. Providing for these peaks is not the only problem: the peaks are followed by troughs: thus, if the race to meet a peak need is successful, there may be 'excess capacity' later. The more rapid the development the greater are the peaks likely to be. The problem thus arises in a particularly acute form in the very rapidly developed overspill estates where the constraint is purely one of construction capacity and careful pre-planning of public utility services. (In the new towns and other schemes where house-building is geared to the growth of employment, this operates as a significant constraint.)

Reducing imbalance in age structure is desirable for other reasons than the avoidance of 'peaking'. The young families who create problems for the social services include the very families who find the cost of living in a new commuter estate a great strain. Middle-age families tend to have higher incomes and be better off in other ways (e.g. they are likely to have more furniture and fewer hire-purchase commitments). The wives of such families are also better able to travel to work since their children are older. This applies even more to middle-aged households whose children have left home and, of course, to the elderly. There is also social benefit in having more elderly and retired households in a new community. Whereas young households centre their interests on making their homes and caring for young children, older households have more time to give to community affairs.

Furthermore, a mixture of household types enables a wide range of dwelling types to be provided, which is of considerable benefit as the community matures and requires small dwellings both for those reaching retirement age and for the new generation of young married couples without children.

This line of thinking—which starts from the social character of the community being created—is the reverse of that which is preoccupied with the needs of a housing list. In physical planning terms, the crucial factor becomes the distribution of dwelling types. The importance of this can be illustrated by reference to a large housing estate built by Birmingham at Castle Vale.[13] In 1967 this consisted of 40 per cent houses and 60 per cent flats; of all dwellings, 26 per cent had one bedroom, 31 per cent two bedrooms, 37 per cent three bedrooms and 5 per cent four bedrooms. This distribution of dwelling sizes was the main determinant of the population structure of the estate.

It is, of course, obvious that household size will vary in dwellings of different sizes. What may not be so obvious is the extent of the variation. In Castle Vale the range was from an average of 1·46 persons in dwellings with one bedroom to 7·16 in dwellings with four bedrooms. Had no one-bedroom dwellings been provided (and assuming no change in allocation policy) the average size of household in Castle Vale would have been, not 3·37 persons, but 4·04 persons. Had the development consisted only of three and four bedroom dwellings the average number of persons per household would have been 4·98. Applying these figures to a hypothetical development of 15,000 dwellings, the resulting population would range from 50,500 (with the Castle Vale size distribution of dwellings) to 74,700 (with only three and four bedroom dwellings).

This analysis, however, relates only to the population at the date of the move. The greater is the concentration of young families, the greater is the population growth likely to be. This growth will also be all the greater the more rapid the rate of development.

So far the discussion has been largely in terms of wholly council developments, though the need for a mixture of tenures has been implied. Again speed of development is a factor. Experience has amply demonstrated that the most efficient type of development (in terms of speed of production) is public sector development wholly for letting to council applicants. Though there are significant signs of change,[14] councils have until recently been able to build at high speed, fully confident that they would have no difficulty in letting their dwellings. Thus there have been good logistic reasons why developments should be entirely, or at least predominantly, public authority. Private building for owner-occupiers can proceed only at the rate dictated by the market: this has not been fast enough for local authorities. Any wider consideration of social balance or of providing a range of alternative housing opportunities has been subjugated to the narrower and more pressing objective of rapid building rates.

Furthermore, given this situation, the pressures for providing attractive developments have come largely from architects and planners—and have been conceived in their terms. With the easing of the general housing situation, councils are having to pay increasing attention to consumer demands. As private sector building increases in response to these demands, the less attractive council estates will increasingly be deserted by those able to buy the type of housing they desire. There will be important implications for the management and improvement of existing council estates. On past experience it is likely that some estates will be rejected by all who can obtain anything better. Already a number of councils are considering major improvements to such estates to make them more attractive. Unfortunately, some are 'tightening' their administrative rules to allow applicants fewer choices and existing tenants fewer opportunities for transfer. The better alternative would be to analyse what people want and to take measures to provide this: which is one of the major objectives of social planning.[15]

SOCIAL PROVISION

The emphasis which is being placed on social structure and character is justified because of the inadequate attention which these issues have received. This, however, is not to deny the importance of social provision: it is simply to assert that social planning is much more than this.

That many new communities have inadequate social provision has been amply demonstrated. Reports from the two official Housing Advisory Committees have underlined the seriousness of the position. The English report on *The Needs of New Communities* referred to one large peripheral housing estate (which was not regarded as being untypical):

A half of the estate's inhabitants are under twenty-one and yet there is no cinema, no dance hall, no bowling alley, no restaurant, not even a coffee bar. Not surprisingly, therefore, many local youngsters have little else to do besides play in the streets. Since the development is compact, large numbers of children inevitably tend to gather on street corners and open plots of land. Less responsible members of the press have seized on this fact to label the estate as 'Kidsville' and 'Mobtown', and gradually the name of the estate and vandalism have become synonymous.[16]

More generally, the Report concluded that 'the real social needs of our times have often been imperfectly assessed and inadequately provided for'.

Similarly, the Scottish report on *Council House Communities* (the irony of the title having apparently escaped the authors) noted that:

A principal reason for building council houses is not only to provide families with the household amenities and space required, but to free them, and the children particularly, from the destructive social influences of living in the slums. The fact that many council schemes impose their own kind of social stresses, often much greater ones, shows that this intention has not always been realised.[17]

Little attention has been given to private estates, possibly because the developing organization is not so vulnerable to complaint and has no continuing local existence, and because private developments are typically on a smaller scale. Be that as it may, social critics have concentrated their attention on publicly sponsored developments where it is (rightly) held that the public authority should be concerned with far more than the provision of houses.

Curiously it is the new towns which have had particular criticism. Yet it is in the new towns that the greatest care, forethought and provision has been made. Whatever the inadequacies of the new towns, these pale into insignificance in comparison with those of the large 'council house communities'.

Part of the problem is that many of these developments take place in contradiction to regional policy rather than in conformity with it. The intrinsic problems of administrative co-ordination and financial planning to which they give rise are thus made much more difficult. Liverpool's Kirkby estate and Birmingham's Chelmsley Wood estate, for example, were both conceded to the Cities after long politico-planning battles in which the Counties (Lancashire and Warwickshire) argued that overspill should go to new and expanding towns beyond the green belt, while the Cities argued (with eventual success) that the urgency of their short-run housing problems admitted of no solution other than peripheral development. As a result, when the developments actually went ahead they did so at an incredibly rapid speed and without the advantage of a sub-regional planning framework. Existing plans had to be hurriedly altered to

131

accommodate a major and unexpected departure from the policy which they had officially embraced.

The development of a major new community raises difficult administrative problems of co-ordination and difficult political problems of determining priorities. Numerous statutory authorities and departments of the 'exporting' and 'receiving' authorities are involved. All these will have their own wider problems and orders of priority. No single body has control over the whole operation. As a result, the major problem of co-ordinating the multiplicity of providers admits of no easy solution. Furthermore, there is abundant opportunity for legitimate argument on who is to provide what and at whose cost. The receiving authority who so bitterly opposed the proposed development in the first place is now called upon to re-allocate resources from its existing electorate in favour of city dwellers being moved into their area.

It is in this uncongenial framework that community facilities have to be provided. Many of these are not directly grant-aided and most are likely to suffer if, as commonly happens, conditions of financial stringency develop. The Report on *The Needs of New Communities* stressed the necessity for a 'social development plan' which would anticipate the needs arising, and establish a planned programme of provision. Here the focus was on techniques of planning and management, but a prior problem is the political one of the allocation of resources. Indeed, perhaps the biggest problem in this type of new community is the low priority which is given to 'non-essential' community facilities. And since so many *old* communities lack adequate facilities there is political justification for not giving them top priority. After all, if an old-established community has been waiting many years for a much-needed facility why should a new community be given it first?

The answer to this is that old-established communities have strengths which a new community lacks. New communities tend to need more support and at least a modicum of provision (e.g. meeting places) to facilitate the building up of a framework of social relationships. Further, the move itself, though providing superior housing conditions can break up established relationships and patterns of activity: help is needed if the new community is to establish itself.

This is appreciated in many new towns which have set up social relations departments (though sometimes belatedly). Such departments are rare within the traditional local government organization, though (as is discussed in a later section) community development programmes are multiplying in relation to specific deprived urban areas. These new town officials carry various titles—a reflection of the uncertainty which attaches to their roles, as well as the varying ways in which these are interpreted.[18] While the term 'social relations' found favour with *The Needs of New Communities* Committee, alternative terms are 'social development', 'liaison', or the more restricted 'community development' and—the narrowest concept of all—'public relations'.

Roles range from full membership of the planning team to press relations and the reception of visitors. The important function, however, is to advise on social matters, to assist in the formation of community groups and activities, and to establish lines of communication between the planners and the planned.

If this is to be a success, the social relations department must be accepted as a power alongside the traditional functional departments of the engineer, the architect, the housing manager and such like. This is a tall order, and such success as has been achieved has been due to the commitment of new town development corporations to social planning and their explicit functions in relation to the comprehensive development of new towns—as distinct from the traditional administrative role of local authorities. This may overstress the differences: local authorities have always had important development functions but, large though these sometimes are, they are typically marginal to their main function of administering local services and developing them incrementally.

THE SOCIAL DEVELOPMENT PLAN

The Needs of New Communities Report contained the recommendation that in addition to a physical development plan each new community should have a social development plan and programme: 'This would be concerned not only with the provision of physical amenities, but also with the staffing of services at both county and district level and with all those functions which are the responsibility in the new towns of a Social Relations Officer and his staff. It would show how the social services and community facilities were to be provided, by whom and when.'[19] The Report only sketched what was meant by 'social development'. (Having accepted the term 'social relations' in reference to new town officials, it might have been more logical to use the phrase 'social relations plan', but this suggests a narrower field of responsibility than was in mind.) 'Social development' was widely defined as 'policies and programmes directed towards meeting social needs'. The Report continued: 'We are concerned with problems of families settling in a new environment, of providing them with education, health and welfare services,

133

community facilities, etc. and with the provision of opportunity and choice.'

Most of the services which would be the concern of a social development plan are frequently the responsibility of agencies other than the one responsible for the provision of housing. This makes the plan an important instrument of co-ordination. The Report stated:

> The plan will be closely concerned with the social provision to be made by statutory authorities, particularly in the case of educational, health and social welfare programmes. Clearly the implementation of these programmes must remain with the responsible authorities* and they will, of course, have their own scale of priorities for the wider geographical area for which they are responsible. It is likely that this will differ from the priorities as seen by the new community, but these essentially political issues can never be planned away. What the plan can do is to ensure that there is adequate co-ordination between the different authorities concerned.

Great stress was laid in the Report on this need for co-ordination (which, after all, is a major element in any planning). Hence, recommendations for development committees, joint development committees, directors of town development and technical organizations at the county level.

The *Plan for Milton Keynes* makes the point clearly:

> The social development programme which the Corporation intends to pursue is essentially a series of actions undertaken to achieve those social goals which require the existence of an appropriate institutional framework or organizational device. In some cases such provision may already be available through the traditional services of the local authority or voluntary services, but where they are not then a function of the social development programme will be to ensure their development. In the majority of cases this function will be fulfilled by ensuring that appropriate authorities as well as employers and commercial interests are alert to social needs and provide for them: in this sense the Corporation does not see its main responsibility as that of providing additional services but more that of acting as a central catalyst of their provision.[20]

---

* This, of course, is not true, except on the pragmatic approach adopted by the Committee. Wisely, they kept clear of these treacherous waters. But there is a case for a developing authority being responsible for as many services as possible. The larger is the number of 'providers' the greater is the difficulty of overall planning.

134

At the time when the Committee was sitting, ideas about 'corporate planning' and 'planning-programming-budgeting systems' (PPBS) were not generally current. Had the Committee sat four years later it is likely that much of the terminology from these approaches would have been employed. Indeed, these approaches are essentially a formalization of the ideas the Committee was wrestling with.

In essence, a social development plan and programme has the objective of making explicit the needs of new communities and the ways in which these are to be met. It could never guarantee that the needs would, in fact, be met but it would ensure that they would not be ignored.

MONITORING SOCIAL POLICY

Surprisingly little attempt has been made to monitor and evaluate the achievements of social policies. It is clear from the previous discussion that some major failures have occurred in the planning of certain new communities. Reasons for these and possible alternative approaches have been suggested, but it must be admitted that, however appropriate these may appear to be, they rest on no assessment of their success in other areas. More alarmingly, there has been little study of the reasons for failure. Indeed, even the failings are very much a matter of description of obvious symptoms of inadequacy. The social commentator and critic has had pride of place over the social analyst.

Increasingly, however, stress is being laid on 'monitoring'. Recent reports of committees of inquiry, research studies, the new structure plan system, and the reorganization of national statistical services have all underlined the need for this. The first issue of *Social Trends*, for instance,describes a long-term project which the Central Statistical Office is undertaking on a 'system' of social statistics:

The aim is to construct a system in which the many statistics bearing on social conditions, social resources and the flows of people through various activities and institutions are brought together coherently and meaningfully. Such a system could, if successful, throw light on the relationships between social investments and changes in social conditions and welfare and on the links between economic changes and social changes. Even if these aims are hard to realize, the system could produce statistical evidence on the way different aspects of social conditions—health, housing, education, income, social care—inter-relate in the lives of people, and to what extent inequalities in one go with inequalities in others.[21]

However, 'social statistics are deficient not only in coverage, but in methods of analysis and interpretation'. It is in this connection that 'social indicators' hold out promise. Social indicators are 'standardized and universally agreed ways of analysing the present large and confusing array of descriptive data so as to arrive at a new set of derived quantities (indicators) which are somehow comprehensively representative of the state of society'.[22] The hope is that a limited number of social indicators will be of direct use in policy formulation. But a major problem is to determine the important issues on which indicators are needed. Most measures relate to deficiencies in environment or some form of malaise. The American *Toward A Social Report* complained that:

> We have measures of death and illness, but no measures of physical vigor or mental health. We have measures of the level and distribution of income, but no measures of the satisfaction that income brings. We have measures of air and water pollution, but no way to tell whether our environment is, on balance, becoming uglier or more beautiful. We have some clues about the test performance of children, but no information about their creativity or attitude toward intellectual endeavour.[23]

In short, we do not know how to measure positively satisfaction, happiness or the quality of life. Instead we have to use, as proxies, 'objective' indicators of inadequacies, ill-health and inequalities. In the present state of the art there is no alternative.

Nevertheless, it is clear that indicators relating to specific issues are not enough. As pointed out in Chapter 1, poverty is a multi-dimensional problem. Families who have inadequate housing or poor health or low income or restricted job opportunities are very different from families who have all of these. Similarly with neighbourhoods it is the combination of deprivations which makes the problem acute— both in terms of what the inhabitants suffer and in terms of devising appropriate policies to deal with the suffering.

Indeed, positive action in relation to one aspect can exacerbate other aspects. Housing improvement, for example, may result in rents (and rates) which cannot be afforded. Area improvement may attract higher income groups to compete for the limited housing available.

Furthermore, the aspects selected for measurement may not be the important ones. Standards of plumbing below those acceptable to middle-class households may be of less (or even no) importance compared with the much more difficult-to-measure community support which a neighbourhood offers. On the other hand, care must

136

be taken not to fall victim to a simple theory of cultural relativity: 'the poor are happier as they are' theory is an easy excuse for doing nothing. In any case, social change is constantly taking place in even the most established neighbourhoods, and what parents (and even more, grandparents) may accept could be intolerable to their children.

The implication of all this is that 'general' national social policies are not enough: people live locally, not nationally, and they experience the strains, stresses and satisfactions of the locality. Effective social policy, therefore, has to be translated into action (and monitored) at the local level.

DEPRIVED AREAS: THE DEVELOPMENT OF THINKING

Thinking first developed on the need for area policies and action in relation to housing. There were two main strands here: one physical and one administrative.

The first was a development of house improvement policy.[24] Initially this was directed towards the improvement of individual houses and gradually changed first to the improvement of areas of housing and then to environmental improvement. Despite a number of social surveys [25] the policy was unashamedly physical: so much so that increasing powers were provided to *compel* reluctant owners and tenants to have improvements carried out. Only recently has attention been focused on the social character and function of areas of old housing.[26]

The second was a response to the problems of controlling multi-occupation and overcrowding in areas of 'housing stress'. The Milner Holland Committee looked favourably on the idea of designating the worst areas as *areas of special control* in which 'some authority might be set up, with responsibility for the whole area and armed with wide powers to control sales and lettings, to acquire property by agreement or compulsorily over the whole area or part of it, to demolish and rebuild as necessary, to require improvements to be carried out or undertake such improvements themselves, and to make grants on a more generous and flexible basis than under the present law'.[27]

Similarly, the National Committee for Commonwealth Immigrants, starting from a concern for the socio-economic problems facing local authorities with substantial numbers of immigrant families, argued for the designation of *areas of special housing need*.[28] Again, the crucial issue was the control over overcrowding, exorbitant rents, insanitary conditions, disrepair and the risk of fire. The N.C.C.I., however, noted that it was not possible to consider areas such as these 'without considering the deficiencies in all other social services that

137

exist within such an area, and the need to rehabilitate these services at the same time as examining housing problems'.

These proposals were not accepted by the Government, though increased powers to control multi-occupation and abuses were provided. Part of the reason for this was that there was considerable doubt as to the efficacy of measures designed to *control*. The N.C.C.I. Report had referred to the need for treating the problems of the stress areas 'patiently and tactfully', for giving the public 'every opportunity to understand the steps which are being undertaken', and for seeking the 'active and willing co-operation' of voluntary organizations and community groups. Indeed, without this they saw the likelihood of their proposed solution creating 'problems almost as serious as those which are being alleviated'.

It was left to the Seebohm, Skeffington and Plowden Reports to probe more deeply into these issues. Before discussing these, it is interesting to note how opinion changed by the turn of the decade. Reviewing the problems of the stress areas, the Francis Report (published in March 1971) flatly stated that 'there is no short term solution to this terrible problem'.[29] Large-scale public acquisition was not even discussed: instead they proposed the designation of areas of housing stress where local authorities should be under a statutory duty 'to give information and advice to landlords and tenants', to check rents, to act in cases of harassment and unlawful eviction, and in extreme cases to temporarily take over the management of individual houses. The value of housing aid centres and legal advice and assistance was underlined.

It is unfortunate that the Committee did not spell out the philosophy underlying their recommendations, but it appears that they were impressed by the limits of public action, the need for preserving a stock of privately rented accommodation and, above all, the need for flexibility, persuasion and negotiation. But no reference was made to non-housing issues: the Committee faithfully restricted its attention to its narrow terms of reference.

Not so the Plowden Committee: appointed in August 1963, 'to consider primary education *in all its aspects . . .*', They reported four years later in very broad terms.[30] They appreciated and underlined the complex of factors which produced seriously disadvantaged areas. Researchers are faced with attempting to abstract and measure the importance of individual factors when 'all other things are equal'. Policy-makers and administrators, on the other hand, 'must act in a world where other things are never equal; this, too, is the world in which the children grow up, where everything influences everything else, where nothing succeeds like success and nothing fails like failure.

The outlook and aspirations of their own parents; the opportunities and handicaps of the neighbourhood in which they live; the skill of their teachers and the resources of the schools they go to; their genetic inheritance; and other factors still unmeasured or unknown surround the children with a seamless web of circumstances.'[31]

This web of circumstances is neatly illustrated in the following further quotation:

In a neighbourhood where the jobs people do and the status they hold owe little to their education, it is natural for children as they grow older to regard school as a brief prelude to work rather than an avenue to future opportunities ... Not surprisingly, many teachers are unwilling to work in a neighbourhood where the schools are old, where housing of the sort they want is unobtainable, and where education does not attain the standards they expect for their own children. From some neighbourhoods, urban and rural, there has been a continuing flow of the more successful young people. The loss of enterprise and skill makes things worse for those left behind. Thus, the vicious circle may turn from generation to generation and the schools play a central part in the process, both causing and suffering cumulative deprivation.[32]

The Plowden Committee recommended a national policy of 'positive discrimination', the aim of which would be to make schools in the most deprived areas as good as the best in the country. Additional resources were necessary to achieve this: extra teachers and special salary increases; teachers' aides; priority for replacement and improvement in the school building programme; extra books and equipment; and expanded provision for nursery education.

The Seebohm Committee had wider terms of reference than the Plowden Committee: 'To review the organization and responsibilities of the local authority personal social services in England and Wales, and to consider what changes are desirable to secure an effective family service.' Of relevance to the present discussion is the Committee's concern for 'social planning' (which is dealt with largely in terms of administrative organization) and their recommendations in relation to *areas of special need*. Unfortunately, the Committee did not suggest how these should be identified in spite of the fact that they recommended that they should be accorded priority in the allocation of resources: 'We are convinced that designated areas of special need should receive extra resources comprehensively planned in co-operation with services both central and local, concerned with health, education, housing and other social needs.'[33]

The Committee ventured a view that areas of special need 'have a

139

profusion of pressing social problems, offer only a dismal and squalid physical environment, are inadequately served by social services and are considered to justify special attention and a generous allocation of resources'. But, beyond a reference to the Plowden Report and *The Needs of New Communities*, the only other comment was that 'recognized *problem areas* appear to lack a sense of community'.

More helpful and perspicacious was their reference to citizen participation, which underlined a point hardly recognized by the Skeffington Committee [34] which was specifically concerned with this issue. It was Seebohm, not Skeffington, who clearly saw that, if area action was to be based on the wishes of the inhabitants and carried out with their participation, 'the participants may wish to pursue policies directly at variance with the ideas of the local authorities ... Participation provides a means by which further consumer control can be exercised over professional and bureaucratic power'.[35]

This rapid review suggests that the concept of areas of multiple deprivation requiring priority action and 'positive discrimination' has become generally accepted, but there is little in the way of guidance as to how these areas are to be identified though, when identified, policies need to be operated with the maximum concern for the feelings and wishes of the people involved.

DEPRIVED AREAS: THE DEVELOPMENT OF POLICY

Three major elements can be identified in the development of thinking on deprived areas: inadequate physical conditions, the presence of a 'large' number of coloured people (usually referred to as 'immigrants'), and a multiplicity of less easily measurable 'social problems'.

In the development of policy the same three elements can be clearly identified. For a very long time there was a preoccupation with inadequate physical conditions. Indeed, British housing policy developed from this [36] and it still remains a major feature of it.[37] The other two elements are of much more recent origin. Legislatively, the important landmarks (modest though they are) are the Local Government Act 1966 (Section 11) and the Local Government (Social Need) Act 1969. These constitute the statutory basis for the Educational Priority Areas programme and the Urban Aid programme. The 1966 Act provided for grants in aid of staff costs involved in 'dealing with some of the transitional (*sic*) problems caused by the presence of Commonwealth immigrants'. The Urban

Programme is broader in concept, 'designed to raise the level of social services in areas of acute social need, and thus help to provide an equal opportunity for all citizens'.[38]

'Areas of special social need' are not defined in the legislation, but Government circulars have referred to 'localized districts, within the boundaries of an urban authority, which bear the marks of multiple deprivation, such as old overcrowded, decrepit houses without plumbing and sanitation; persistent unemployment; family sizes above the average, a high proportion of children in trouble or in need of care; or a combination of some or all of these'.[39]

It is easy to criticize the inadequacies of these first approaches to a reorientation of policy,[40] but the inadequacies are recognized by the central departments as well as by academic critics. It is a very different matter to devise operational programmes which are directed to the relevant areas and which can overcome the administrative separatism which characterizes local government organization. Initial policies were conceived largely in terms of local authority action, but increasingly attention is being redirected towards supporting 'local unofficial effort'.[41]

The identification of areas of special social need and the devising of appropriate programmes is still at a primitive stage, and it is not at all clear on what issues policies should be concentrated. An experimental Community Development Project is under way aimed at finding 'ways of meeting more effectively the needs of individuals, families and communities, whether native or immigrant, suffering from many forms of social deprivation'.[42]

It is early days yet to assess the impact and efficacy of these programmes, and published material is scanty. Nevertheless, it is clear that policy is shifting markedly from 'capital projects' to community action. What remains unclear is how community action is to be organized, by whom and with what objectives. Unfortunately the available indices relate predominantly to physical deficiencies, rather than social deprivations and the potential for social development.

Research undertaken by John Edwards at the Centre for Urban and Regional Studies at the University of Birmingham, confirms the importance which is, in practice, given to physical factors. Following an analysis of the variables used by public authorities in identifying 'stress areas', he concluded:

The most frequently occurring variables by far are those relating to the dwellings in an area whether in terms of age, condition, amenity, crowding, etc. Variables of this type are mentioned some

141

forty times in the source material, compared with twelve times for the next most frequent group [social class, economic status and income], and a total of fifty mentions for *all* other groups together. Clearer evidence of the nature of the bias prevalent in notions of urban stress would be difficult to come by.[43]

This is a far cry from the cumulative social deprivation concept of the Plowden Committee, even though their concept includes physical factors. Without denying the importance of these in conjunction with economic and social factors, the danger of concentrating upon them is twofold. First, areas which rank high on a physical assessment (e.g. some of the 'new communities' already discussed) tend to be overlooked. Secondly, action in relation to physical inadequacies may ignore more difficult socio-economic problems, or even exacerbate them.

There is certainly recognition of these problems, but they are more difficult to identify and measure. Nevertheless, attempts are being made: Edwards lists a wide range of factors which are included in the various indices of stress: a high proportion of wage-earners in social classes IV and V, low wages, truancy, poor school attendance, high teacher turnover, persistent unemployment, high mortality and morbidity, children in need of care, incomplete families, and so forth. Each of these are indicators of particular social needs, but in combination they point to cumulative deprivation which is the *raison d'etre* of 'priority action'.

Much work remains to be done in this field, not only in relation to the assessment of deprivation, but also in relation to the means by which social improvement can be achieved. This involves a development of local community programmes of a character which is relatively new to Britain—with a high degree of local direction and control within a supportive statutory framework of social service education, training and income-maintenance. The Seebohm Committee's comment that 'recognized problem areas appear to lack a sense of community' has already been quoted. But it is more likely that the 'sense of community' is unrecognized, ignored or even overridden in normal programmes. Areas of deprivation are deprived not only in the ways already discussed, but also in power. Powerlessness is both a result of poverty and a major force exacerbating it. The needs of deprived neighbourhoods cannot be met by the 'provision' of services alone. Extensive research and heart-searching on American programmes has convincingly demonstrated that an essential ingredient of success is 'the organization of people in a community for mutual help and the development of democratically based system of co-operation which can among other things increase the effectiveness of governmental and other programs'.[44]

A major element in social planning is to determine the areas of competence for social action by statutory services, voluntary bodies and local community groups. Each of these has a different role to play: and only the first can be 'planned' in the usual sense of the term. The others can be assisted—though only if it is accepted that they may have objectives which differ from those of governmental bodies, or may wish to achieve shared objectives by 'unconventional' means.

There is, however, a limit to effective community action. Only a much broader social planning approach can, for instance, deal with 'social polarization'. This term is achieving currency in contemporary debates on both social and physical planning policies. It is useful to discuss it in a wider context.

SOCIAL POLARIZATION

It is relatively simple to demonstrate the flows of population between regions and from urban areas to their commuter hinterlands. The gross effects of these movements on population structure and growth can also be shown. It is a very different matter to analyse the socio-economic character of the complex of movement, or to establish its importance to the socio-economic structure of different areas. Studies undertaken before the availability of data from the 1961–66 Censuses indicated that while rural depopulation was predominantly a migration of young unmarried people, outward movement from urban areas was mainly of married people. Further, 'Unlike the migrants of the last century who built up the great industrial cities, the migrants out of these cities into the suburbs and residential towns during this century have been of relatively high socio-economic status.'[45] There was also a strong suggestion that mobility varied within broad occupational groupings by family size. Manual workers with three or more children were (in 1959–60) almost 50 per cent less mobile than those with no children. Non-manual workers with three or more children, on the other hand, were twice as mobile as those with no children.[46]

There was, thus, an indication that economic difficulties (e.g. in obtaining suburban housing and jobs, or facing high journey-to-work costs) were preventing manual workers from following the more affluent non-manual workers to the suburbs (though sociological factors may also have been important). In fact the situation is much more complex, but there was a growing fear in the sixties that urban areas were losing their more 'prosperous' and 'vigorous' people, to

143

the detriment of community life and the health of local government in the towns. Thus, the Local Government Commission for England stated:

> The county boroughs, representing the main urban centres, are losing population to the peripheral areas, where more land is available for building and people can get a house with a garden. Among the population which is lost in this way are the younger families, because these need accommodation with more space for children, and, more generally, the higher income groups. As a result, the county boroughs . . . are beginning to lose variety in the social and economic make-up of their populations. . . . This is all the more unfortunate in that we are concerned not with a small minority, but with a very broad-based section of the rather more prosperous and go-ahead people—people who might be expected to take a vigorous interest in housing and other problems in the big town.[47]

Using published and unpublished data from the 1961 and 1966 Censuses, the research staff of the Royal Commission on Local Government in England carried out a study of this issue.[48] They pointed out that there is also a movement of the 'prosperous' and the 'vigorous' *to* urban areas and that it was, therefore, the resultant balance which needed to be analysed. More fundamentally, any analysis required the use of more precise concepts. This was not discussed at any length, but available data determined the use of the 'professional and managerial' socio-economic groupings of the General Register Office [49] for 'prosperous', and the age group 25–44 for 'vigorous'[50] (though some data was available only for the 15–44 age group). In both cases the analysis had to be restricted to males.[51] Using these two indices, the study clearly supported the contention that there was a growing social imbalance between the county boroughs and their surrounding county areas.[52]

The concern here was, of course, with local government boundaries, and the conclusion that town and country are now interdependent was supported by migration and commuting figures. A further conclusion that there was a 'long term weakening effect on the socio-economic character of the major centres' can also be accepted in this limited context. But even if all local government boundaries were changed to embrace meaningful areas of common socio-economic interest, the socio-economic distribution would be untouched. Local authorities would have more sensible areas and would probably be financially stronger, but this would not, in itself, alter the fact that more of the 'prosperous' or 'vigorous' live in the suburbs and fewer of them live in the inner areas. Concentrations of deprivation—and of affluence—are not affected by changes in boundaries (though they may put a local authority in a better position to take more effective action).

The issue was also examined by the South East Joint Planning Team. It could hardly be expected that social polarization would occur over such large areas as that of Greater London, however extreme it might be at particular places within Greater London. It is not, therefore, surprising that the team concluded that 'evidence of polarization at the moment is either lacking or, at best, inconclusive'.[53] Much more usefully the team discussed the *concept* of polarization.

Social polarization is a strong force. People of similar socio-economic position like to live near to each other. In any case, the widespread desire for more space, fresher air and congenial surroundings, combined with differing income constraints inevitably leads to a degree of homogeneity. This is a positive force which both the private and the public sectors have accommodated on a large scale, with very real social benefit. This 'positive' social polarization is, however, very different from the 'negative' polarization which traps people in areas of cumulative disadvantage and lack of opportunity. Poor housing (by no means necessarily cheap), poor employment opportunities (with little opportunity for advancement), poor schools (or adequate schools lacking the social stimulus to educational achievement) all reinforce each other.

It is doubtful, however, how far the term 'social polarization' is useful. Indeed, it may be positively unhelpful in that it may imply first, that there is something inherently bad about people living in socially homogeneous areas, and secondly, that the answer to the problem is some form of imposed social heterogeneity. Of course, since the concentration of disadvantage itself increases that disadvantage, the problems are compounded, but the root of these problems lies elsewhere.

Yet this is not all there is to the issue. Much of the confusion which characterizes the debate on social polarization emanates from a lack of agreement (or even clarity) on the geographical scale which is at issue. (Problems can be manufactured as well as hidden by the choice of particular boundaries.) There is a presumption—to put it no more strongly—that there is a scale of homogeneity which is problem-creating. (The problem relates, in practical terms, only to homogeneity at the lower end of the socio-economic scale. This is only to ignore—not to deny—the fact that 'too many' of the rich in a particular area may present its own problems, particularly of

145

'external relations': of comprehension and of willingness to contribute to the wider good.)

The threshold scale will differ: at one extreme will be 'problem families', while at the other will be 'the working classes'. In all cases, the threshold is that point at which social improvement is held back by the scale of the concentration. Put thus, it is apparent that dispersal is only part of the solution if the scale is large. Indeed, since dispersal is most probably selective it can itself lead those who are left behind to be further socially disadvantaged. To the extent that this is the case, the real answer must lie in increasing the opportunities *within* the socially homogeneous area. But can this be done without introducing more heterogeneity? If educational attainment, for example, is significantly restrained by the low-class social character of an area, is it possible to change the situation except by removing the constraints, i.e. by enticing higher social classes to move in? This is one important implication that can be drawn from the observation that 'the children of less privileged parents have a greater chance of educational success and hence of social mobility when they go to schools which draw children from a wider range of social backgrounds than they would have if they were to go to schools which tap a segregated area'.[54] Careful determination of school catchment areas (even if demo- cratically possible) obviously cannot be a solution where the scale of homogeneity extends beyond conceivable catchment areas. The alternative of 'bussing' (with all the social upheaval this causes) is limited in both practical and policitical terms and, in any case, is a reflection of the inadequacy of earlier policies and, at best, a tempor- ary solution.

The SEJPT report does not go so far (or at least so explicitly) as to suggest attracting higher socio-economic groups into areas of low socio-economic status. It does, however, talk of 'social mix' and stresses the crucial importance of the future occupational structure. Logically, emphasis is also placed on the priority allocation of resources to education. But is this enough? And might it not be self- defeating? Policies (which are eminently desirable) aimed at facilitat- ing social mobility may also (certainly on current experience) lead to geographical mobility. Those who climb the socio-economic ladder will aspire to the appropriate socio-economic areas. To the extent that they succeed, the social polarization of the area they leave will, if anything, be increased. On the same line of argument, a 'socially improved' employment structure will hardly, *of itself*, attract higher status residents.

The alternative is housing development and environmental im- provements aimed at attracting new residents. This is likely to be as popular with local authorities and their electorates as providing homes for incoming workers in areas of housing shortage. General experience of 'key workers' housing underlines the difficulty of providing houses for 'strangers' in areas where large numbers of 'locals' are in need of housing. Nevertheless, the scheme has had some success even in housing pressure areas since the employment benefits are clear. This situation is likely to be very different with a policy deliberately and explicitly designed to give some degree of priority to affluent strangers over poorer locals.

The Plowden Report underlined the complex of factors which produce seriously disadvantaged areas.* Of particular relevance to the argument being put forward in this chapter is a reference to the need to attract teachers to live in these areas:

> Priority areas are not the kind of place where teachers normally live, yet those whose homes are near their pupils' can often do a better job than those who travel greater distances. They belong to the same community; they can understand their background better. What is more, the creation of vast one-class districts from which all professional people are excluded is bad in itself. Sustained efforts ought to be made to diversify the social composition of the priority areas. Many professional workers feel the need to start buying a house early in their careers because mortgage terms may be more favourable, and because once they own a house it is easier for them to secure another if they move elsewhere. Their needs should be recognized by the housing and planning authorities. There should be a mixture of houses for renting, for owner-occupation and for co-ownership and cost-rent schemes run by housing associations . . .
>
> The housing needs of families in badly overcrowded places are likely to be more urgent than those of teachers; but their children will not get the education they deserve if teachers are systematically excluded from the locality.[55]

The same point, in a wider context, was made in the Central Housing Advisory Committee's Report on *Council Housing* [56]: 'If the needs for education, health and other social and community services are to be adequately met, local authorities must ensure that those who man these services have opportunities of finding homes within the areas they serve. . . . These needs must be the responsibility of local authorities, though actual provision may be made in a variety of ways.'

We must, however, heed Gans' warning that the planner has only limited influence over social action and that 'sizeable differences,

* See above, p. 138.

especially with regard to fundamental social and economic interests, are not erased or set aside by the mere fact of living together'.[57] Nevertheless, two points need to be made. First, the experience of American cities, with their fragmented administrations and (by British standards) archaic tax systems, is not necessarily relevant to Britain.[58] Secondly, Gans is referring particularly to social contacts and more particularly to heterogeneity at the very local ('block') level. He explicitly rejects the 'neighbourhood' both as a meaningful social unit ('since the significant face-to-face relationships occur on the block') and as a relevant unit (since 'it is not a political unit, and, thus, cannot make decisions about its population composition'). In the context of the current argument it is not this very local level which is relevant.

But it is not necessary to go into the finer points of this debate to accept the major point: that a community which is so heavily *un*-balanced that it is repellent to those needed for the community services of the area and to the potential local leaders, suffers extreme cumulative deprivation which becomes increasingly difficult to ameliorate. Whatever the impracticability or unacceptability of attempting to achieve 'socially balanced' communities, there is a strong case for attempting to prevent highly *un*balanced communities.

THE NATURE OF SOCIAL PLANNING

It is apparent from this discussion that 'social planning' is not a discrete activity which can be allocated to a specific department. The emphasis in *The Needs of New Communities* on social relations officers, social relations departments and social development plans is, perhaps, unfortunate in that it might be taken to suggest the opposite. In fact, the Report was at pains to stress that '" Social thinking" and "awareness" is not—and should not—be delegated to one individual. It should permeate all the work undertaken for or by a new community.' A proposed 'social development plan' was in reality a plan for social services and community facilities. The functions of a social relations officer were set out under four headings: social planning and advice; public relations; community development; and research and information. Nevertheless, the Committee clearly had difficulty in determining how these functions were to relate to the functions of other officials and departments concerned with a new community. In existing communities—which constitute the majority—the position is even less clear.

Given the wide range of relevant issues it is impossible to conceive an all-embracing 'social planning' department. More important, any

148

attempt to do so would be misconceived. Social planning is an *aspect* of planning. It is concerned with social goals and the ways in which programmes and plans can be elaborated in an attempt to meet these goals. As such it is an approach, a way of thinking, which should permeate all planning. It should not be separated from 'physical' planning or any other type of planning since these are all aspects of a total activity.

Further, it is more than assessing the social implications of a physical planning operation. It is concerned with the explicit formulation of the goals which these operations are to be instrumental in achieving, and the means by which they are to be achieved.

In this wider context the term is perhaps misleading. A more embracing term might be 'societal planning', defined by Gans as the evaluation of social goals and the development in broad outline of the kinds of programme required to achieve the chosen goals.[59] This is a useful approach since it subordinates the differently labelled types of planning to their proper place as *means* to given ends.

Terms such as 'physical planning', 'economic planning' and the like in practice tend to reflect departmental responsibilities and professional skills as well as means. Problems are seen and analysed in narrow terms. Means become ends in themselves. Alternative means are rejected because they conflict with other means which have become regarded as ends. The clearest example of this is, perhaps, the current debate on economic growth.[60]

Gans has argued that the dichotomy between social and physical planning is meaningless:

> . . . the terms *social* and *physical* are inaccurate labels. Zoning is considered a physical planning method, but an ordinance which determines who is to live with whom and who is to work next to whom is as much social—as well as economic and political—as it is physical. So is a transportation scheme which decides who will find it easy to get in and out of the city and who will find it difficult. Conversely, social planners who urge the construction of more low-rent housing, or argue for scattered units rather than projects, are proposing physical schemes even while they are ostensibly doing social planning. Since all planning activities affect people, they are inevitably social, and the dichotomy between physical and social methods turns out to be meaningless. Moreover, in actual planning practice, no problem can be solved by any one method or any one skill. In most instances a whole variety of techniques are needed to achieve the goal.[61]

This is unconvincing and misleading. While it is true that physical

149

planning measures have social implications, the important issue is whether these are anticipated or unexpected, desirable or undesirable, or, indeed, whether they have ever been considered. Similarly, while social planners may recommend certain physical solutions, these are to social problems which they have defined in terms very different from those of the physical planner. It is certainly true that no problem *should* be approached by any one method or any one skill, but the fact remains that all too frequently this is precisely what happens.

Fortunately, there are signs of changes in thinking (and, perhaps more important in the long run, also in professional education). Physical planning documents decreasingly deal solely with urban form, land use, the layout of roads and the juxtaposition of buildings. In one sense, of course, they never have: land is not 'used' by buildings but by human activities. What distinguishes the trend in physical planning is its direct and explicit concern with human activities, needs and aspirations. The implicit aim of improving social well-being is becoming more explicit.

This is nicely illustrated by comparing the London Plan for 1951 with its more recent 1970 equivalent. The former dealt predominantly with the allocation of land for particular uses while the latter covers a very wide field of social, environmental and economic issues: the functions of London, the needs for increasing choice, issues of social structure and polarization, trade and industry, preserving existing and creating new amentities, costs and resources, and so on. Of particular interest in the present context is a section which discusses 'The Planner in Society':

> (The Planner) was once a maker of physical designs which the builder had to translate into a series of structures. In fact a Planner was an Architect.
>
> In the society of the present time, and the future, the Planner is much more than that. He is still concerned with the physical environment, but he is equally deeply involved with the efficient functioning of the economy, the growth of communities, and the correct use of scarce resources for which there is competition from many directions.[62]

It is also interesting to note that despite the relatively high 'social content' of the Plan, much of the current debate is focused on extending this. For instance, the Centre for Environmental Studies has stressed the importance of changes taking place in London to particular groups. One illustration can be given from the evidence of this Centre to the Inquiry into the Plan. The Greater London Development Plan aims:

(1) to improve the whole quality of the environment throughout the crowded and more decayed parts of London;
(2) to improve the housing conditions of the worst housed people;
(3) to ensure an adequate labour supply for the enterprises that are essential for London's economic health;
(4) to prevent a loss of the more highly skilled and paid people from London, the segregation of one social class from another, and the growing concentration of poorer people (or the richest and poorest) in London.

These are noble aims, but as the CES evidence points out:

It is when these aims are brought together that dilemmas emerge. If the environment of inner London is to be improved, densities must be reduced and many people must move out; since it is the richer, the more skilled and the younger families who move out, their departure hastens tendencies to social segregation and polarization. The enterprises most characteristic of central London include service trades and small businesses paying low or widely fluctuating wages; such work does not enable people to pay the costs of better housing and a high quality environment, yet to move these workers out may destroy industries on which London's economy depends and leave people under-employed in suburbs and new towns where there are inadequate opportunities for the untrained. If the worst housed people are to be given overriding priority for subsidized Council housing in inner London, then others must be somehow compelled to leave this housing, the local authorities must reduce rents and may have to reduce building standards in order to house the poorest tenants, and massive social ghettos may be created in the process.[63]

This is not the place to enter into a discussion of the Greater London Development Plan.[64] Sufficient has been outlined to demonstrate the difficulties to which a broader planning approach leads. A multiplicity of agencies, interests and skills are involved. Any 'plan' to operationalize one set of goals highlights conflicts with others. A totally agreed set of goals (except at a level of meaningless abstraction) and a totally agreed plan for achieving these are inconceivable; but this does not mean that the attempt should not be made. On the contrary, the identification and pinpointing of inherent conflicts is the first stage in the development of adequate political debate. The 'planning solutions' set out in published plans

151

have typically avoided all this. It has been assumed (at least by implication) that questions of 'who gains?' and 'who suffers?' can be obviated by the application of professional skills to defined problems.

The issues raised by a consideration of social planning thus take us far afield. The crux of the matter is seen to be more than the opposing viewpoints of physical and social planning technicians: it is essentially political.

Advance on this front stems from new recognition of the multi-faceted nature of human problems: The recognition comes on the part of politicians who (by definition laymen) are not constrained by professional training and on the part of those practitioners who see advance by way of crossing professional and disciplinary boundaries. But as society becomes more complex and inter-dependent, and as the tempo of change increases, so the character of social, economic and environmental problems change. Indeed, problems are not 'solved': they are merely changed.

In this constant state of flux clear guidelines are impossible. What is clear is that continuous debate is needed—within professional groups (where a generation trained to deal with the problems of yesterday need retraining to cope with those of today); between professional groups (whose constantly changing boundaries need recognition and acceptance); between experts and politicians (neither of whom can be effective without the other); and between the planners and the planned (since planning is essentially a political process in which public awareness, support and participation are crucial elements).

For the 'expert' perhaps the biggest difficulties lie in appreciating, first, the contribution to be made by other experts, and secondly—much more difficult—the key role to be played by the politician whose expertise lies in deciding what action is desirable, appropriate and acceptable to the people he represents. The most important issues can be dealt with and decided upon only in political terms.

How far politicians do, in fact, play this role, and how it relates to citizen participation and community action, are questions which are only beginning to be asked.

References and Further Reading

1. I. Lowry, 'Housing' in T. Pascal (ed.), *Cities in Trouble: An Agenda for Urban Research*, The Rand Corporation, 1968.
2. *Parliamentary Debates*, Vol. 188, Col. 949, 12 May 1908.
3. G. C. M. M'Gonigle and J. Kirby, *Poverty and Public Health*, Gollancz,

1936. For further discussion see A. E. Martin, 'Environment, Housing and Health' *Urban Studies*, Vol. 4, No. 1, February 1967, pp. 1–21.

4. A wide-ranging review is Alvin Schorr's *Slums and Social Insecurity*, English Edition, Nelson, 1964.

5. But see *Private Housing in London: People and Environment in Three Wates Housing Schemes*, Shankland Cox and Associates (undated).

6. See S. A. Ruddy, *Industrial Selection Schemes*, University of Birmingham, Centre for Urban and Regional Studies, Occasional Paper No. 5, 1969; and F. A. Gee, *Homes and Jobs for Londoners in New and Expanding Towns*, Office of Population Censuses and Surveys, Social Survey Division, Report SS. 452, HMSO, 1972

7. See, for example, R. Thomas, *London's New Towns: A Study of Self-Contained and Balanced Communities*, PEP Broadsheet 510, April 1969 and B. J. Heraud, 'Social Class and the New Towns', *Urban Studies*, Vol. 5, No. 1, February 1968.

8. This issue is further discussed in Vol. 1, Chapter 2.

9. Harlow Development Corporation: Twenty-Fourth Annual Report, 1971, (p. 189) in *Reports of the Development Corporations, 1971*, H.C.P. 550, Session 1970/71, HMSO, 1971.

10. This statement needs qualification since it begs questions on the determination of acute housing need and the ability of those in such need to afford the costs of commuting.

11. *Report by a Joint Working Party on Community Problems*, Corporation of the City of Glasgow, 1968.

12. See Vol. 1, Chapter 1, p. 37.

13. The figures are taken from an unpublished report on a study carried out by the Centre for Urban and Regional Studies at the University of Birmingham.

14. See Chapter 2.

15. It may be objected that what people want is to live in one-class communities among people of similar backgrounds and interests. This is, however, a misleading formulation of the issue: a matter which is discussed later in this chapter.

16. Central Housing Advisory Committee, *The Needs of New Communities*, HMSO, 1967, p. 12.

17. Scottish Housing Advisory Committee, *Council House Communities*, HMSO, 1970.

18. See B. Goodey *et al.*, *Social Development in New Communities*, University of Birmingham, Centre for Urban and Regional Studies, Research Memorandum No. 12, 1972.

19. Quotations are from *The Needs of New Communities*, op. cit., Chapter 5.

20. Milton Keynes Development Corporation, *The Plan for Milton Keynes*, 1970, Vol. I, p. 19.

21. C. A. Moser, 'Some General Developments in Social Statistics', *Social Trends*, No. 1, 1970, HMSO, 1970, p. 9.

22. Ibid., p. 10.

23. U.S. Department of Health, Education and Welfare, *Toward A Social Report*, U.S. Government Printing Office, 1969, p. xiv.

24. See J. B. Cullingworth, *Town and Country Planning in Britain*, Allen & Unwin, 4th Edition, 1972, pp. 268–269.

25. See, for example, MHLG, *The Deeplish Study: Improvement Possibilities in a District of Rochdale*, HMSO, 1966 and MHLG, *Barnsbury Environmental Study*, MHLG, 1968.

26. See particularly DOE, *New Life in Old Towns*, HMSO, 1972.

27. *Report of the Committee on Housing in Greater London* (Milner Holland Report), Cmnd. 2605, HMSO, 1965, pp. 122–123.

28. National Committee for Commonwealth Immigrants, *Areas of Special Housing Need*, N.C.C.I., 1967.

29. *Report of the Committee on the Rent Acts* (Francis Report), Cmnd. 4609, HMSO, 1971, p. 212.

30. Department of Education and Science, Central Advisory Council for Education (England), *Children and their Primary Schools*, HMSO, 1967, (Vol. 1: *The Report*; Vol. 2: *Research and Surveys*).

31. Ibid., Vol. 1, para. 131. This must not be interpreted as a lack of concern for research. On the contrary, it reinforces the need for research, to which Volume 2 of the Report is eloquent testimony.

32. Ibid., para. 132.

33. *Report of the Committee on Local Authority and Allied Personal Social Services*, Cmnd. 3703, HMSO, 1968, p. 150.

34. *People and Planning* (Skeffington Report), HMSO, 1969. See Chapter 6 below and Chapter 4 of Volume III.

35. Seebohm Report, op. cit., pp. 151–156. The issue is discussed further in Chapter 6 below.

36. See M. Bowley, *Housing and the State*, Allen & Unwin, 1944 and J. B. Cullingworth, *Housing and Local Government*, Allen & Unwin, 1966, Chapter 1.

37. See Chapter 2.

38. Home Office, *Urban Needs in Britain*, Mimeo, Home Office, 23 June 1970.

39. Loc. cit. (For further discussion see Chapter 1).

40. See R. Holman, 'Combating Social Deprivation', Chapter 4 of R. Holman (ed.), *Socially Deprived Families in Britain*, Bedford Square Press, 1970.

41. See Home Office *Circular No. 51/1971*.

42. See Home Office, *Community Development*, Mimeo, 1969 and *Community Development Project: Objectives and Strategy*, Mimeo, 1969.

43. Unpublished Working Paper.

44. T. Gladwin, *Poverty U.S.A.*, Little Brown, 1967, pp. 163–164.

45. D. Friedlander and R. J. Roshier, 'A Study of Internal Migration in England and Wales, Part II: Recent Migrants—Their Movements and Characteristics', *Population Studies*, Vol. 20, 1966, pp. 47 and 50.

46. Ibid., p. 54.

47. Local Government Commission for England, Report on the *West Midlands Special Review Area*, para. 47.

48. Royal Commission on Local Government in England, *Volume III: Research Appendices*, Cmnd. 4040–II, HMSO, 1969, Appendix 3, 'Migration between Major Centres and their Surrounding Areas'.

49. The Professional and managerial socio-economic groups are:

No. 1: Employers and managers in central and local government, industry, commerce, etc.—large establishments.

No. 2: Employers and managers in industry, commerce, etc.—small establishments.

No. 3: Professional workers—self-employed.

No. 4: Professional workers—employed.

No. 13: Farmers—employers and managers.

50. Though noting that it would be absurd to suggest that those of other ages could not be 'vigorous', it was thought that the 25–44 age group 'did seem an especially vital part of the working population, excluding as it did the youngest,

apprentice elements, many of whom would not be fully into their stride with relatively new jobs, but including the majority of people in the productive prime of their lives'.

51. Females were excluded because of the methodological difficulty in allocating appropriate socio-economic status to the very large female category of housewives.

52. A 'very small and highly tentative' inquiry in Glasgow produced evidence that was 'consistent with the hypothesis that children from overspill families are significantly more able than those of non-migrants'. The evidence was the higher than average scores in intelligence tests, position in the class, and marks in English and arithmetic of a small number of children of families who moved to overspill areas from the Govan and Partick areas of Glasgow. G. Jahoda and M. Green, 'Does Glasgow Overspill Cream off the More Able?' *Scottish Journal of Political Economy*, November 1965, pp. 293–296.

53. South East Joint Planning Team, *Studies Vol. 2: Social and Environmental Aspects*, HMSO, 1971, para. 1.98.

54. Ibid., para. 1.99(iv).

55. *Children and their Primary Schools*, op. cit., para. 162.

56. MHLG, Central Housing Advisory Committee, *Council Housing: Purposes, Procedures and Priorities*, HMSO, 1969, para. 63. See also Seebohm Report, op. cit., para. 490.

57. H. Gans, *People and Plans*, Basic Books, 1968, p. 170.

58. Ibid., The following passage underlines the point: 'Many suburban communities today are split over the question of school expenditures. Upper-middle and middle-class residents, for whom high quality schooling is important regardless of price, cannot often find a common meeting ground with lower-middle-class residents, who may have different definitions of quality, and place less urgent priority on getting their children into a 'good' college, or with working-class residents for whom tax economy is often—and of sheer necessity—the most important consideration' (p. 170).

59. Ibid., p. 85.

60. See, for example, J. K. Galbraith, *The Affluent Society*, Hamish Hamilton, second edition, 1969; E. J. Mishan, *The Costs of Economic Growth*, Staples, 1967, and *Growth: The Price We Pay*, Staples, 1969; and W. Beckerman, 'Why We Need Economic Growth', *Lloyds Bank Review*, October 1971.

61. H. Gans, op. cit., p. 245.

62. Greater London Council, *Tomorrow's London: A Background to the Greater London Development Plan*, 1970, p. 44.

63. The full statement is reproduced in Volume 3, Chapter 3.

64. See J. Hillman, *Planning for London*, Penguin Books, 1971 and Town and Country Planning Association, *London Under Stress*, TCPA, 1970.

Chapter 6

Planning in a Democratic Society

PLANNING AS A PROCESS

A recurring theme in this work has been the essentially political nature of planning. Few problems have a 'right' answer even where there is an agreed framework within which the issues are posed. Moreover, 'problems' are seldom solved: they merely change. Planning should be conceived, therefore, not as the identification of problems and their resolution, but as a process of balancing conflicting claims on scarce resources, of deciding who is to benefit and who is to bear the costs of planning decisions, and of achieving compromises between conflicting interests. If this is accepted, it follows that a main focus of debate should be the planning process itself.

The better the process, the better it will be able to deal with the types of problems which are discussed in these three volumes. But what are to be the criteria of 'better'? Though no definitive answer to this question can be given here, two major elements can be identified. First, the process will be better to the extent that it can take all the relevant issues into account. Secondly, it will be better to the extent that those whose interests are affected by the operation of the process are able to influence it.

These two elements are inter-related. The greater the amount of public involvement, the more likely is it that relevant issues will be considered; or, to use an alternative formulation, the more likely is it that relevant issues will be seen as such. On this line of argument 'relevant' means 'the people affected'. This formulation does not, however, take us very far. It implies the need for citizen-participation but does not define it; nor does it help in defining the point at which participation must give way to wider social considerations. It implies that local government areas should be drawn in a way which reflects community of interest, but it does not help in determining how wide this 'community of interest' should be. It implies that local government should be responsible for determining local policies but does not identify the point at which local policies must be over-ridden by regional or national considerations.

156

There is no neat resolution to such questions. Nevertheless, a review of some of the issues raised in the preceding chapters suggests a number of pointers. In this final chapter the discussion focuses on the relationship between public opinion and government action, citizen-participation, and the role of research and technical opinion in the planning process.

PUBLIC PRESSURE AND GOVERNMENT ACTION

In the first chapter of Volume I the general complacency on population growth was noted. The major focus (like the major debate) was on internal migration and its impact on the regions, together with the implications of population increases for housing programmes and the social services. Britain has never had a population policy: politicians, uncharacteristically, exhibit a reluctance to interfere with 'natural forces'. The same impotence was expressed in the inter-war years towards the 'natural' economic forces which created vast unemployment and economic and social distress. The latter was overcome by the impact of war and changed public opinion. A quiet revolution took place when all political parties committed themselves to a policy of 'full employment' (though vestiges of the previous attitude occasionally manifest themselves). It would be foolhardy to suggest that a similar transformation of political attitude towards population growth will take place, but signs of marked changes in opinion are becoming apparent. The matter is no longer confined to academic circles: learned discourses on *The Optimum Population for Britain* [1] are now accompanied not only by alarmist writings such as *The Population Bomb* [2] (dealing with world overpopulation) but by sombre Committee reports: one of the four working parties set up by the Secretary of State for the Environment to prepare reports for the United Kingdom delegation to the United Nations Conference on the Human Environment has this to say:

> The government must develop a policy to stabilize our population through education and persuasion. As a first step it should provide substantial funds for both state and voluntary organizations to publicize the facts and dangers of population growth and to provide a free comprehensive service in family planning. The mass media and the world of education must be prepared to give real space and thought to population stabilization.[3]

Lady Dartmouth's group, who produced another of the four reports, is less sure-footed:

> We do not share the views of the prophets of doom who point to

the lesson of the Gadarene Swine, and who try to make us feel guilty every time we eat or procreate ... But any trend which will put increased pressure upon the facilities and services which are a vital part of our habitat is a serious cause for concern. We await with interest the results of studies now in progress by the Population Panel, set up by the Government in late 1971.[4]

What is significant is not the difference in emphasis between the two reports, but the fact that both see 'the population question' as one for study and discussion. The Population Panel which was established without any marked sign of enthusiasm is likely to ensure that the debate develops.

The underlying factor here is a heightened public awareness of the relevance of the issue. (Perhaps further evidence of this is provided by a recent film entitled *Zero Population Growth*.) In no sense can it be said that this increasing debate is fostered by Government: on the contrary, it has developed in spite of clear Government reluctance to tackle a 'delicate' issue. It seems likely that this debate will grow, though what action Government can take is by no means clear.

Much clearer is Government action in response to the 'rediscovery' of poverty first among the elderly and then later among the low paid (Chapter 1 of this volume and Chapter 7 of Volume III). The elderly, of course, attract greater public sympathy than the low-paid and, in any case, their problems are easier to deal with. (The basic issue is that of finding acceptable ways of making appropriate transfer payments.) The problems of the low paid are more intractable and, in the last resort, involve structural changes for which (currently at least) there appears to be both insufficient public support and insufficient political leadership. The 'pressure' is being exerted by a very small public.

Nevertheless, these 'small publics' can grow. This is very evident with the extraordinary growth of public concern about the environment, the impact of the motor car on the urban fabric, and pollution. As was pointed out in Chapter 4 of Volume I, controls over traffic which were thought, in 1963, to be unacceptable to a car-owning electorate are now well within the ambit of practical possibility. Similarly, environmental issues now loom very much larger than they did ten years ago in planning decisions. Examples abound: at the time of writing (June 1972) a particularly illustrative case is that of the office block being built on the site of the Queen Anne's Mansions. This was 'accepted' by the Royal Fine Art Commission in 1964, but had the case come up in 1972 'the Commission thinks it would not have succeeded—at any rate without a great public showdown'.[5]

Similarly, in the Lords' Debate on this issue, Lord Sandford, the Under Secretary for the Environment, in explaining the limited grounds on which planning permission could be revoked and the liability for compensation which would be involved, stressed that the Secretary of State had to be satisfied that such revocation was 'expedient'; nevertheless, he continued: 'The expediency must relate to planning considerations, and the undoubted change in public attitude about the environment and the change in environmental policies since 1969, would come within that term.'[6]

Public demand to be informed and to be involved in the decision-making process on issues such as this is mounting: 'The more information that is put before the public, the more articulate opinion will embody a real collective sensibility and not simply be tiresomely obstructive.'[7]

A more general comment is apposite: governments rarely have time to do more than to cope with problems which are forced upon their attention by political processes. Even then they are reluctant to act unless there is a strong body of opinion to convince them that action (as distinct from deliberation) is appropriate. A well-informed electorate is an essential pre-requisite of this.

GOVERNMENT ACTION WITHOUT PUBLIC SUPPORT

Contrariwise, when governments act in response to specific pressures, but without the advantage of full public debate, valid policies may fail. Political leadership (or, at least, political initiative) may then go beyond 'the art of the possible'.

This is, arguably, one of the factors which has prevented any long-term solution to the problems of land values, compensation and betterment outlined in Chapter 5 of Volume I. It was there suggested that it was the lack of public understanding, debate and support which was responsible for the failure of both the 1947 and the 1967 attempts to solve this issue. But that is not all: these failures have diverted attention to alternative 'solutions' which are inherently inadequate and which, if adopted, will do more harm than good. In this particular case the alternative solution being proposed by Government is a 'streamlining of planning procedures'. It is not planning procedures which are at fault, but a basic weakness in the planning system which can be removed only by the resuscitation of a system similar to that which was incorporated in the 1947 and 1967 Acts. This will not be politically possible until there is greater public understanding of the issues involved.[8]

Failures of 'political communication'[9] are also apparent in the long-standing political unpopularity of family allowances [10] and in the mounting distrust of the population census and other forms of government inquiry. In both cases public understanding is inadequate. The issues have received insufficient political debate and public attention is focused on side-issues such as 'abuse'.

Yet another example is provided by the long drawn-out uncertainties and vacillations of central government on local government reform.[11] In England at least this has become entirely a matter of compromise between the possessors of political power: public debate has been restricted to local issues of boundaries and losses of responsibility. Perhaps it is naive to expect anything more when such articulate and powerful organizations are embroiled in battle.[12] Nevertheless, the tragedy is that the resulting organization of local government (at least in England) may be singularly inappropriate to cope with the tasks which lay before it. The difficulties are already very apparent in the reorganized system of local government in Greater London, particularly in relation to planning [13] and housing.[14]

The problems have been discussed at length elsewhere [15]: here it is sufficient to note that political limits to reform are set not only by the pressures of those directly involved but also by the quantity and quality of more general public debate. This is one aspect of 'citizen participation' which has received too little attention.

CITIZEN-PARTICIPATION

Though citizen-participation is now officially embraced as a desirable element in the planning process, there is surprisingly little debate on its meaning. Yet if it means more than consultation, it necessarily involves a transfer of power—from professionals who have the technical skills deemed appropriate for dealing with problems and from politicians whose function it is to determine the use to which these skills are put in the public interest. But to whom is the power to be transferred? Is there not a danger that citizen-participation could lead to the triumph of narrow sectional interests over broader social considerations? Can 'democracy by participation' take over from 'democracy by consent' in a complex inter-dependent society? Though there are no simple answers to such questions, a useful approach is to inquire how pressures for citizen-participation change the way in which planning problems are viewed. A good starting point is transport.

Except for some touring traffic, roads have value only in so far as they connect points of activity. Nevertheless, as Melvin Webber has noted, three ideas have dominated transportation engineering and planning:

(1) Transportation investments tend to be seen primarily as capital investments, i.e. as investments in physical plant, in physical facilities, rather than in transport services.
(2) The function of transportation facilities tends to be seen as *connecting geographic places*, rather than as connecting people.
(3) The primary test of goodness of our geographic network of facilities over another has tended to be *least cost*, i.e. least input of resources, rather than the largest output of benefits.[16]

On this approach transportation planning has been conceived in terms of inputs, aimed at providing a network which connects geographical locations at the least cost. But, if one thinks in terms of how people are affected by transport systems and in terms of the provision of services for diverse groups of the community whose interests differ, the problems appear very differently (most obviously between those who use an urban motorway and those who live in the area through which the motorway passes). Such an approach is much more complicated, but it leads to the right questions being asked: above all, who is to be serviced? Once this type of question is raised, we are forced to think in terms of who benefits and who loses. Given that diverse (and conflicting) interests are involved, we are immediately concerned with the distributional effects of planning or, to use the more homely language of the CES evidence to the Greater London Development Plan Inquiry, 'who gets the goodies?'.[17] And so finally we come to the crucial question 'who decides who gets the goodies?'.

The importance of this lies not only in the intrinsic value of participation in the decision-making process (which, as we shall see, has its own problems and costs), but in the fact that planning policies and decisions are not a matter of *the* public interest, but of deciding between different interests. Moreover, though some of these interests have spatial dimension (i.e. there is a community both of interest and of location), some of them are non-spatial (those of the elderly, the disabled, birdwatchers and lovers of old buildings, for example). Of course, planning proposals can themselves create new communities of interest (just as a threatened rent increase can give life to the dormant community spirit of a council estate). Nowhere is this more in evidence than in relation to urban motorway proposals. But here there is (at least potentially) an alliance between geographical

161

communities and interest communities. What then is the planner to
do? Webber poses part of the difficulty:

> Transport routes are by nature lines that cross geographies. Some
> communities do comprise persons who occupy a single place. High-
> way lines cross those sorts of places in getting from here to there,
> and the outcries from those types of communities are a familiar
> sound. . . . More difficult still are the culturally heterogeneous
> mixtures of communities that occupy a common place. They pose
> a rather different problem to the transport planner, for each of
> these citizen groups has a somewhat different set of transportation
> preferences from the others. Because transport routes are in-
> herently geographic, it is difficult indeed to please all inhabitants of
> a single geographic place when their wants differ widely. Thus it
> must seem to the transport planner who hears objections to every
> proposal that he makes that 'the local community' doesn't know
> what 'it' wants. He is understandably perplexed when the would-be
> spokesmen for the local community say one thing and their
> 'followers' say something different. The joker is that there is
> seldom 'a local community'. People who live next to each other are
> not necessarily like each other, nor are they necessarily a communal
> group with common likes and dislikes. Persons who present them-
> selves as representatives of 'the local community' are frequently
> self-elected. At best, they can represent themselves and perhaps a
> sub-group from the larger collection of local groups. In the face of
> this sort of ambiguity, what is the responsible public official to do?
> How is he to know what's right.[18]

Clearly, simplistic ideas of the 'over-riding public interest' do not
fit into this complex human reality. Neither can cost benefit
analysis circumvent the intrinsic issues of equity. The professional
naturally attempts a technical solution in terms with which he is
familiar: he talks of traffic flows, gravity models, modal splits and the
like which are incomprehensible to those who enter the lists as
objectors.

Indeed, the increasing sophistication of the planning professions
and their academic colleagues (both those who support them and
those who challenge them) adds to the problems of communication—
without which 'participation' lacks any base whatsoever. More
dangerously, the elected representatives whose function it is to
determine the policy to be implemented by the professionals are,
themselves, increasingly unable to perform their essential role. The
increasing emphasis on research (which is much needed) can serve to
exacerbate the problems. Research workers and officials may develop

mutual understanding and share concepts and vocabulary, but the politicians are left bemused and the public at large estranged.

THE SKEFFINGTON REPORT

Concern with—and even interest in—citizen-participation has not been a particularly obvious strength of British local government and it will be even more difficult to achieve with the larger authorities which are currently being established. With little experience to build on it was perhaps inevitable that the Government should appoint a committee 'to consult and report on the best methods, including publicity, of securing the participation of the public at the formative stage in the making of development plans for their area'. The Committee was set up, under the chairmanship of the late Arthur Skeffington (then Joint Parliamentary Secretary to the Minister of Housing and Local Government), in March 1968, and published its report *People and Planning* in July 1969.[19]

The Skeffington Report made a number of rather obvious recommendations which do not carry us a great deal further, for example:

people should be kept informed throughout the preparation of a structure or local plan for their area;

local planning authorities should seek to publicize proposals in a way that informs people living in the area to which the plan relates;

the public should be told what their representations have achieved or why they have not been accepted;

people should be encouraged to participate in the preparation of plans by helping with surveys and other activities as well as by making comments.

The mundane nature of many of the recommendations is testimony to the distance which British local government has to go in making citizen-participation a reality.

Unfortunately, the report does not discuss many of the really crucial issues, though passing references suggest that the Committee were aware of some of them. For instance, it is rightly stated that 'planning' is only one service 'and it would be unreasonable to expect the public to see it as an entity in itself'. The report continues: 'Public participation would be little more than an artificial abstraction if it became identified solely with planning procedures rather than with the broadest interests of people.' This has major implications for the internal organization and management of local authorities. So have the proposals for the appointment of 'community development officers ... to secure the involvement of those people who do not join organizations' and for 'community forums' which would 'provide local organizations with the opportunity to discuss collectively planning and other issues of importance to the area', and which 'might also have administrative functions, such as receiving and distributing information on planning matters and promoting the formation of neighbourhood groups'.

What is conspicuously lacking in the debate on citizen-participation is its political implications. The Skeffington Report noted that it was feared that a community forum might become the centre of political opposition: but the only comment made was 'we hope that that would not happen; it seems unlikely that it would, as most local groups are not partly political in their membership'. The issue is not, however, one of *party politics*: it is one of local policies, pressures and interests. Citizen-participation implies a transfer of some power from local councils to groups of electors. It is power which is the crucial issue—not in any sinister sense, but simply in terms of who is to decide local issues. The Department of the Environment does not want to be concerned with these (except where they have ramifications over a larger front: hence central approval of structure plans). This will be a matter of intimate concern for local councillors—and officials as well.

The transfer of considerable statutory powers from central to local government will show only too clearly that planning is essentially a political process—a fact which has been confused by the semi-judicial procedures with which the Department has become so preoccupied.

None of this is to argue that the philosophy underlying the new legislation is misplaced: far from it. The intention is to demonstrate that the real problems of citizen-participation and local democratic control go far deeper than issues of formal procedures, of social surveys and public exhibitions. If the new system works it will have a major impact on British political processes; and it will not be confined to 'town and country planning'.

Curiously, it was not the Skeffington Committee but the Seebohm Committee [20] which highlighted another related issue (and one which the proposed community development officer would particularly face):

the participants may wish to pursue policies directly at variance with the ideas of the local authorities and there is certainly a difficult link to be forged between the concepts of popular participation and traditional representative democracy. The role of the social worker in this context is likely to give rise to problems of conflicting loyalties. The Council for Training in Social Work suggest in evidence that if community work is to be developed by the local authority, then the authority 'will need to recognize the fact that some of its staff may be involved in situations which lead to criticism of their services or with pressure groups about new needs. The workers themselves will need to be clear about their professional role and this will depend upon their training and the organizational structure within which they work . . .' Participation provides a means by which further consumer control can be exercised over professional and bureaucratic power.

A further problem in citizen-participation is that of determining how representative are the views expressed by participating citizens. As the Skeffington Report implies, the views of the 'non-joiners and inarticulate' are as important as those of 'the actively interested and organized'. One of the difficult issues raised by any discussion of citizen-participation is the plight of those who are not able to participate because they lack the knowledge, sophistication or ability to make their views known, or who are totally bewildered by what is happening. Direct citizen-participation, more thorough social research and better understanding of the effects of planning decisions will help, but more is needed if we are to solve the problems of, for instance, the low income family trapped in an inner urban area with poor public and social services, low educational opportunity and declining employment opportunities.

It is by such an analysis that the inter-relationships between the varied issues discussed in this book and accompanying volumes are to be seen. There is no simple answer to the problems of equity and justice with which the machinery of planning is so vitally concerned. The debate on citizen-participation cannot lead to a solution of these wider problems, but it highlights their importance. Moreover, given an acceptance of the principle of citizen-participation it is impossible to confine it to limited issues defined in advance. Such limitations are appropriate to consultation, not to participation.

There are difficult dilemmas here. On the one hand, if every small issue is widened to encompass major issues of social policy the result will be disillusionment and excessive delay. On the other hand, adequate consideration of an issue may well lead to a highly appropriate redefinition of it. A further dilemma arises in determining at what stage in the development of a proposal citizen-participation will be most fruitful. At 'too early' stage it may be difficult to arouse and sustain widespread interest; while at a later stage there may be objection that the major decisions have already been made.

165

PARTICIPATION AND CONSULTATION

It is frequently commented that the typical citizen is not interested in broad planning issues: his concern is with issues which he sees as directly affecting him. The published reactions to the Consultants' proposals for Warrington New Town are illustrative [21]:

The public were principally concerned about issues affecting their property or their day-to-day existence. Nevertheless, the opportunity was not lost to comment on wider issues. In reply to questions concerning the principal benefits that would accrue from the Proposals, many people thought that the environment would be cleaner and more attractive, and that the New Town would be 'better and safer for children'. Much importance was attached, particularly amongst the young, to the prospect of more jobs and a wider range of job opportunities. Many hoped that there would be an improvement in housing standards and design, and a departure from the 'council house image'. Many also expected a major improvement in shopping and public transport, and in sports, recreation and open space provision. There was concern at the possible loss of the Town's 'character', at the source and type of the incoming population, at problems of relocation from renewal areas, and at the encroachment on agricultural land. Taken altogether, about two-thirds of those who answered the questions seemed generally satisfied with the intention. There was an emphasis on the need to get things moving and to keep them moving.

It was clear that there was some confusion at the multiplicity of authorities involved; many people were not sure where responsibility lay. The Corporation subsequently issued a Brief Guide to clarify the position.

Of what use, it may be asked, is all this? It may accord with the Skeffington Committee's recommendations, but does it provide any basis for action? Does 'a departure from the council house image' really mean that the citizens of Warrington want higher standards of design; or merely that they do not want the types of design which are associated with council houses? (In which case, should 'architect-designed' housing give way to 'builder-designed' housing?) What does the lay public mean by the Town's 'character'? And what of 'the source and type of the incoming population' (the 40,000 Mancunians which the Consultants' Proposals were aimed at accommodating)?

This is not to heap scorn on the Development Corporation's efforts. Far from it: a good attempt was made to arouse public interest and to

166

take serious account of the views expressed. But is this what is meant by public participation?

Much more tangible were the objections to road proposals: but the Corporation and the Council could 'see no acceptable alternative' to the general alignment to the North–South Expressway—and the High Level Bridge. Similarly, the alternative route suggested by the Lambs Lane Ratepayers' Association could not 'in traffic engineering terms, provide a true alternative' to the Distributor Road proposed by the Consultants. Again, the objections to the siting of a refuse tip resulted in conditions being imposed to minimise loss of amenity, but the proposal could not be modified.

Again, does this amount to citizen-participation? Is it not more a matter of information, publicity and consultation? The final paragraphs of the relevant section of the Outline Plan, suggest that this is so:

> Most people are concerned about the immediate effect on themselves of the Proposals. The Corporation hope, in this respect, that their staff have helped to clarify such matters as the law concerning compensation for the compulsory acquisition of land and the assessment of rateable values . . . An Information Service has been set up which, with the participation of the County Borough Council and the two Rural District Councils, will be expanded. This Service provides a valuable two-way channel of information between the public and the Corporation. It will be linked to the monitoring and review process . . . The Corporation recognize a continuing obligation to the public and proposes, when this present Report is issued, not only to employ the customary methods of publicity but to distribute, to every household in the Designated Area, a brochure describing the outline and the intentions of the Plan, the function of the various Authorities and the current stage of progress.[22]

The fact of the matter is that different types of decision have to be taken at different levels. The regional strategy for the North-West is a matter for the central government in consultation with the local authorities of the Region. The sub-regional stragegy for the Warrington area is essentially a matter for the local authorities, subject to the approval of the central government (who are concerned with any wider implications this strategy may have). The Outline Plan for Warrington New Town is similarly the major responsibility of the local authorities concerned. It is when one comes to the level of Local Plans that something more than publicity and consultation is involved, though even here some decisions must rest with the local authority (no local community will welcome the siting of a refuse tip in its area). It is at this local level that it is possible to have true participation in the sense of effective power to directly influence what is to happen to the area, what developments should be prevented and what developments should be encouraged. At the street or neighbourhood level there is scope for considerable community decision and action. It is here that planners may be controlling matters which are of purely local interest and from which they should withdraw.

This, of course, is to take a geographical area approach. There is also an interest approach. A minority of citizens will be concerned with the preservation of historic buildings, or with services for pre-school children or the elderly. Such organized groups have a role to play in the planning process. Indeed, it is only through organizations that such interests can be effective.

There is, moreover, the further issue of 'objections'. It is of the essence of a democratic society that individuals whose personal interests are affected by social action shall have the right to object and the right to a fair and open hearing. It may frequently be neces sary for individual interests to be subjugated to the wider public good: indeed, on occasion, the outcome of an inquiry may be a foregone conclusion, but this can never be taken for granted.

The line between objections relating to individual property rights and wider 'community' objections and views is not always easy to draw in practice. But in principle they are very different. If they are confused, participation can become what the County Planning Officer for Buckinghamshire (Mr F. Pooley) has termed 'a matter of mass private intervention'. On this argument, there is a danger of participation 'defeating its own ends through self interest rather than total involvement'. The result could be a paralysis of the planning process which in turn could lead to a sudden collapse of planning controls: 'This kind of participation is building a dam of twigs and sticks against development. The day will come when public pressure for more houses will burst the dam, and a flood of development will be released which will wash away proper planning constraints'.[23]

That this is more than a plaintive *cri-de-coeur* from a professional planner who has to operate within the widening framework of public participation is evidenced by the proposals put forward by the Minister for Local Government and Development in response to the 1972 land shortage issue, briefly discussed earlier.[24]

Pooley suggested that the current proliferation of amenity societies was not the answer to the problem since 'they tended to be concerned with their own special corner'. In his view, 'a new focal point must be found for a second force in planning, possibly a Council for the Protection of Urban England'.

However, such an organized machinery for protest fails to recognize the variety of opinion which can exist on a planning issue. More fundamentally, it denies the conflicts of interest which arise among those affected. These conflicts cannot be rationalized in a single voluntary organization. Indeed, it is the function of the statutory authorities to decide how conflicts are to be resolved and compromises reached.

Citizen-participation is not a means for achieving consensus. On the contrary it is a means of establishing conflicting views. As the Stevenson Working Party unequivocally put it: 'Since planning will always involve choices between irreconcilable alternatives—as to the allocation of resources, etc., it would seem to us that the more people there are involved in the decisions and the better informed those people are, the greater will be the discord. Greater dissemination of information and expertise should lead to a better definition of the issues, but it is unlikely to lead to greater harmony.'[25]

This is the justification for the proposal for the official encouragement of pressure group activity and grant aid to voluntary bodies: if protest is to make its mark it has to be adequately financed. Sometimes voluntary bodies can raise sufficient money, but this is by no means always the case. To quote the Stevenson Working Party again:

At present it is likely to be a matter of pure coincidence whether any particular issue is discussed in depth at an inquiry, depending on whether it is in the financial interest of anyone to put forward a particular planning argument. Otherwise it will only happen if:
  (i) two authorities with different views happen to be involved; or
  (ii) there is sufficient public feeling to generate the funds necessary to mount a full scale case; or
  (iii) there happens to be someone around who feels strongly about a particular issue and has the expertise and time to develop a case himself.[26]

In their evidence on this issue to a Select Committee, the Scottish Civic Trust suggested that a scheme similar to that of Legal Aid and Advice might be appropriate.[27] But this is to confuse protest to safeguard personal rights with community involvement in the discussion of planning issues.

NEW STYLE PUBLIC INQUIRIES

One proposal which is worthy of further consideration has been put forward following the publication of the Town and Country Planning (Amendment) Bill which, at the time of writing, is before Parliament. The provisions of this Bill are particularly relevant to the present discussion and a summary of them is, therefore, appropriate.

The Bill includes provision for a new type of more informal inquiry on major issues arising in structure plans. The intention is that structure plans would be submitted to the Secretary of State together with a statement of (i) the publicity given to the proposals before they were included in the plan, (ii) the public reaction to these, and (iii) the authority's 'consideration of representations'.[28] Objections to the structure plan which the authority could not satisfy would be submitted to the Secretary of State who would select those which he thought should be examined in public. He would also determine which organizations and individuals would be invited to participate in the examination.

It is envisaged that the 'examination' would be in the form of a 'probing discussion' between the panel which would be established for the purpose, the local authority and the participants.

Issues requiring detailed analysis or technical advice might be referred by the panel to their supporting secretariat for 'examination in depth'. Moreover, the panel might provide opportunities for participants to 'test the authority's case and where necessary actively to assist interested parties in so doing'.

The object of this new system is to concentrate discussion on key strategic issues such as employment, population, housing and transport. The 'participants' in the 'examination' are, therefore, not necessarily 'objectors'.[29] They will consist of those who wish to discuss the major issues involved and to participate in a 'probing' examination.

This new system is not yet finalized, but it represents an attempt to surmount the problems which the Inquiry into the Greater London 'structure plan' have shown to be clearly insoluble in the context of a more traditional type public 'inquiry'.[30] Though it is obviously premature to assess its adequacy, pressures are already evident for an extension of this particular approach to other types of planning issue. If a public discussion of 'selected' crucial issues is appropriate in relation to structure plans, is it not similarly appropriate to a wide range of planning issues? The Stevenson Working Party have already (before the Bill is even passed) suggested that it might be extended to cover other 'pre-inquiry' issues including, not only matters of policy, but also 'the disclosure of necessary information and the award of grants or legal aid in suitable cases'.[31]

The question of 'information' is an important one. If there is a 'public inquiry' (as distinct from a 'public examination'), the authority whose proposals are the subject of the inquiry may feel that their case would be jeopardized if they revealed all the facts in their possession —particularly when these are of a technical nature.[32] Yet this is to give an inquiry a legal character which is quite inappropriate. The question should not be one of 'which side' is to win, but one of deciding what is the best solution to particular problems in the light of a full consideration of all the relevant issues. It follows that all relevant information should be shared: without this, profitable debate is not possible.

None of this is likely to make the life of planners or their political masters easier: on the contrary, it is explicitly directed towards making their decisions more difficult.

THE TEMPO OF CHANGE

The tempo of change in modern society is unprecedented. The best laid plans founder on the quicksand of change. It is this which has led to the increasing demand for flexibility in planning. But at what point does flexibility degenerate into expediency? The discussion (in Chapter 2 of Volume I) on regional policies amply demonstrates that this is not a rhetorical question. Curiously, but very significantly, the major changes which were not forseen were the facts and implications of increasing affluence and increasing relative poverty. This theme is developed at length in Chapter 1 of Volume III. Here it is appropriate to note that, with the speed of socio-economic change, 'problems' must be constantly redefined. The 'regional problem' is a nice case in point.

Since increasing affluence rests on economic development it implies increasing insecurity. Social security thus becomes a means of accommodating change in a socially acceptable way. It is not a matter of carrying casualties, but of equitably distributing the fruits of affluence and of easing the paths of change. In this context the regional problem becomes more than a historical legacy: it is re-defined in terms which accept that the whole is simply the sum of the parts. It is no longer a matter of the 'regional social problems' attendant upon national economic development. A malaise in a part is a malaise in the whole.

Governments have been slow to acknowledge this, and policy has vacillated. The intransigence of the problems in the further-flung

171

regions has resulted in increasing demands for regional devolution,[33] though (desirable as it may be) it is no panacea, as the experience of Northern Ireland painfully demonstrates.

Governments cannot, however, be accused of inactivity. The 1968 and 1969 Planning Acts have introduced new approaches to physical planning at the 'structure' and 'action' levels. Local government is being reorganized. Major changes have taken place in the organization of passenger transport in the conurbations, and even more radical changes are in view for water, rivers and sewerage. Further changes are to come in hospitals and local health services. New fields of planning endeavour have been opened up by the establishment of Regional Planning Boards and Councils, the NEDC, the Countryside Commissions, the Highlands and Islands Development Board, the Sports Councils and the Tourist Boards. Major changes have taken place in the organization of central government.

The contemporary scene is thus one of major institutional change. On the other hand, the techniques of planning have altered little and regional physical and economic planning is still at an embryonic stage. Those who are to work in the new organizational structures have no ready-made new ways of tackling the problems with which they are confronted, though their widened areas of responsibility will inevitably lead to the reframing of questions, a desire for new types of knowledge and a development of new ways of thinking. Mistakes have been made in the past, and there is no certainty that they will not be made, on a grander scale, in the future.

THE ROLE OF RESEARCH

One response to this has been a major increase in research effort. Again it is institutional change which is the most apparent: the establishment of the Social Science Research Council, the Centre for Environmental Studies and the (Rowntree) Centre for Studies in Social Policy are all institutional innovations at the national level. Centres of research in the Universities have proliferated. In local government, the number of research and intelligence units is growing.

Another response has been the large growth of training and retraining programmes for local and central government staffs (though little as yet for elected representatives). Here, attempts are beginning to be made to forge effective links between those who undertake research and those who have to apply its results in the planning and implementation of services.

The utilization of social research has not yet had the successes which have been achieved in industrial research and development, and much more effort is required in this field.[34] But the problem is much more than one of facilitating the use of existing research. A great deal of current research is not usable in any clear-cut sense since it is not designed to be so. Much of it is on too small a scale, is repetitive, or haphazard (rather than systematic), and has little in the way of direct implications for policy-makers and administrators. It addresses itself to questions which are different from those seen as important and relevant by those concerned with policy.

This, in essence, was the gravamen of the Rothschild Report [35] though this suffered greatly by a remarkable lack of consultation with the research world and an extraordinary absence of argument supporting the recommendations.[36]

The difficulties of policy-orientated social research should not, however, be underestimated. To Rothschild there is no problem: 'The customer says what he wants; the contractor does it (if he can); and the customer pays.' On this view the policy-makers identify a problem on which they see the need for some objective research; they pose a number of questions to which the research attempts to provide the answers; and, finally, the policy-makers take the research results and determine their policy in the light of them. But posing the questions in a useful and valid way is often a major part of a research exercise. Poverty is a clear illustration of this, as Chapter 1 has demonstrated. Similarly, with the determination of the relevant questions on transportation planning: as the discussion earlier in this chapter shows, the answers to questions posed in terms of traffic flows are very different from answers to questions posed in terms of groups of people to be serviced. Who, indeed, is the 'customer' who is to say 'what he wants' from research?

Moreover, interpretation and judgement play a large role in social research, and the techniques employed frequently need careful scrutiny before 'conclusions' can be accepted as such. The Bethnal Green studies of Young and Willmott are a nice case in point.[37] Their survey in the 'Greenleigh' overspill estate involved interviewing only forty-seven families. This enabled a fairly intensive study to be made but, as the authors pointed out (and as has been consistently ignored), their conclusions 'are bound to be impressionistic'. Further, the Greenleigh sample was deliberately chosen so as to consist solely of parents with at least two children. This was done in order to provide a comparison with a sample interviewed in Bethnal Green, but the results obtained by a survey so designed cannot give a picture of the reactions of all types of household. Again, Greenleigh was developed as a dormitory estate: at the date of the survey it was seriously deficient in amenities, and the majority of earners travelled daily to work in London. It was the very antithesis of a new town where people can both live and work, and where, moreover, it is possible for elderly parents to move out with their married children.

Thus, to the extent that the results of studying forty-seven families were valid they were so only for a particular type of family living in a particular type of housing estate. Few 'users' of this research have made such a qualification.

This is a matter of properly using research findings, but there is also the question of interpretation. In relation to the Bethnal Greeners, for example, Young and Willmott concluded that 'very few people wish to leave the East End. They are attached to Mum and Dad, to the markets, to the pubs and settlements, to Club Row and the London Hospital.' But an alternative interpretation notes that the population of Bethnal Green fell by 59,000 (from 117,000 to 58,000) between 1921 and 1951 and concludes that 'the enormous movement of population out of areas such as Bethnal Green will not stop until they are made attractive places to live in'.[38]

The Young and Willmott study is quoted not because of any peculiar shortcomings which it may have (all studies have some shortcomings: most more than this one), but because of its widespread use in the debate on 'overspill'.

The number of people who wish to move from slum clearance areas will vary between areas—according to the physical state of the area, its social and economic structure, the available alternatives and so forth. The number who wish to move from any particular area can theoretically be established, simply by asking them: but the answer will depend on a range of uncertain factors—the method of inquiry, the organization undertaking the inquiry, the questions asked, the assumptions made by those answering the questions, the alternatives posed and the way in which the 'results' are interpreted.

In all such cases the mere presentation of results is totally inadequate. The methodology adopted needs rigorous evaluation and the conclusions need interpretation.

But there is an even bigger issue: at what point in a decision-making process is research to be undertaken? And, what is to be its scope? Are families in an area of old housing to be asked for their views about the area *before* it is decided whether or not to demolish it, or are they to be asked for their views on moving from the area *after* it has been decided that clearance is the right policy?

The issue is probably even clearer with improvement area policies. An official Circular [39] is interesting in this context:

Along with the planning future and the physical potential of an area the authority should consider as a third governing factor the attitude of the inhabitants and owners. This they may wish to discover either from house to house visiting or by public meetings. This is something they will need to know when deciding whether to declare an area to be a general improvement area and is the sort of information which may often help them to decide on one area as against another on the grounds that the people in it are more likely to welcome and co-operate in a scheme of improvement.

This clearly sets social research into the framework of decision-taking. But there are real difficulties about this—quite apart from those already raised about establishing the 'facts of the situation'.

It is highly unlikely that all the people in a given area will share the same views. What happens if they split 50/50? Suppose that all the owner-occupiers want the area to be improved, but all the tenants want it to stay as it is?

Clearly 'interpretation' of any study of the area will be required. The character of this interpretation will depend very much on who makes it. A physical planner will tend to see the issues very much in physical terms, though not untypically he will couch his analysis in social terms: e.g. that in the future families will find the area inadequate unless it is improved. An economist will talk of costs, rents and prices, though he may begin to trespass on the sociologist's domain by suggesting that improvement to the area will attract higher income groups. The sociologist will tend to be more concerned with what would become of the displaced lower income groups if this happened. He is also likely to talk in terms of community values.

With increasing concern for citizen-participation these issues will become more than matters for academic debate. The new planning system being introduced under the 1968 Town and Country Planning Act actually makes citizen-participation a statutory requirement. Further, Local Plans prepared within the framework of an approved Structure Plan, are to be approved not by the Secretary of State, but by the local authority. If their 'research' is inadequate the political implications could thus be very significant. At the least, there will be a far greater dependence upon local action-orientated research than has been normal in British local government.

Worthwhile research cannot be constrained by pre-determined questions. This is particularly so with research which is concerned with assessing need. As social research increases the understanding of 'need' so it highlights the relevant issues—which may be very different from those originally envisaged. Numerous local studies have demonstrated that 'local' needs are a reflection of wider needs which can be dealt with only on a wider scale. Indeed, a focusing of attention on local problems can divert attention from more important broader approaches.

The evolution of the Coventry Community Development Project nicely illustrates the point.[40] The initial stages of this led to an increasing awareness of the fact that though the project area had problems, for example, of poverty, environmental deficiency, and restricted educational opportunity which were the legitimate subject for local community action, 'the Project's exclusive preoccupation in the early phase with short-term remedies tended to lead to over-concentration on the relatively marginal features special to Hillfields at the expense of more systematic analysis of the causes of the under-lying problems'.

Following a reappraisal of the situation, emphasis is shifting to key areas for 'longer-term action-research consideration'. The project is adopting:

(i) an approach to the study area not so much as a self-contained 'problem area' as a laboratory for the study of problems which have their origins and implications beyond any one neighbourhood, in processes which are city-wide and nation-wide.

(ii) a preventive rather than a remedial strategy.

(iii) a focus on organizational and operational change at the level of local and central government rather than at the neighbour-hood level alone.

(iv) an operation which involves integration of action and research rather than independent action followed by research evalua-tion; and

(v) a longer time-perspective deriving from planned action-research programmes with clear objectives rather than from short-term ad hoc action responses.

The key areas have been selected in the light of issues which residents, fieldworkers and researchers have identified during the first phase of the Project. There are six of these: income maintenance; housing and environment; community education; the transition from school to work; the needs of the elderly; and 'social priority planning'.

Each of these fields requires not only 'study', but also 'dialogue' with all the relevant agencies and decision-makers in local and central government. It is at this point that the relationships between 're-search', 'citizen-participation' and 'policy' become apparent. Social research is part of a process by which social problems are identified and appropriate policies formulated. The operation of policies and the framework within which they operate are not separate from the 'problems' with which the researcher is concerned: they are part of the 'problems'. Deprivation is not something which can be isolated from wider social, economic and political forces: it is a result of these forces.

COST–BENEFIT ANALYSIS

Nevertheless, research cannot provide the answers to political issues, even though it can improve the quality of the debate on them. Indeed, if research does attempt to provide answers it will not only prejudice the political process, it will also lose its credibility and its power to contribute effectively to political debate. Social scientists have for long faced this problem and have frequently been tempted into areas of judgement which are beyond their competence.[41] The development of cost–benefit analysis has highlighted the issue.[42]

Given a clear definition of the framework within which cost–benefit analysis should operate and an understanding of its limitations and assumptions, it can be a useful tool, but no more. Its value lies particularly in the attitude of mind which it engenders: 'that of defining a problem, seeking alternatives and identifying the effects on all sectors of the community'.[43] In practice, however, cost–benefit analysis tends to be concerned with *overall* costs and benefits, and this can be insensitive to the fact that the individuals who lose are different from those who benefit.

With the 'lowest level of decision-making'[44] this issue is relatively unimportant: the question is a largely unpolitical one of choosing between, e.g. dustbins and papersacks, though even here there are a surprising number of intangibles.[45] But with major issues, such as the siting of the third London airport, questions of equity which should loom large in the decision-making process, may become submerged in pseudo-scientific calculations. Moreover, those who lose are often not compensated for their loss. As Mishan trenchantly puts it:

> If indeed, the business tycoons and the Mallorca holiday-makers are shown to benefit, after paying their fares, to such an extent that they *could* more than compensate the victims of aircraft spillover, the cost–benefit criterion is met. But compensation is *not* paid. The former continue to enjoy the profit and the pleasure; the latter continue to suffer the disamenities.[46]

This is not the place to enter into an extended discussion of cost–

benefit analysis: in any case, this has been well done by others.[47] There is a number of immediately relevant points. First, cost–benefit analysis has a limited role as an aid to policy in defined areas which are appropriately encompassed by its methodology. This excludes issues such as the 'valuation' of Stewkley church (put at £51,000 by the Roskill team). Secondly, issues of the distribution of benefits and costs (essentially issues of equity) cannot be summed: they can only be indicated.[48]

Thirdly, and most important of all, the essentially political nature of important questions must not be allowed to be submerged under sophisticated techniques such as cost–benefit analysis or, indeed, any academic or semi-judicial inquiry. The Roskill Commission (with the exception of Buchanan) were content to hear all the evidence, to make an overall 'impartial' assessment, and to come to a conclusion. But semi-judicial inquiries, cost–benefit studies and research projects are no substitute for political judgement.

Unfortunately, particularly after the Roskill Report (following which the Secretary of State for the Environment rejected the recommendations and made an overtly political decision in favour of Foulness), cost–benefit analysis has taken on the nature of a religion: some believe in it, others do not. Thus, a tool of analysis which is of use (albeit limited) as an aid to policy has become discredited. Had fewer claims been made for its utility and validity, this would not have happened.

Part of the problem is that cost–benefit analysis (like some transportation studies and economic studies of the housing improvement *versus* redevelopment—to mention but two examples) has become so complex, that it is not only not understood, it is also not believed. Were these approaches infallible this would be most unfortunate: but they are not, and thus other 'experts' are called upon by objectors to provide not only different conclusions, but also different evidence.

This is a healthy reaction since it shows that the public is not prepared to accept 'professional' judgements. Instead, there is a demand for debate on the issues which are seen as important by the 'man in the street'. To put the issues on to a 'technical' plane which is incomprehensible to him (and to the elected members of local and central government who represent him) is to deny the democratic nature of our institutions.

The basic issue is not one of 'costs' and 'benefits', but of values. As Max Nicholson has put it:

Welcome as it is to find public opinion awakening to the value of outdoor environment in town and country, we have to face the fact that frustration and disillusionment await us unless sweeping changes can be achieved in the attitude and sense of values of both individuals and society. For example, well-intentioned efforts to determine by the crudest kind of cost–benefit how to decide planning issues may well be bracketed by our descendants with the arguments of medieval theologians over the number of angels who could dance on the point of a needle?[49]

Of course, some of the issues are difficult to understand. Public support and participation demand an increasingly sophisticated electorate. But this means that strenuous attempts must be made to translate technical issues into a language which can be generally understood. If this is not done, there will be a strong suspicion that political issues are being masked by technical mumbo-jumbo. And (though the professionals may be very reluctant to admit it) this may well be the case. Or, at the least, issues will be defined in terms which brook no interference from the non-professional.

Such an attitude is incompatible with the increasing demand for citizen-participation. The citizen can participate only if he understands what he is participating in. If he cannot, he will press for the issues to be redefined. As we have seen with transport planning this can be a very useful corrective to the blinkered approach of the professional. But alternatively the result can be the abandonment of attempts to provide a solution to difficult problems. It was suggested in Chapter 5 of Volume I that this has been the case with the compensation-betterment problem.

Lack of public understanding can also lead to the false posing of issues. Perhaps the clearest contemporary example of this is that of economic growth *versus* the quality of life.

ECONOMIC GROWTH AND THE ENVIRONMENT

All governments are committed to policies of economic growth and, in this, they have the support of their electorates. But without management and foresight severe environmental problems can result. The development of nineteenth century public health policy, and of twentieth century policies in relation to such issues as town planning, clean air, mineral workings, derelict land and noise, all emanate from an appreciation of this. In every case these policies have recognized the undesirability of uncontrolled growth.

Increased public concern for the quality of the environment has given this traditional concern a new twist. Rather than regulating growth there are arguments now put forward for abandoning it. Essentially the issue is that the side-effects of growth are reaching such enormous proportions that 'space ship earth' (to use one of the terms from the new ecological vocabulary) is heading for disaster. The 'limits to growth' are in sight: without a major reorientation in policy (encompassing a 'blueprint for survival') current trends will lead to 'the breakdown of society and the irreversible disruption of the life-support systems on this planet, possibly by the end of the century, certainly within the lifetimes of our children'.[50]

The arguments of the 'ecodoomsters' have been given political urgency by the dire warnings of the former Secretary-General of the United Nations,[51] and academic credibility by the 'world model' produced at the Massachusetts Institute of Technology.[52]

This macro-ecological movement has attracted a great deal of interest and support: so much so, in fact, that to reject it, or even disagree with it, is to run the risk of appearing to be materialistic and ostrich-like. Indeed, the lobbying of the 'Club of Rome' is having an impact (or at least apparently cannot be ignored) in the world's centres of political power. The Club of Rome (which sponsored the MIT Report [53]) is an informal international association, limited to one hundred members, who have an 'overriding conviction that the major problems facing mankind are of such complexity and are so inter-related that traditional institutions and policies are no longer able to cope with them, nor even to come to grips with their full content'.[54]

Yet, even where the basic cause for concern is accepted, any objective analysis of the writings of the Club of Rome (or of the prestigious group who 'supported'—though 'without endorsing every detail'—the Blueprint for Survival) shows it to be a hollow piece of sophistry. The model which it espouses lacks empirical content and ignores the 'feedback' which would be set up by the price increases which would follow from the postulated future scarcity of raw materials.

The matter could be viewed as an exercise in science fiction if it did not carry the danger that of diverting attention from the real problems: i.e. those of so directing economic growth that its benefits are equitably shared and are not offset by its costs. On an international scale the issue was nicely put in context by Mrs Gandhi at the Stockholm Conference when she passionately declared that 'Poverty is the greatest polluter of all'. Indeed, the Stockholm Conference showed how widespread was the feeling among 'developing countries' that the environmental issue was 'a devious excuse for the rich countries to pull up the ladder behind them'.[55]

Exaggerated prophecies of doom bring the response of equally

180

exaggerated statements of complacency. In fact, the time is premature for optimism, defeatism or complacency. What is required is sober assessment. This is not facilitated by horror stories of world disaster.

More immediately relevant to the present discussion is the elevation of debate to a level beyond the comprehension of normal political debate. If population growth needs to be restrained, it can be effected only by the general support of the public at large. If ecological disaster is on the horizon, prevention depends on public understanding and acceptance. A computer programme is particularly ill-suited to this:

> The depressing thing is that the crisis the computer describes is a very real one, but that by turning it into numbers that have at best a tenuous connection with reality, the programmers have been influenced more by the limits of computation than those of the real world. If there is a solution to the environmental crisis, it will have to come from human not mechanical brains. Not even a compassionate computer can point the way.[56]

And so we return to the issue of citizen-participation and informed public debate.

THE FRAMEWORK FOR CITIZEN-PARTICIPATION

Citizen-participation can be effective only if the statutory framework within which it can operate is appropriate. Essentially this means that the organization of government should be such that decisions can be taken at the right level. Matters of purely local concern should be decided at the local level. Matters involving wider issues should be decided at a higher level.

The extremes are easy to exemplify: the positioning of a pedestrian crossing or the provision of a toddlers playground are essentially local issues which should be decided at the community level. The location of the third London airport (and the question as to whether there should be one at all) is a national issue which should be decided at the national level. There are, of course, important regional and local considerations involved in the latter, and these must be taken into account in arriving at a decision, but the decision itself can only properly be taken by the central government.

The majority of issues, however, are not as clear as this and there is wide scope for argument. Moreover, matters which may appear to be purely local in importance may have broader implications and may raise wider issues of equity.

As Amercian experience shows, citizen-participation can lead to strong demands to keep an area 'white', to exclude public authority housing, and to safeguard local amenities at a high cost to the larger community. It is not every community which is best placed to assess its needs in relation to a wider area.

On the other hand, public involvement in local problems can lead to a questioning of (and a demand for a change in) national policies which have an impact on a locality.

Debates on such matters are, of course, the essence of the political process, and there is no simple formula which provides the 'correct' answer. What is important is that local and regional government is appropriately structured and has appropriate powers.

It is here that we see the unresolved dilemma of present regional policies. Regional planning means different things to central and local government. As Senior has put it: 'What *central* government means by "regional planning" is primarily the correction of economic imbalance *between* one "region" and another; and it is only with reluctance that central government is reconciling itself to the fact that this purpose—crucial to its central function in the economic field— necessarily involves the making of investment decisions *within* "regions" on a territorial as well as a functional basis. What *local* government means by "regional planning", on the other hand, is primarily the expression of national policies in terms of a comprehensive long-term strategy for economic and physical development *within* each provincial-scale "region", in the context of which local planning authorities can work out meaningful structure plans for their own areas.'[57]

This gap cannot be bridged until there is a regional planning machine designed for the job. At present central government can channel (or block) resources to regions, but there is no machinery for rationally distributing resources *within* regions on the basis of a comprehensive strategy. The Department of the Environment has a role and powers quite inadequate for this; and in any case, it is not a proper task for central government—it is essentially a regional matter. Any plan involves the submerging of some interests in favour of others. At national level the priority given to development areas is a clear case in point. But at the regional level there is no system for determining priorities. Each local authority has the interests of its ratepayers at heart and development needed for a wider benefit is jeopardized. Thus (for instance), if a conurbation authority sees industrial overspill as having undesirable effects on its rateable value and a potentially good overspill authority sees development as an intolerable local burden, an overspill policy is killed at birth, even if

PLANNING IN A DEMOCRATIC SOCIETY

it is in the wider interests of the region as a whole. To quote Senior again:

Any plan which seeks to guide development in the interest of the region as a whole must call for the concentration of investment in particular parts of it and the prevention of development in others. But so long as the region is divided between different implementing authorities, one of them is bound to find that it is being called upon to bear more than its share of the cost and get less than its share of the benefit of giving effect to particular provisions of the overall plan: if this were not so there would be no need for such a plan. And it would be not only altruistic, but positively undemocratic, for that authority thus to subordinate its own ratepayers' interests to that of its neighbour's ratepayers. It is quite unreasonable to expect a wrongly organized local government structure to behave as it would automatically tend to do it were it rightly organized, when the wrong organization automatically produces a different incidence of the costs and benefits of acting in the interest of the region as a whole.[58]

There has been little serious *public* debate on local government reorganization. The issue has been a battle between highly articulate local government pressure groups concerned essentially with the effect of reorganization on their interests. Yet public debate would have redefined the problem and, paradoxically, may well have resulted in a more powerful system of truly local government. Instead, the new system will inevitably involve the central government in controlling (or, at least, attempting to control) the policies of local authorities in order to safeguard the wider interests which are denied by the boundaries of the new authorities and the division of responsibility between the countries and the districts.

Serious doubts must therefore remain as to the effectiveness of the new system of local government. What is clearly demonstrated by the discussion in the earlier chapters is that central government will continue to have a major role to play in the determination and operation of major urban policies. At the same time, the increasing demand for public involvement in the planning process and for much more sensitive urban policies may well involve the central government in an extension of its quasi-judicial functions. Increasingly these will be concerned not so much with physical planning proposals *per se* but with their social implications.

Moreover, strong expressions of public opinion on a wide range of local issues—motorways, office blocks, improvement areas, 'dispersal' of coloured people, soaring house prices, 'pockets of poverty', social provision and the like—will inevitably lead to a reassessment of national policies. All that can be said with certainty is that the re-organized systems of 'town and country planning' and local government will rapidly need review in the light of changing and increasingly articulate public opinion.

The pressures for citizen-participation are no longer simply a reaction against the results of planning: they reflect a mounting desire from the public to be involved in the formulation and execution of policy. The citizen pays heavily by way of taxation for the pro-vision of services. Increasingly he is demanding a greater role in the decision-making process than is provided by the opportunity of registering blanket approval or disapproval on election days. Well-established lines of authority are now being questioned: the rules of the political game are changing. The issue is not only one of what is to be decided, but of how the decisions are to be taken and by whom. Planning is not a technical means to a political end: it is itself part of the political process.

References and Further Reading

1. L. R. Taylor (ed.), *The Optimum Population for Britain*, Academic Press, 1970.

2. P. R. Ehrlich, *The Population Bomb*, Ballantine Books, 1971; see also J. Barr (ed.), *The Environmental Handbook: Action Guide for the U.K.*, Ballantine—Friends of the Earth, 1971.

3. *Sinews for Survival: A Report on the Management of Natural Resources*, HMSO, 1972, p. 5.

4. *How Do You Want to Live?: A Report on the Human Habitat*, HMSO, 1972, pp. 12–13.

5. *The Times*, 28 June 1972.

6. *House of Lords Debates*, 4 July 1972.

7. *The Times*, 28 June 1972.

8. See Volume I, Chapter 5 for further discussion.

9. The phrase is Sir John Walley's: see Chapter 9 of D. Bull (ed.), *Family Poverty*, Duckworth, 1971.

10. See Chapter 1 of this volume, p. 33.

11. See the author's *Town and Country Planning in Britain*, Allen & Unwin, 4th edition, 1972, pp. 132–141; and J. Morton, *The Best Laid Schemes?: A Cool Look at Local Government Reform*, Charles Knight, 1970.

12. Cf. the arguments put forward by New Town Development Corporations and local authorities on the future ownership of housing in the new towns: J. B. Cullingworth and V. A. Karn, *The Ownership and Management of Housing in the New Towns*, HMSO, 1968.

13. See P. Self, *Metropolitan Planning: The Planning System of Greater London*, London School of Economics and Weidenfeld and Nicolson, Greater London Papers No. 14, 1971; J. Hillman (ed.), *Planning for London*, Penguin Books, 1971;

and Town and Country Planning Association, *London Under Stress: A Study of the Planning Policies Proposed for London and Its Region*, TCPA, 1970.

14. See my *Report to the Minister of Housing and Local Government on Proposals for the Transfer of G.L.C. Housing to the London Boroughs*, 2 vols., MHLG, 1970.

15. See the sources quoted in the previous two references.

16. Melvin M. Webber, *Alternative Styles of Citizen Participation in Transport Planning*, University of California, Berkeley, Institute of Urban and Regional Development, Centre for Planning and Development Research, Working Paper No. 143, January 1971, pp. 2–3. This section of the chapter leans heavily on this very useful paper.

17. See Chapter 3 of Volume III.

18. Melvin M. Webber, op. cit., pp. 7–8.

19. *Report of the Committee on Public Participation in Planning: People and Planning*, HMSO, 1969. See also P. Levin and D. V. Donnison, 'People and Planning', *Public Administration*, Vol. 49, Winter 1969, reproduced as Chapter 4 of Volume III of the present work.

20. *Report of the Committee on Local Authority and Allied Personal Social Services*, Cmnd. 3703, HMSO, 1968.

21. Warrington New Town Development Corporation, *Warrington New Town Outline Plan*, 1972, p. 91.

22. Ibid., p. 92.

23. The *Guardian*, 3 July 1972.

24. See Volume I, Chapter 5, p. 168. The proposals envisaged the replacement of planning applications by notices of 'intention to develop'. Development would not require planning permission, but it would be incumbent upon local planning authorities to take action to prevent development if they considered it to be undesirable.

25. *50 Million Volunteers: A Report on the Role of Voluntary Organizations and Youth in the Environment*, HMSO, 1972, p. 64. See also the evidence given by the Scottish Civic Trust to the Select Committee on Scottish Affairs, Session 1971–72, *Land Resource Use, Minutes of Evidence, 12th April, 1972*, H.C. 53–xi, HMSO, 1972, pp. 217–220.

26. *50 Million Volunteers*, op. cit., p. 66.

27. Select Committee on Scottish Affairs, loc. cit.

28. It should be stressed that, at the time of writing, the Bill is still before Parliament. Furthermore, the way in which the Bill, when passed into law, is to be operated is still under discussion. The quotations are from a 'consultation document for a code of practice' and are taken from the *Greater London Council Minutes*, 21 March 1972, pp. 173–175.

29. Cf. the evidence of the Centre for Environmental Studies to the Greater London Development Plan Inquiry, reproduced in Chapter 3 of Volume III.

30. See the comments at the end of Chapter 3 in Volume III.

31. *50 Million Volunteers*, op. cit., p. 66.

32. See Select Committee on Scottish Affairs, op. cit., p. 217.

33. See, for example, J. P. Mackintosh, *The Devolution of Power: Local Democracy, Regionalism and Nationalism*, Chatto and Windus and Charles Knight, 1968; and M. Slesser, *The Politics of Environment: A Guide to Scottish Thought and Action*, Allen & Unwin, 1972.

34. See, J. K. Friend and W. N. Jessop, *Local Government and Strategic Choice: An Operational Research Approach to the Processes of Public Planning*, Tavistock, 1969.

35. Published, together with the Dainton Report and a curiously insensitive

Government memorandum, in *A Framework for Government Research and Development*, Cmnd. 4814, HMSO, 1971. See also, Select Committee on Science and Technology, *Minutes of Evidence*, 26 January 1972, H.C.P. 114–i (Session 1971–72), HMSO, 1972.

36. See First Report from the Select Committee on Science and Technology, Session 1971–72, *Research and Development*, H.C. 237, HMSO, 1972.

37. M. Young and P. Willmott, *Family and Kinship in East London*, Routledge, 1957.

38. J. B. Cullingworth, *Housing Needs and Planning Policy*, Routledge, 1960, p. 168.

39. MHLG Circular 65/69, *Housing Act 1969: Area Improvement*, HMSO, 1969, para. 11.

40. This section is based upon (and quotations are taken from) Coventry Community Development Project, *C.D.P. in Coventry: The Second Phase Strategy and Key Areas of Need*, Working Paper 2/72.

41. See the author's *The Politics of Research*, reprinted in Volume III.

42. There is a large and growing literature on cost-benefit analysis, of which the following represents only a small selection:

R. Dorfman, (ed.), *Measuring Benefits of Government Investments*, Brookings Institution, 1965.

G. H. Peters, *Cost-Benefit Analysis and Public Expenditure*, Institute of Economic Affairs, 1966.

A. R. Prest and R. Turvey, 'Cost-Benefit Analysis: A Survey', *Economic Journal*, Vol. LXXV, December 1965, pp. 683–735.

A. Williams, *Output Budgeting and the Contribution of Microeconomics to Efficiency in Government*, Centre for Administrative Studies, Occasional Paper No. 4, HMSO, 1967.

H. G. Walsh and A. Williams, *Current Issues in Cost-Benefit Analysis*, Centre for Administrative Studies, Occasional Paper No. 11, HMSO, 1969. See also references quoted below.

43. Institute of Municipal Treasurers and Accountants, *Cost-Benefit Analysis in Local Government*, IMTA, 1969, p. 16.

44. Loc. cit.

45. Ibid., pp. 53–62 and 91–106.

46. E. J. Mishan, 'What is Wrong with Roskill?', *Journal of Transport Economics and Policy*, Vol. 3, No. 4, September 1970, p. 234.

47. See, for example, H. G. Walsh and A. Williams, op. cit.

48. As is done in the 'Planning Balance Sheet' technique developed by Professor Lichfield. See, for example, N. Lichfield, 'Cost Benefit Analysis in Urban Expansion: A Case Study: Peterborough', *Regional Studies*, Vol. 3, 1969, pp. 123–155; N. Lichfield and H. Chapman, 'Cost Benefit Analysis in Urban Expansion: A Case Study: Ipswich', *Urban Studies*, Vol. 7, 1970, pp. 156–179; N. Lichfield and H. Chapman, 'Cost Benefit Analysis and Road Proposals for a Shopping Centre: A Case Study; Edgware', *Journal of Transport Economics and Policy*, Vol. 2, 1968, pp. 280–320; and N. Lichfield and H. Chapman, 'Financial Analysis', in G. Ashworth, 'Environmental Recovery at Skelmersdale', *Town Planning Review*, Vol. 41, 1970, pp. 282–287.

49. *How Do You Want to Live? A Report on the Human Habitat*, HMSO, 1972, p. 185.

50. *The Ecologist*, Vol. 2, No. 1, January 1972.

51. 'I do not wish to seem overdramatic, but I can only conclude from the information that is available to me as Secretary-General, that the Members of the

United Nations have perhaps ten years left in which to subordinate their ancient quarrels and launch a global partnership to curb the arms race, to improve the human environment, to defuse the population explosion, and to supply the required momentum to development efforts. If such a global partnership is not forged within the next decade, then I very much fear that the problems I have mentioned will have reached such staggering proportions that they will be beyond our capacity to control.' U Thant (1969), quoted in the Introduction to D. H. Meadows *et al.*, *The Limits of Growth*, Earth Island, 1972, p. 17.

52. J. W. Forrester, *World Dynamics*, Wright-Allen Press, 1971.

53. Ibid. See also D. H. Meadows *et al.*, *The Limits of Growth*, Earth Island, 1972.

54. D. H. Meadows, op. cit., pp. 9–10.

55. A. Crosland, 'Pollution—or Poverty', *The Sunday Times*, 25 June, 1972.

56. F. Arnold, 'The Compassionate Computer', *The Times*, 1 April, 1972. See also J. Maddox, *The Doomsday Syndrome*, Macmillan, 1972.

57. Royal Commission on Local Government in England, Vol. 2, *Memorandum of Dissent by Mr. D. Senior*, Cmnd. 4040-1, HMSO, 1969, para. 471.

58. Ibid., para 58.

Index

189